The Psychology And Dynamics of Human Energy

How Understanding your Energy can Transform your World

CP
THE CHOIR PRESS

First published in the United Kingdom in 2026 by
The Choir Press

ISBN 978-1-78963-564-5

Dedication

This book is dedicated to those talented people around the world who are using The GC Index to change the world for the better. We call them GCologists!

The contributors to this book are: educationalists, coaches, family therapists, counsellors, well-being gurus and psychologists.

They all share the same drive: to help people to be the best that they can be in the world.

Acknowledgements

Special thanks to:

Teresa Shaw for continued *Play Maker* inspiration.

Nicole Rogers for continued *Polisher* perseverance.

Gemma Roszkowski for unfailing *Game Changer* creativity.

Nigel Evans for his *Strategist* understanding of the world of neurodiversity and how we can understand it through the lens of The GC Index.

Manon Frazer for the *Implementer* energy that she brought to making our neurodiversity project happen.

All the wonderful GCologists in our community and their unfailing commitment to changing people's lives for the better.

About the Authors

Dr John Mervyn-Smith

John is one of the UK's leading psychologists. He is a co-creator of The GC Index. He is an author, broadcaster and keynote speaker with an expertise that reflects a hybrid career as an academic, clinical and occupational psychologist. He has published on subjects from leadership to well-being.

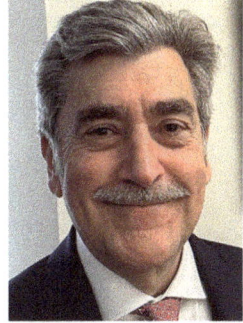

Leticia Dollennga

Leticia is the founder of Leve Connect, where she empowers leaders and organisations through strategic development, cultural transformation, and leadership impact. With extensive experience in executive coaching and business strategy, she helps companies enhance leadership, foster innovation, and drive sustainable change. A certified Somatic Experiencing facilitator, she takes a body-centred approach to resilience and transformation. Passionate about human potential, Leticia believes in the power of collective action to create lasting impact, combining strategy and people development to help businesses and leaders thrive.

Jon Crocker

Jon works with young people and professionals, focusing on transferable skills. With three decades in international education, he specialises in innovative learning and thrives on challenging conventions. Passionate about potential, he helps individuals and teams grow, adapt and make a meaningful impact.

John and Natalie Franklin-Hackett are the co-owners of Frankly Farm Tours in Broseley, Shropshire – an open farm tourist attraction established in 2022. John is an accredited GCologist and has been working with The GC Index in the context of his other career as a consultant since 2016. Natalie was previously an assistant headteacher in an inner city primary school in Coventry.

Nikki Finucan

Nikki Finucan is a Transformation Architect who thrives on bold ideas, deep human connection, and unlocking untapped potential in leaders and teams. A 'recovering accountant' turned organisational Game Changer, she re-energises workplaces by aligning purpose, people, and performance. Nikki's magic lies in helping leaders move from overwhelm to impact, using energy for action, trust, and courageous transformation.

John Frost

John is a professional leadership coach, GCologist and the bass player in Rebel and the Banned. He has delivered leadership development programmes across different cultures in Europe, North America and Asia. He has a particular interest in enabling personal, team and organisational impact using the leadership lenses of consciousness, connection, curiosity, collaboration and compassion.

Helen Rivero

Helen is the founder of Your Future Impact and co-creator of The Young People Index, a revolutionary assessment tool designed to help young people discover their unique impact and contributions in a team, helping them make better-informed choices about their futures. With a passion for unlocking potential, Helen has dedicated her career to re-imagining how the next generation prepares for the world of work – guiding them towards careers where they can thrive, feel fulfilled, and make a meaningful impact.

Simon Phillips

Simon is the founder of The Change Maker Group and is known as The Change Man by his clients. He specialises in helping executives, teams and organisations to thrive on change and transformation. He has written and contributed to seven books on personal development and change and supported clients globally during his time with Accenture and independently.

Reem Prakkash

Reem, an MSc graduate with Distinction in Organisational Psychology and Psychiatry from King's College London, is passionate about workplace dynamics and mental health. Guided by her passion for Positive Psychology, she strives to leverage her expertise to promote well-being and drive meaningful change in professional environments.

Teresa Shaw

Teresa has, in recent years, concentrated her efforts in the academic world, lecturing, presenting and researching in her specialist field of performance anxiety. Her pioneering master's research in this area was published in *Frontiers in Psychology*. An established classical vocalist, much of her early career was spent performing as a soloist in the UK and Europe with an extensive concert and an operatic repertoire.

Renée Smith

Renée Smith is a researcher, writer, speaker and Loving Leader who makes the business case for love. She leads the consultancy, A Human Workplace, and co-founded the non-profit Center for a Loving Workplace to bring the innovative technology of love to the world. She lives with her husband in Tacoma, Washington.

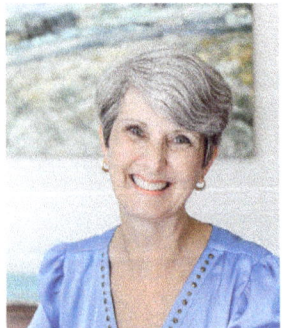

Dr Judith Mohring

Dr Judith Mohring is a psychiatrist, trainer and coach with over 25 years clinical and organisational experience. She trained at Cambridge and London universities and is an honorary lecturer in organisational psychiatry at King's College. She is an expert in ADHD and trains clinicians and the public in the understanding and management of adult ADHD. She founded www.adhded.co.uk in 2025 which provides evidence-based psychoeducation and group coaching for adults with ADHD and the professionals who help them.

Contents

Life changes always put us under pressure to adapt and they test the resilience of our relationships. This chapter follows *John and Natalie Franklin-Hackett's* inspirational journey from despair to joy as they went through a dramatic transition in their lives.

John Frost picks up this theme of energy in relationships in this chapter, which tells the story of a rock band and the ways in which they work to maintain their cohesion and creativity, making their collective energy work for them. At the heart of this exploration is the view that great art 'connects' with people and to do so, those making that art must feel connected to each other.

If you lead people in any sphere of life, from CEO to parent, you will find this chapter a compelling read. *Simon Phillips* and *Renée Smith* give us a very practical approach to the otherwise complex challenge of leading others through periods of change.

Reem Prakkash and *Dr John Mervyn-Smith* present their leading-edge research findings in this chapter that highlights an intriguing relationship between ADHD and dyslexia and Game Changer energy.

Introduction

By Dr John Mervyn-Smith

'Radiators and drains'

Like many 16-year-old boys I was restless, easily bored and more at home on the sports field than in the classroom. As you might imagine then, the thought of being stuck in a drab assembly hall on a sunny summer's day for the school's annual prize-giving filled me with dread. We have probably all experienced the mind-numbing boredom that such events can induce.

With low expectations set, my headmaster did not disappoint, droning on for what seemed like an eternity. However, what was to follow was startling, an epiphany perhaps. The guest speaker was also a head teacher, and her message was compelling, her energy infectious.

Her message was:

> 'There are two types of people in this world, "radiators and drains".'

I can't remember the details of her proposition; her energy and presence was enough to convince me. It's a statement that has stayed with me even though I'm generally not seduced by binary views of the world.

I got the message, and it was a challenge of a sort. She wanted each and every one of us to recognise that we have the capacity, and potential, to generate energy in our world and for others around us, and, equally, to drain others of energy. She wanted us to see that we have a choice in this.

This view of energy and how we choose to use it, has fascinated me ever since; in some ways it seems so simple and yet, with thought, becomes complex.

The simple bit: we all seem to know when we have energy and, conversely, we all seem to know when we haven't. Over time, and with growing self-awareness, we may come to recognise our own idiosyncratic manifestations of energy.

As we will see in the coming chapters, recognising and understanding individual differences when it comes to the manifestation of energy has been a preoccupation of many psychologists. You will have your own 'markers' of when you have energy and when you don't.

And then the concept of energy starts to become a bit more complex: we may begin to recognise those experiences and situations that 'give' us energy and those that 'deplete' us, but we don't always know why.

We may recognise when we're 'pretending' to have energy when we don't, and what this 'costs' us, or indeed, when we are 'suppressing' energy when we consider it inappropriate to express it.

The chapters that follow will shed some light upon the complex ways in which human beings express their energy within the workplace and present the reader with a framework and language – The GC Index – for understanding how people can manage and develop these expressions as they seek to have an impact within their world.

Section 1:
Understanding Energy for Impact

Psychologists have taken an interest in the theme of energy for over a hundred years: the ways in which it is manifest as neuroses, how it shapes our personality, our motivation and our approach to learning, to surviving, adapting and thriving.

In Chapter 1 of this section, Dr John Mervyn-Smith gives a brief history of some of the most significant thinking in this area that culminated in the development of The GC Index, which he goes on to describe in Chapter 2.

The GC Index takes our thinking on a step as it describes individual differences when it comes to Energy for Impact: the ways in which we seek to channel our energy when it comes to surviving and thriving in our world, and making an impact.

The GC Index gives us a very practical framework, built on science, that helps us to explore the ways in which energy is manifest.

Chapter 1

A Psychological Perspective on the Expression of Human Energy from Freud to the Present Day

A brief overview of the history of the most significant thinking in this area and how this culminated in the development of The GC Index.

Dr John Mervyn-Smith

An evolutionary perspective

Let's go back to basics and ask the question 'why do human beings need energy?'

The pregnant mother will often delight at the first kicks of her child to be. She is bringing a new life into the world and what could be more confirming of that life.

The relevance of these kicks become more apparent when the newborn begins to crawl, their leg movements propelling them across the floor. These movements are instrumental in developing spatial awareness and the precursors of standing, walking and running.

Observing young children learning to walk illustrates a strong drive for potency: they get up, flop back down and then get up again. Without this drive the infant is vulnerable: the world would become a very threatening place without these very basic actions needed for 'flight' and 'fight'.

Humans have the luxury of mastering these actions over many months while giraffes, for example, are walking upon wobbly legs within an hour of being born. Giraffes, like many other animals, are 'prey animals' and they need to be able to move with the pack, especially when they are under attack. The survival imperative means that they have evolved to act with speed and this takes energy.

With human beings, this drive for mastery continues and many will delight in seeing the extent to which the complex action of walking becomes a Florence Griffith Joyner or a Usain Bolt, setting world records for running fast. Their actions, ultimately, give us collective hope in the ability of the human species to survive and thrive. Thriving, excelling, is a demonstration of the human potential to survive through developing our capabilities, learning from, and adapting to, a changing world.

These actions of fight and flight are key to humans surviving and thriving, and these actions are fuelled by energy channelled into what we would typically call drive or motivation.

The paradox, of course, is that this human drive for mastery may come to destroy the human species: we can become complacent in our belief in our collective ability to master our world with science and technology, and we are witnessing this with our global management of a climate crisis rapidly reaching a point of no return but with a view that someone will come up with the magic answer.

Fight and flight are designed then, to help us to manage and eliminate threat and can be evidenced as energy for action fuelled by biochemical, physical and physiological changes.

These behaviours in the animal world can be quite dramatic when we witness, for example, the stampedes on the African Savanna as zebras are being pursued by cheetahs. And the energy that is required to fuel these behaviours seems obvious when we conjure up images of buck deer locking horns to determine mating rights.

We also know that 'flight' doesn't always work; it doesn't always eliminate the threat in a way that 'freeze' behaviour can.

This YouTube video provides a dramatic example of the benefits of 'freeze' behaviours in the animal kingdom: https://www.youtube.com/watch?v=-QgglTik6G4

For human beings these behaviours of fight, flight and freeze are usually more subtle – shaped by social and cultural norms and expectations – and not always manifest as action even though that suppression of action will take energy. Moreover, these behaviours can be both adaptive and maladaptive for people in terms of the ways in which they support survival and nurture thriving.

In Table 1 (see overleaf) I have presented some examples of human 'fight', 'flight' and 'freeze' behaviours in a work context with possible consequences. You will note that, dependent upon circumstances, behaviours could fit into more than one category: they can be adaptive in the short term but maladaptive in the long term and, potentially, vice versa.

Charles Darwin sought to capture the principle inherent in the relationship between these behaviours and survival with this paraphrase:

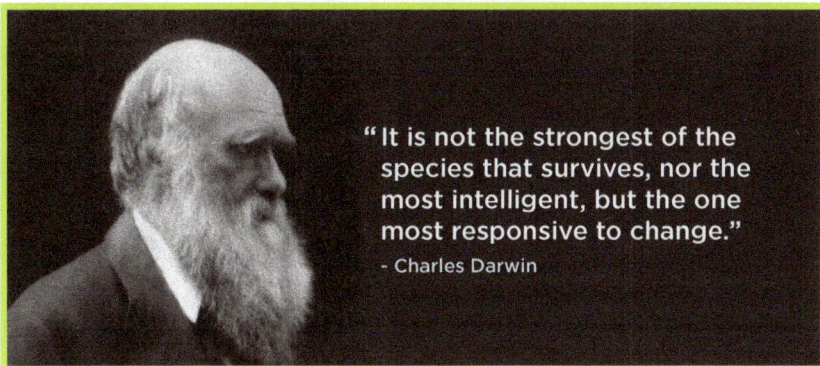

"It is not the strongest of the species that survives, nor the most intelligent, but the one most responsive to change."
- Charles Darwin

BEHAVIOURS	ADAPTIVE	MALADAPTIVE
'FIGHT'	• Leading with visions of success. • Building alliances with others. • Learning new skills and acquiring new knowledge as a way to meet the demands of a job. • 'Putting in the hours' in order to meet expectations of performance. • Competing for profile and recognition. • Getting promoted. • Working at being indispensable.	• Working harder but not 'smarter'. • Winning at other's expense: getting to the 'top' of the organisation makes us less vulnerable, we're in charge, or are we? • Bullying: showing someone 'who is boss'. • Empire building: protecting ourselves from the threat of others. • Taking credit for others work/ideas.
'FLIGHT'	• Getting away from 'toxic' cultures that undermine self-esteem. • 'Cutting losses' when there is a misalignment of expectations.	• Avoiding conflict and confrontation. • Avoiding dependence upon others. • Passive aggressive behaviours such as 'switching off' in meetings. • Avoiding 'being seen'.
'FREEZE'	• Avoiding change for the sake of change?	• Hypervigilance when it comes to getting things wrong. • Not speaking out; standing out. • Procrastination.

Table 1: Fight, flight and freeze behaviours

Given the complexity of these behaviours, it is not surprising that the ways in which human energy is shaped, and manifest, has received attention from some of the great minds in the world of psychology over the last 100+ years and their influence remains with us today.

A psychodynamic view of energy

In 1874, the concept of 'psychodynamics' was proposed with the publication of 'Lectures on Physiology' by German physiologist Ernst Wilhelm von Brücke.

Influenced by the physicist Hermann von Helmholtz, one of the formulators of the first law of thermodynamics, he presented the view that all living organisms are energy systems and governed by this principle.

In 'Lectures on Physiology', he went on to propose the then radical view that the living organism is a dynamic system to which the laws of chemistry and physics apply.

At this time, Brücke was tutoring a first-year medical student at the University of Vienna called Sigmund Freud. Freud, in turn, was influenced by this new 'dynamic physiology'.

In 1920 Freud presented his views on the now familiar model of the Id, Ego and Superego in the essay 'Beyond the Pleasure Principle'. He went on the develop his thinking in a 1923 publication: *The Ego and the Id*.

Like much of Freud's work, his proposal was compelling, controversial and, as we will see, influential.

Freud describes the Id as 'the great reservoir of libido', the energy of desire, usually seen as the energy of sexual desire, that underpinned the drive for constant renewal of life or more broadly we might argue, the survival of the species. His view of a death drive or instinct, Thanatos, came later.

On the assumption that the Id, in social animals such as humans, needs to be regulated by social norms if it is to find acceptable expression, Freud described the regulators of this expression as the Ego and Superego, functions of the psyche developed through socialisation.

Moreover, this approach to understanding the ways in which the expression of energy is shaped, underpins much of our thinking about the nature of individual differences in the form of personality.

Freud's thinking was criticised by those who saw the model as beyond scientific confirmation. Nonetheless, others were influenced by his thinking.

In that same decade Carl Jung published 'On Psychical Energy' (1928) in which he presented his views upon how individual differences – 'personality' – are a reflection of the ways in which activities differentially give us energy or deplete us.

The Myers-Briggs Type Indicator grew from this view and, necessarily, the many subsequent derivatives of the MBTI.

In 1957 Eric Berne presented his model of ego states – 'Parent', 'Adult', 'Child'. Berne trained as a psychoanalyst and his thinking clearly reflects this and, within it, Freud's influence.

His model of ego states underpins Transactional Analysis, an approach to therapy that readily maps onto Freud's model of Id, Ego and Superego: Id = Free Child; Ego = Adult; Superego =Parent.

Berne's model has provided a very practical and enduring approach to focusing upon developing adaptive behaviours in relationships, as well as a framework for thinking about the origins of maladaptive behaviours; those behaviours that lead to dysfunction and emotional distress. Coaches, counsellors and psychotherapists for the last six decades will have found value in Berne's approach.

Energy as motivation

Maslow's (1943) 'Hierarchy of Needs' gives us a contrasting view of how human energy is shaped. It focuses, in a positive way, upon the human drive to channel energy into meeting basic and aspirational needs in contrast to the psychodynamic view of energy distorted and/or suppressed in ways that can lead to pathological outcomes.

Nonetheless, what the psychodynamic and Hierarchy of Needs approaches share is the view that energy not requited can lead to the subjective experience of frustration, a sense of deprivation. The notion that frustration is 'energy that can't go where it wants to' also features below in the exploration of the practical applications of The GC Index.

Maslow's Hierarchy of Needs is often portrayed in the shape of a pyramid (see Figure 1 below), with the most fundamental needs at the bottom, and the need for 'self-actualisation' at the top.

Essentially, the idea is that an individual's most basic needs must be met before they become motivated to achieve higher-level needs. Even though the ideas behind the hierarchy are Maslow's, the pyramid itself does not exist anywhere in Maslow's original work.

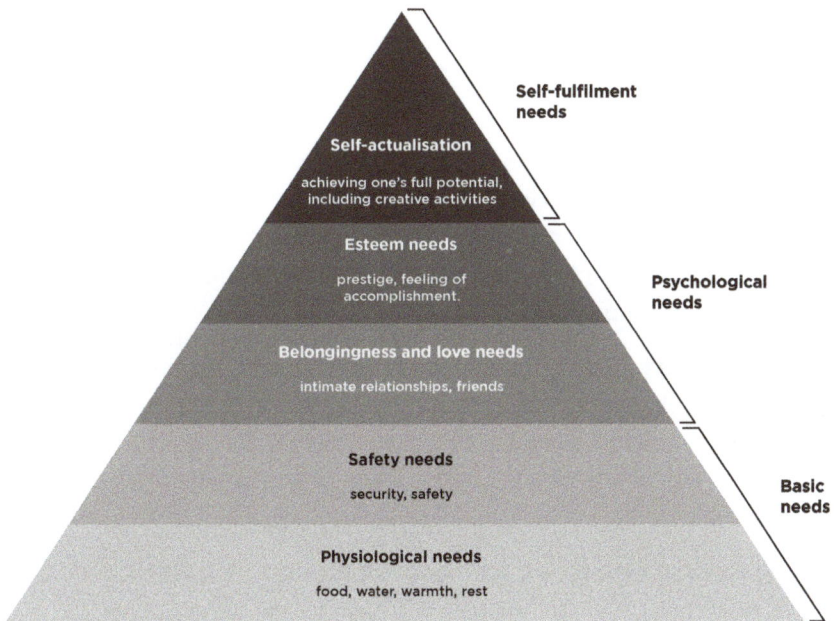

Self-fulfilment needs

Self-actualisation
achieving one's full potential, including creative activities

Esteem needs
prestige, feeling of accomplishment.

Belongingness and love needs
intimate relationships, friends

Safety needs
security, safety

Physiological needs
food, water, warmth, rest

Psychological needs

Basic needs

Figure 1: A representation of Maslow's Hierarchy of Needs

The most fundamental four layers of the pyramid include what Maslow called 'deficiency needs' or 'd-needs': esteem, friendship and love, security, and physical needs. If these 'deficiency needs' are not met the individual will, the argument goes, feel anxious and tense.

Deprivation is what causes deficiency, so when one has unsatisfied needs, this motivates them to fulfil what they are being denied. Maslow's idea suggests that the most basic level of needs must be met before the individual will strongly desire (or focus motivation upon) the secondary or higher-level needs.

This is then a model that describes the journey from surviving to thriving, and the overlaps between this and the 'fight-flight' approach to understanding human behaviour are evident. It adds to our understanding of how human beings channel their energy in ways that shape behaviour.

In the next chapter we will see how Maslow's view of self-actualisation has much in common, conceptually, with a GC Index view of Energy for Impact.

Herzberg's 'Motivator-Hygiene Theory' (1987) develops Maslow's thinking within a work context.

Herzberg's Motivator-Hygiene Theory, also known as the 'Two-factor theory of job satisfaction', proposes that 'hygiene factors' don't motivate people per se, but if they are not in place, they can undermine motivation. These factors could be anything, from clean toilets and comfortable chairs to a reasonable level of pay and job security.

The model takes a view of satisfaction and dissatisfaction that arises in jobs, and which are not affected by the same set of needs, but instead occur independently of each other. Herzberg's theory challenged the assumption that 'dissatisfaction was a result of an absence of factors giving rise to satisfaction'.

So motivational factors will not necessarily lower motivation but can be responsible for increasing motivation. They include, he suggests:

Intrinsic factors:

> *'Orientations toward money, recognition, competition, and the dictates of other people, and the latter includes challenge, enjoyment, personal enrichment, interest, and self-determination.'*

Extrinsic factors:

> *'Doing something because it leads to a distinct outcome, something external you expect to receive, and the latter refers to doing something because it is inherently interesting or enjoyable, an internal reward.'*

Herzberg's 1968 publication 'One More Time: How Do You Motivate Employees?' had sold 1.2 million reprints by 1987 and was, at that time, the most requested article from the *Harvard Business Review*.

Herzberg's drivers or motivators readily equate to Maslow's needs for esteem and self-actualisation presented in a work setting; we see in his thinking the ways in which energy is channelled into making work satisfying and fulfilling.

Moreover, the approach brings a practical focus to understanding what 'self-actualisation' means to an individual in their world of work.

Similar thinking will have shaped the emergence of the concept of 'the psychological contract' and employee engagement surveys; theories and practice designed to support and develop the engagement and motivation of people at work in the hope of increasing productivity and retention.

While this thinking can bring a practical approach to shaping an individual's Energy for Impact, it also highlights the complexity of human motivation, the number of intrinsic and extrinsic variables that can play a part in motivating or demotivating all of us.

Energy channelled into learning and adaptation

To revisit Darwin's proposal noted above:

> *'It is not the most intellectual of the species that survives; it is not the strongest that survives; but the species that survives is the one that is able best to adapt and adjust to the changing environment in which it finds itself.'*

Darwin (1859)

Given Darwin's emphasis upon the importance of adaptation for survival in a changing world, it's not surprising that the themes of learning, adaptation, change and growth have been the subject of enquiry for many psychologists and philosophers.

The equation is this:

- Survival requires the efficient and effective use of energy, energy fuels survival.
- This efficient and effective use of energy is reflected in the human ability to learn, adapt and master the world.
- That process of learning is shaped by many variables that humans experience as thinking, feeling and doing.

For the American psychologist George Kelly part of the complexity of how we learn is a product of how we make sense of our world. Efficient learning, in part, assumes the potential to make sense of patterns and trends in our world and to use our understanding to make predictions about future events. This assumption of causality is the basis for learning, adaptation and, potentially, growth.

In 1955 Kelly published *The Psychology of Personal Constructs*. The main thrust of his proposition was that human beings can be likened to 'amateur scientists' who seek to make sense of our social world. This 'making sense' then, would be more likely to be experiential and unique rather than wholly derived.

Given this, our view of others would be unique, meaning that the perception of another's personality would be 'in the eye of the beholder' and this unique view would shape our predictions about others and our interactions with them.

Take, by way of illustration, the theme of trust. Making judgements about whether or not we can trust someone can be key to both surviving and thriving.

We may base that judgement on a few, very superficial constructs such as the shape of someone's ears having 'learned' that people with certain shaped ears cannot be trusted. This approach to learning is limiting in terms of missed opportunities and leaves the learner vulnerable should this view of causality not be reliable.

A complex set of constructs using, for example, eight constructs to determine someone's trustworthiness, may also be less than optimal, leading to indecision and passivity, not the basis for thriving.

It's possible to see, from this very brief description, how Personal Construct Theory lends itself to a range of psychotherapeutic interventions, cognitive behavioural therapy (CBT) for example. People could, given the theory, potentially, change their view of the world and in so doing change the way they interact with, think about and feel about others and their reactions to them.

This very positive view of human nature takes on a broader horizon in the world of enquiry known as Social Learning Theory.

Social Learning Theory was influenced by the work of behavioural psychologists in the 1950s and 1960s and was pioneered by Albert Bandura. For Bandura the question went beyond 'how do people make sense of the world?' to 'how does sense-making shape the ways in which people learn?'

Bandura rejected the simplistic behaviourist notion that human learning could be explained by the processes of Pavlovian or operant conditioning alone. His view was that learning needed to take account of the complexities of human cognition.

As with Freud's notion of Id, Ego and Superego, we have seen how Social Learning Theory has developed, not surprisingly perhaps, into a very complex area of enquiry.

From Bandura's early thinking developed the concept of 'self-efficacy', a key variable that influences the individual's approach to learning and acting upon that learning.

The essence of Bandura's thinking is captured in this quote:

'The development of a sense of personal agency begins in infancy and moves from the perception of the causal relationship between events, to an understanding that actions produce results, to the recognition that they can be the origin of actions that effect their environments. As children's understanding of language increases, so does their capacity for symbolic thought and, therefore, their capacity for self-awareness and a sense of personal agency.'

Bandura, 1997

So, the basic premise of self-efficacy is that 'people's beliefs in their capabilities to produce desired effects by their own actions' are the most important determinants of the behaviours people choose to engage in and how much they persevere in their efforts in the face of obstacles and challenges.

This view echoes the famous Henry Ford quote:

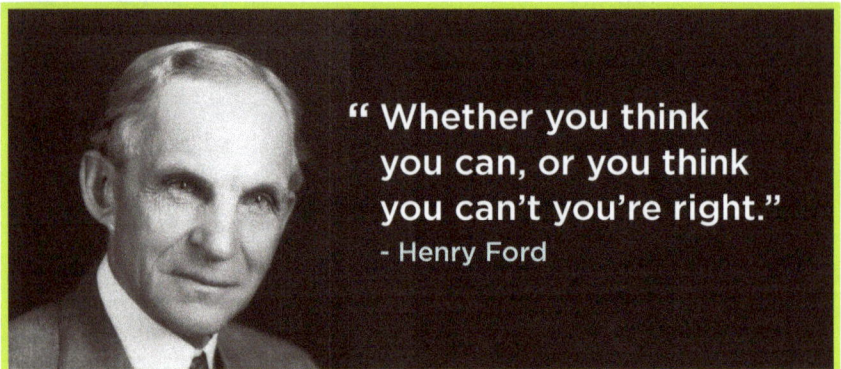

" Whether you think you can, or you think you can't you're right."
- Henry Ford

The relevance of this thinking for the ways in which people survive and thrive in their world is evident. Social Learning Theory broadly, helps us to understand the ways in which energy is channelled into learning.

Not surprisingly, this concept has been the subject of a good deal of research with the suggestion that perceptions of self-efficacy play a role in psychological adjustment, psychological problems, and physical health.

Self-efficacy then, seeks to understand the relationship between how someone responds to events based upon their anticipation of those events. Individual differences when it comes to learning from past events has been the subject of enquiry known as attribution theory and as we might expect, it has proved to be a fascinating challenge for researchers to discern how anticipatory beliefs develop from past experiences.

In psychology, the term attribution has two meanings: the first refers to explanations of behaviour; the second refers to inferences.

'What the two meanings have in common is a process of assigning: in attribution as an explanation, a behavior is assigned to its cause; in attribution as inference, a quality or attribute is assigned to the agent on the basis of observed behavior.'

Malle, 2011, p. 17

Put simply an attributional and explanatory style is the way in which an individual explains their circumstances to themselves and, in this sense, it's easy to see the influence of George Kelly's work on Personal Construct Theory (1963) on this line of thinking.

The theory has developed over time, shaped by influential psychologists such as: Heider (1958), Rotter (1966), Kelley (1972), Weiner (1972, 1985), Maier and Seligman (1976).

In its most developed form, attribution theory highlights three variables that will shape an individual's assumptions of causality, why events happen in their world. These are:

1. **Internal vs External Locus of Control**
   Locus of Control was originally proposed by Rotter (1966) as a generalised and enduring belief about how responsive and controllable our environment is.
   Locus of control is a continuous scale; at one end are individuals who attribute success or failure to things they perceive that they have control over, at the other end are those who attribute their success or failure to forces outside of their control: to luck and/or 'powerful others'.

2. **Stable vs Unstable (Permanence)**

   This dimension is the degree to which we attribute outcome causality to temporary or temporally fixed factors. Weiner (1972) drew a distinction between stable versus unstable causes. A stable attribution occurs when an individual believes an outcome will persist indefinitely. An unstable attribution occurs when an outcome is attributed to a transient factor, specific to a period of time.

3. **Global vs Specific (Pervasiveness)**

   This dimension was introduced by Kelley (1972) who focused on attributions of global versus specific causes for events. The globality dimension indicates a tendency to generalise events, with the expectation that these events will continue to occur in other aspects of life.

Here's an example of how these variables can play out in the real world: when my son failed his first driving test, he declared that he was 'unlucky' (External Locus of Control) on that particular day (Unstable and Specific). When he passed his second test, his announced that he was the best (Internal Locus of Control; Stable) driver in the world (Global).

The work of Overmier and Seligman (1967) is significant for the purpose of this book in a very particular way. They explored the role that 'Explanatory Styles' can play in mediating positive and negative mental states and, in doing so, formulated a model of 'Learned Helplessness'. This thinking evolved with the work of Abramson, Semmel, Seligman, & Von Baeyer (1978) who took the view that the attributional variables of locus of control, stability versus instability and global versus specific, would be influenced by the predispositions of optimism and pessimism.

Energy channelled into potency: Energy for Impact

The 'Learned Helplessness' model supports the evolutionary view, described above, of the importance of energy for survival. The model and associated research demonstrate the dramatic consequences that can come from believing (attributional and explanatory styles) that we cannot have an impact upon our world: that we behave as if helpless, that we lack energy and that we 'feel' depressed.

So, how can we understand energy channelled into impact, channelled in ways that leave individuals feeling potent in their world rather than helpless?

The following chapter presents that next step in this journey of enquiry into human energy with the history and development of The GC Index. The GC Index profiles individual differences when it comes to Energy for Impact, the ways in which human beings seek to have an impact in their world.

Chapter 2

The GC Index and Energy for Impact

The history and science behind the development of this ground-breaking organimetric profiling individual Energy for Impact.

Dr John Mervyn-Smith

A note about this chapter

The chapters that follow will present the ways in which The GC Index has been used to understand the varied manifestations of Energy for Impact.

This chapter will give you an understanding of how The GC Index model works but you may want to use it for reference as you read subsequent chapters.

Research phase 1: understanding 'Game Changers'

The GC Index journey started in 2012.

Nathan Ott, director at the time of the London-based search firm eg1, had several client organisations who had expressed an interest in recruiting people who could 'drive transformational change' within organisations and as consultants to others. They wanted to know more about these individuals; how to identify, recruit and retain them.

These organisations were still suffering the after-effects of the 2008 banking crisis and wanted to find a 'competitive edge' within their markets. 'Game Changers' as they had tagged them, were seen as a possible solution.

In an evolutionary sense, this quest made sense: organisations, like all living organisms, survive and thrive when they have the capability to develop, change and adapt; Game Changers were seen as those people who could drive transformational change through creativity and innovation.

This view was also consistent with the Darwinian view of surviving and thriving discussed in Chapter 1.

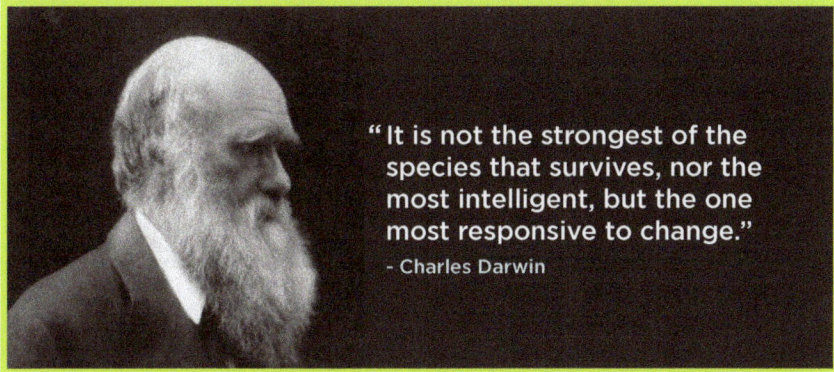

" It is not the strongest of the species that survives, nor the most intelligent, but the one most responsive to change."
- Charles Darwin

We might argue that there was enough anecdotal evidence to support the view that these people existed; the Apple video – 'Here's to the crazy ones' is an example of such evidence.

So too, was the story of Paul Buchheit, a Google engineer in 2001. It illustrates the potential and power of people to make a game-changing, transformational impact on organisations. He started using his '20% time' (the one day a week Google allowed staff to work on new projects) to develop a new product. Initially codenamed Caribou, the product was, after nearly three years of development, released as Gmail and would reinvent the entire web-based email category, capturing 53% of the market.

Gmail, at the time, was one of Google's most successful products and was not an idea formulated by management and developed in a classic top-down waterfall manner. Developing an email product was not even part of Google's corporate strategy at the time. It was one engineer's 'passion project', driven by the belief that email services should be better.

It is an example of how one Game Changer can positively transform the destiny of not just one organisation but an entire industry.

Nonetheless, inherent in this interest were the assumptions that these individuals existed in the 'real world of work' and given the tag of Game Changer, that they had defining and differentiating characteristics.

These two questions became the focus for a series of research projects funded by eg1 and supervised by me.

The methodology for this research was influenced, in part, by the work of researchers like Warren Bennis and Burt Nanus who developed our understanding of leadership and, specifically, what leaders actually do with an emphasis upon observation and deduction.

This approach seeks to understand the world as it actually is, rather than seeks to impose conceptual models upon it. It's an approach that allows data to shape our understanding rather than have our understanding shape the data.

Given the broad methodological approach then, our questions for exploration were:

- Do these individuals who drive transformational change through creativity and innovation – people tagged as Game Changers – exist in the corporate world?
- If they do, what characteristics differentiate them from their colleagues?
- Can we assess these characteristics in a meaningful way, a way that can support the identification, recruitment, retention and development of these individuals?

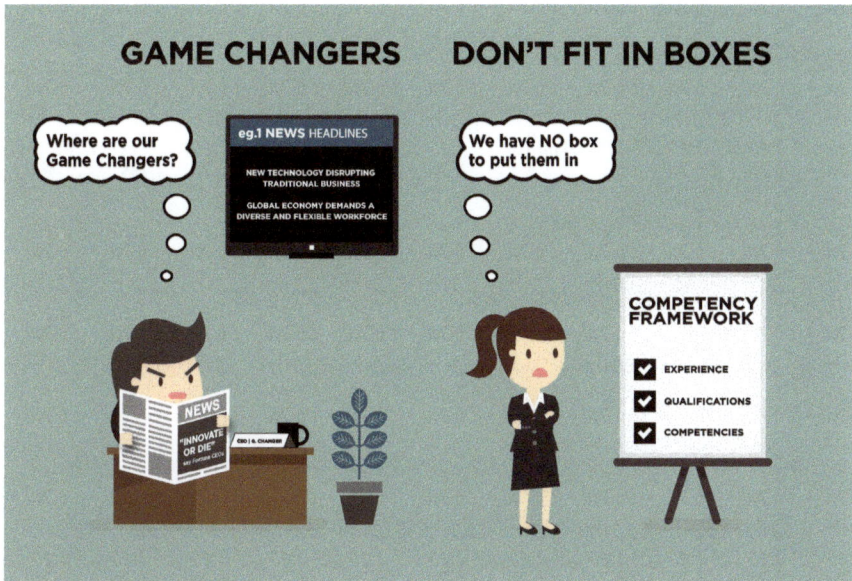

The research methodology together with the full results are described in the study: 'The DNA of a Game Changer'. It can be downloaded from www.TheGCIndex.com.

In brief, and consistent with a belief in a deductive approach to scientific endeavour, we gathered data from hundreds of 1:1 interviews using a data capture methodology based upon a repertory grid approach that reflects the essence of George Kelly's Personal Construct Theory. We wanted to capture people's experience of Game Changers, if, indeed, they had them!

The key findings to emerge from this first phase of our research, and presented in Duke University's Corporate Education Journal *Dialogue* were as follows:

1. Game Changers do exist in the corporate world, working at all levels of an organisation; this was what our interviewees reported.
2. Game Changers are different: they have characteristics that differentiate them, in a statistically significant way, from colleagues described, in our interviews, as 'high potentials' and successful senior executives. Our interviewees' descriptions of Game Changers created a convergent and coherent picture.

The characteristics described by our interviewees seemed to 'cluster' into two main constructs: imagination and obsession.

- Imagination: a capacity for original ideas; the ability to see possibilities that others don't.
- Obsession: an obsessive, compulsive nature that drives them to turn ideas into reality.

You may recognise these qualities in people you know or have worked with, or perhaps yourself. We did at the time of doing the research: James Dyson's book *Against the Odds: An Autobiography* (1997) certainly brought these qualities to life.

Dyson challenged all the rules to achieve success and, in his words:

> *'The key to success is failure ... not other people's failure but how you respond to failure yourself.'*

Giving up was never an option for Dyson; he believed in something and was going to make it happen.

There was also Maxine Clark in our thoughts. She was the founder of Build-A-Bear Workshop who features in *The Transformative CEO: Impact Lessons from Industry Game Changers* by Jeffrey J. Fox and Robert Reiss.

Maxine talked about how she followed her dream with passion. She says:

> *'When a 10-year-old girl innocently asked, "Why can't we make our own teddy bears?", the lightbulb flashed. My dream for Build-A-Bear Workshop was born. Every adult I asked about the idea said it would not work.'*

So, the headline view from 18 months of research suggested that Game Changers were imaginative and obsessive! Not a surprising outcome perhaps, but in line with my experience of science in the sense that, more often than not, it supports a 'common sense' view rather than reveals a counter-intuitive truth.

A trawl of the literature also revealed that much had been written on the topic of imagination and much on the topic of obsession. Of more interest was the fact that we didn't come across any research that gave us a picture of how these constructs interacted. We were left with the view that it was possible to be imaginative but not obsessive and vice versa and with only anecdotal views, like those above, of how the constructs 'came together'.

Moreover, one aspect of the original challenge on understanding Game Changers remained: 'how could we help organisations to identify, recruit, manage and nurture them?' It was not enough to say that they are imaginative and obsessive, we wanted to find a more sophisticated way of measuring these characteristics.

Consistent with the tradition of psychological research, we sought a way of measuring these individual differences through subjective self-report; a questionnaire.

Our literature review helped Nathan Ott and I to prepare a series of questions designed to measure these two constructs. We wanted to test the hypothesis that Game Changers would see themselves as imaginative and obsessive and, if they did, shed more detail upon associated characteristics.

Research phases 2 and 3: the emergence of The GC Index

With a set of 58 questions for reliably measuring the two key constructs of imagination and obsession, our approach was to gather data from a sample of 400 volunteers in order to examine the distribution of responses to the questions set. This revealed a diverse set of responses: within this large group, people saw themselves differently in terms of imagination and obsession.

This initial exploration then, suggested that we may be measuring real differences. While we persisted with the hypothesis that Game Changers would see themselves as imaginative and obsessive our presentation of these data to learning and development specialists encouraged us to consider other patterns within the data. 'What does it mean,' they asked, 'if someone does not see themself as obsessive and/or imaginative?'

These questions led to a third phase of research, which consisted of adding data to our sample in order to see if we could we make any meaningful sense of why people score 'low' on imagination and/or obsession.

At this point The GC Index model developed from a factor analysis of data from an initial sample of 1000 people which was subsequently re-examined with a sample of n = 7880.[1]

These statistical analyses revealed an underlying structure within our data with four factors emerging, grouping responses of people together who saw themselves as:

- Imaginative and obsessive
- Imaginative and not obsessive
- Not imaginative but obsessive
- Neither imaginative nor obsessive.

We needed then to explore the question: does this statistical map reflect the real world? Our initial examination of the four factors suggested a tentative description of each factor that gave us a starting point for this enquiry. These were:

- Factor 1: describes people who are imaginative and obsessive who we called 'Game Changers'.
- Factor 2: describes people who are obsessive but not imaginative and who we called 'Polishers'.
- Factor 3: describes people who are imaginative but not obsessive and who we called 'Strategists'.
- Factor 4: describes people who are neither imaginative nor obsessive and who we called 'Implementers'.

---

[1] This was the beginning of The GC Index framework and its technical development, which is described in more detail in 'The GC Index: The Technical Story So Far' which is available via info@thegcindex.com on request.

This representation of the data at this point in our research is presented in Figure 1 below.

The Evolution of The GC Index Proclivities

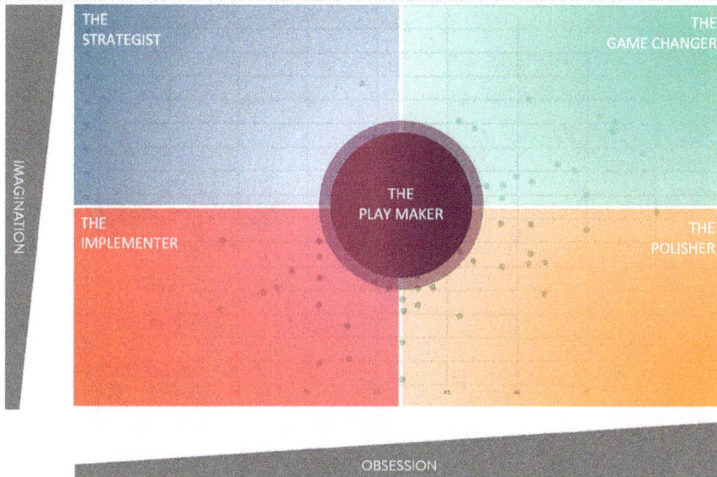

Figure 1: The GC Index model at the end of research phase 2

Phase 3 of our research consisted of series of focus groups which were then used to test the veracity of the model. More specifically we invited groups of people to review their profiles to emerge from the questionnaire; to explore its accuracy and to add comments to the ways in which these constructs were manifest in their day-to-day lives. From these focus groups we learned:

1. There was a high degree of convergence between their profiles and the ways in which they behaved day to day; people saw their profiles as accurate.
2. The ways in which people described the manifestation of the characteristics led to the view that, in broad terms, the instrument was measuring individual differences when it comes to Energy for Impact: the ways which people like to make an impact upon their world. I will discuss this finding in more detail below.
3. That the model was incomplete. A number of individuals whose profiles plotted midway on both dimensions of imagination and

obsession, described the influence of their relationships upon the manifestation of their energy in these areas. Whether or not they were imaginative or obsessive or a mixture of both, they described how these characteristics would be shaped by a need for a degree of harmony in their relationships, a need for cohesion and groups and often manifest as an inclusive and involving approach to working with others. Given their descriptions, we called these individuals 'Play Makers'.

Figure 2 below was the culmination of these early phases of research. We, along with The GC Index community, have continued to develop an understanding of the ways in which the five GC Index proclivities are manifest. This understanding is the focus for the remainder of this book.

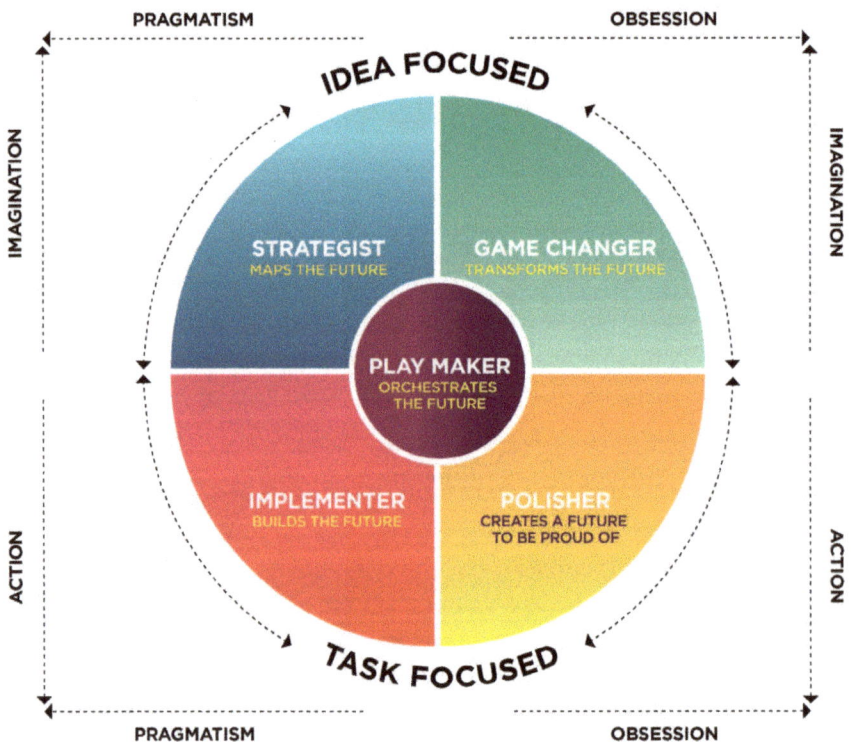

Figure 2: The GC Index model at research phase 3

The framework describes five proclivities that reflect individual differences when it comes to channelling energy, the basis for making an impact.

The GC Index then, measures proclivities not competence.

These five proclivities suggest individual differences in the following ways:

Strategists

- Bring energy to making sense of patterns and trends in events and data, looking for causal relationships.

Game Changers

- Bring energy to new ideas and possibilities, to original thinking.

Play Makers

- Bring energy to seeking consensus in groups that leads to a sense of cohesion.

Implementers

- Bring energy to delivering tangible outcomes.

Polishers

- Bring energy to review, learning, continuous improvement, and the pursuit of excellence.

Energy for Impact

Consistent with the nature of scientific enquiry perhaps, a journey that started with a desire to understand Game Changers led to an understanding of the expression of human energy. As noted in Chapter 1, this interest in human energy is not a new one but this research gave us a new perspective. This evolving view of our understanding is presented in broad summary on page 28.

An Historical Context:
Understanding the Psychology of Energy

PSYCHODYNAMIC ENERGY	ENERGY AS PERSONALITY	ENERGY AS MOTIVATION	ENERGY AS SELF EFFICACY	ENERGY AS WELLBEING	ENERGY FOR IMPACT
The energy of neuroses	Approach and avoidance behaviours	'Surviving and Thriving'	Learning and adaptability	Energy correlates of mental health	Energy for Impact
Freud (1923)	Jung Berne	Maslow Herzberg	Bandura Rotter Dweck	Seligman	The GC Index (2013)

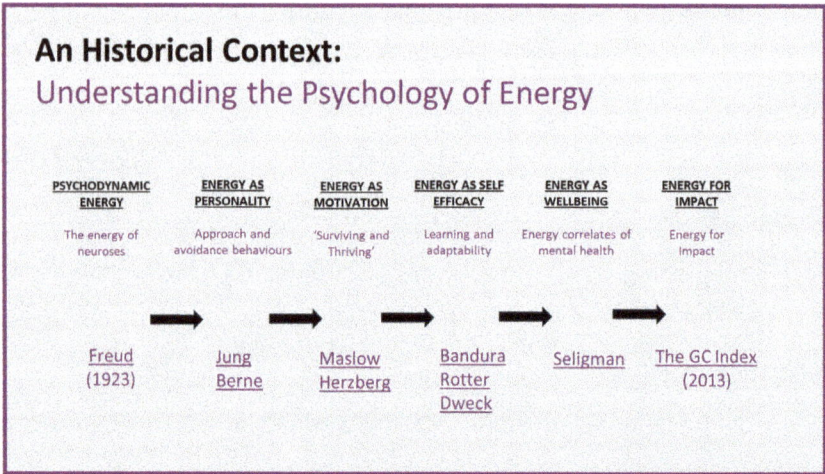

The GC Index framework then measures and describes five proclivities: five different ways in which people are inclined to make an impact and contribution.

These five proclivities are described in more detail below. As you read about the behaviours associated with each proclivity, bear in mind that these behaviours are a product of an individual's assumptions about the world, their values and beliefs, 'internal dialogue' – what people say to themselves about their actions and impact upon the world. See Figure 3 below.

The Strategist - 'The Past Shapes Our Future'

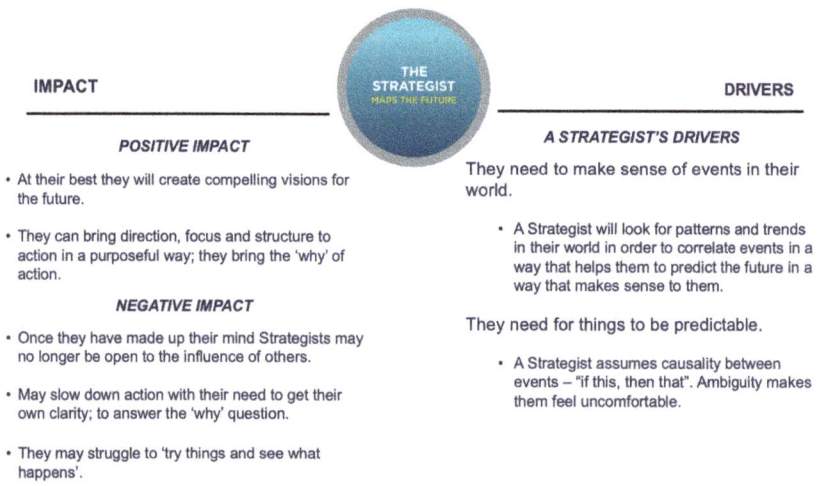

THE STRATEGIST
MAPS THE FUTURE

IMPACT

DRIVERS

POSITIVE IMPACT

- At their best they will create compelling visions for the future.

- They can bring direction, focus and structure to action in a purposeful way; they bring the 'why' of action.

NEGATIVE IMPACT

- Once they have made up their mind Strategists may no longer be open to the influence of others.

- May slow down action with their need to get their own clarity; to answer the 'why' question.

- They may struggle to 'try things and see what happens'.

A STRATEGIST'S DRIVERS

They need to make sense of events in their world.

- A Strategist will look for patterns and trends in their world in order to correlate events in a way that helps them to predict the future in a way that makes sense to them.

They need for things to be predictable.

- A Strategist assumes causality between events – "if this, then that". Ambiguity makes them feel uncomfortable.

The Game Changer - 'Freedom is the Oxygen of Possibilities'

IMPACT   **DRIVERS**

POSITIVE IMPACT

A GAME CHANGER'S DRIVERS

- They are possibility-centred. They see possibilities in ways that others often don't.

- Generate original ideas that can be creative, supporting transformational change.

- They can help organisations to reinvent themselves with their creative ideas.

The need for creative expression; to express their ideas, thoughts and feelings in an uncensored way.

- They see possibilities which might seem unrealistic or intangible to others.

NEGATIVE IMPACT

The freedom to be expressive in a way that can bring about change.

- May see things with such clarity that they can become fixated with turning an idea into a reality.

- Might struggle to accept that an idea may not be relevant or timely.

- They can lose interest and become visibly bored.

- Game changers work best in a 'safe to fail' cultures that encourages experimentation in innovation and creativity.

The Play Maker - 'One for All and All for One'

IMPACT   **DRIVERS**

POSITIVE IMPACT

A PLAY MAKER'S DRIVERS

- Building cohesion in a way that is inclusive and involving.

- Encourage consensus in a way that drives collective performance through collaboration.

- They can challenge colleagues to be at their best and having the 'tough conversations'.

They take responsibility for building cohesion in teams.

- Play Makers have strong values about the importance of the group: inclusivity, collaboration and cohesion.

NEGATIVE IMPACT

Valuing others.

- Sometimes failing to align the needs of the individual with the needs of the group.

- Seeking cohesion even if it is built upon an illusion of harmony rather than healthy conflict.

- Play Makers care that people are valued for the contribution they can make and the contribution that they could make.

The Implementer - 'Just Do It!'

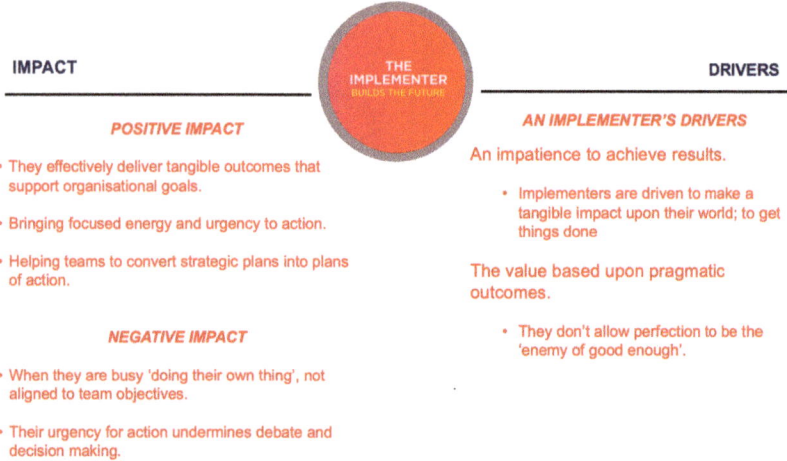

IMPACT

THE
IMPLEMENTER
BUILDS THE FUTURE

DRIVERS

POSITIVE IMPACT

- They effectively deliver tangible outcomes that support organisational goals.

- Bringing focused energy and urgency to action.

- Helping teams to convert strategic plans into plans of action.

NEGATIVE IMPACT

- When they are busy 'doing their own thing', not aligned to team objectives.

- Their urgency for action undermines debate and decision making.

AN IMPLEMENTER'S DRIVERS

An impatience to achieve results.

- Implementers are driven to make a tangible impact upon their world; to get things done

The value based upon pragmatic outcomes.

- They don't allow perfection to be the 'enemy of good enough'.

The Polisher - 'If a Job's Worth Doing, It's Worth Doing Well.

IMPACT

THE
POLISHER
CREATES A FUTURE
TO BE PROUD OF

DRIVERS

POSITIVE IMPACT

- Focusing upon innovation through continuous improvement and the 'pursuit of excellence'.

- They can inspire others to greater things when they set high standards for themselves and others.

- Often they are role models for review, learning and development.

NEGATIVE IMPACT

- May inhibit others with a critical and demanding nature.

- They can allow 'perfection to be the enemy of good enough'.

A POLISHER'S DRIVERS

That things can always be better.

- Polishers struggle to settle for 'good enough' and will set high standards for themselves.

'If I'm going to do this, I'm going to do this brilliantly'.

- Polishers have energy for review, learning, continuous improvement and the pursuit of excellence.

Figure 3: The GC Index proclivities

We have with The GC Index then, a more detailed and refined way of understanding the ways in which human beings channel energy but a way that is consistent with the core principles described above, namely that the human need to be potent – to survive and thrive – takes different and definable forms.

Energy for Impact, learning, motivation and personality

So, The GC Index view of Energy for Impact has grown from, and is consistent with, over a 100 years of enquiry in the world of psychology into the nature of human energy.

If we use this understanding of people as a starting point, it also helps us to link the model to past-thinking on personality and motivation. This relationship is presented in Figure 4 below, reproduced with permission from its creator Shantonu Chundur.

This example will help us to explore the point here: two individuals have similar GC Index profiles; they both have a strong Implementer proclivity: they bring energy and urgency to getting things done in a task-focused way. Can we assume that their Implementer actions reflect the same motives? The diagram below highlights that actions are the product of a complex set of motives, and this is the picture that has emerged from exploring with people the underlying drivers of their GC Index proclivities.

More specifically, our two Implementers may *look alike* and while they will often report some shared drivers, they will also report different ones. So, for example, while Implementers will often report shared values such a belief in 'good enough' delivery or valuing the 'tried and tested' one might report that they are motivated by a strong sense of responsibility, another needs for control or 'personal glory'.

With all five proclivities we can speculate about the underlying drives and motivations. Our interest was in describing behaviours, so The GC Index is presented as an organimetric which measures Energy for Impact. We feel this is a critical difference when comparing to typical psychometrics measuring personality. Moreover, we shall see in coming chapters the relevance to organisations of being able to measure the collective Energy for Impact of teams and groups.

Energy for Impact as a product of motivation, learning and personality*

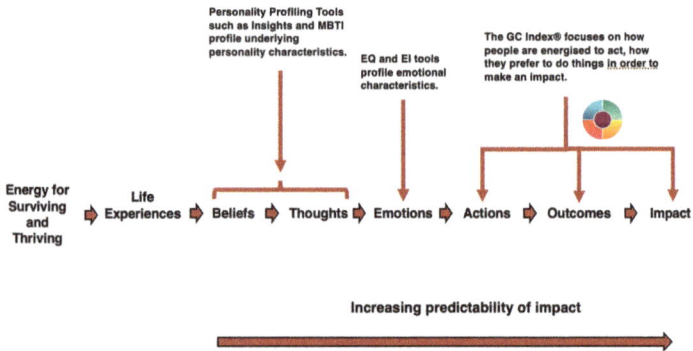

Figure 4: A representation of the relationship of GC Index Energy for Impact with aspects of personality

An example of The GC Index profile

At this point an example profile may help you to crystallise your understanding of The GC Index and give you a more concrete sense of how it works.

The mechanics of a GC Index profile: in the profile for Joanna (below) you will see a score in the 1–10 range (a STEN score) for each of the five proclivities. The scores are based upon a normal distribution of raw scores responses to the 58-item questionnaire and are, largely, independent of each other. This means that there are 80,000+ different combinations of scores.

The scores reflect the strength of that proclivity: a high score suggests a strong Energy for Impact for that proclivity; a low score suggests a weak Energy for Impact for that proclivity. The scores do not reflect competence.

In Figure 5 (opposite) I have presented Joanna's profile. She is in the early stages of her career in a customer-services role in an energy company. She had thrived in her previous role trouble-shooting high-profile customer complaints: she had enjoyed the pace of the action (Implementer) and the contribution that she was making to the company's visionary purpose (Strategist).

She enjoyed the pressure to come up with creative solutions to practical problems (Game Changer/Implementer); she was thriving and seen as a future company leader. In her new role she was struggling. Rather than being 'out and about' fixing problems, she was working on her own in an office, focused upon checking detailed customer-service contracts. The role, which would lend itself to a Polisher proclivity, was depleting her, not feeding her.

Her manager was concerned by her loss of energy for the job but she, and Joanna, used her profile to understand what was happening and find a practical solution. Joanna's story is not an untypical one and demonstrates the utility of The GC Index for understanding Energy for Impact.

In the chapters that follow you will be presented with a number of different GC Index profiles reflecting the many and varied manifestations of human beings' Energy for Impact.

Figure 5: Joanna's GC Index profile

Bibliography and References (Chapters 1 and 2)

Abramson, L. Y., Seligman, M. E. P., and Teasdale, J. D., 'Learned Helplessness in Humans: Critique and Reformulation', *Journal of Abnormal Psychology*, 87, 1978, pp. 49–74

Bandura, A., *Self-Efficacy: The Exercise of Control*, W. H. Freeman, New York, 1997

Bennis, W., and Nanus, B., *Leaders: The Strategies for Taking Charge*, Harper & Row, New York, 1985

Berne, E., 'Ego States in Psychotherapy', *American Journal of Psychotherapy*, 11 (2), 1957, pp. 293–309

Dyson, J., *Against the Odds: An Autobiography*, Orion Business, 1997

Freud, S., 'Beyond the Pleasure Principle', *Standard Edition*, Vol. 18, Hogarth, London, 1920, pp. 7–64

Heider, F., *The Psychology of Interpersonal Relations*, John Wiley & Sons Inc., 1958

Herzberg, F., 'One More Time: How Do You Motivate Employees?', *Harvard Business Review*, 46, 1968, pp. 53–62

Herzberg, F., Mausner, B., and Snyderman, B., *The Motivation to Work,* (2nd edn), John Wiley & Sons Inc., New York, 1959

Jung, C. G., 'On Psychical Energy', A paper in: Jung, C. G., *Contributions to Analytical Psychology*, Harcourt, Brace and Company, 1928

Kelly, G. A., *A Theory of Personality: The Psychology of Personal Constructs*, W. W. Norton, 1955

Kelly, H. H., *Causal Schemata and the Attribution Process*, General Learning Press, Morristown, NJ, 1972

Malle, B. F., 'Attribution Theories: How People Make Sense of Behavior', Chadee, D. (ed.), *Theories in Social Psychology*, Wiley-Blackwell, 2011, pp. 72–95

Maier, S. F., and Seligman, M. E. P., 'Learned Helplessness: Theory and Evidence', *Journal of Experimental Psychology*, 105, 1976, pp. 3–46

Maslow, A. H., 'A Theory of Human Motivation', *Psychological Review*, 50, 1943, pp. 370–396

Mervyn-Smith, J., and Ott, N. O., *Coaching Me Coaching You*, self-published, 2018, The GC Index Ltd, ISBN-13: 978-1-5272-2713-2, ISBN: 1-5272-2713-8

Overmier, J. B., and Seligman, M. E. P., 'Effects of Inescapable Shock Upon Subsequent Escape and Avoidance Learning', *Journal of Comparative and Physiological Psychology*, 63, pp. 23–33, 1967

Rotter, J. B., 'Generalized Expectancies for Internal Versus External Control of Reinforcement', *Psychological Monographs*, 80 (1), 1, 1966

von Brücke, E. W., 'Lectures on Physiology', 1874

Weiner, B., *Theories of Motivation: From Mechanism to Cognition*, General Learning Press, Morristown, NJ, 1972

Weiner, B., *An Attributional Theory of Motivation and Emotion*, Springer Verlag, New York, 1985

Section 2:

'Why do you make me feel like that?': How Energy for Impact Shapes our Relationships

And then there's the expression of energy in our relationships.

We are all likely to have memories of those relationships that 'drain' our energy and, perhaps, wonder why we persist with them. We will also have people in our lives that we seek out, people whose company we enjoy, people who 'give' us energy rather than take it.

What does the expression of energy in relationships tell us about whether or not those relationships will be successful, productive, satisfying, fulfilling?

Chapter 3

Making our Special Relationships Work: How Energy for Impact Shapes Couple Dynamics

Dr John Mervyn-Smith and Teresa Shaw discuss the ways in which an understanding of energy differences can help couples to thrive and grow.

We've come together later in life. We've been 'around the block' in terms of relationships and experienced separation. Separation is always painful; unexpected separation is particularly painful. No one commits to another person expecting things not to work out.

So, when we came together there was, as some would put it, 'baggage' and fear about repeating the patterns and outcomes of the past. Life has taught us some lessons but how could we put them into practice?

We've been influenced by the pioneering work of John Gottman and Nan Silver (1999) and the profound wisdom of Will Schutz (1979).

We've taken on board the prosaic:

> *'You know you are in love when the two of you can go grocery shopping together.'*
>
> Woody Harrelson

And the poetic:

> *'Let there be spaces in your togetherness,*
> *And let the winds of the heavens dance between you.*
> *Love one another, but not make a bond of love:*
> *Let it be rather a moving sea between the shores of your souls.*
>
> Kahlil Gibran, The Prophet

But we needed a way to share and understand our past, to see and value each other: our differences and our uniqueness; we wanted to feel a sense of security in knowing each other and how to grow together.

We know from experience that relationships are dynamic; they must be because people change. To paraphrase Muhammad Ali:

> *A person who views the world the same at 50 as they did at 20 has wasted 30 years of their life'.*

Influenced by our own experiences and the work of couple experts such as John Gottman and Nan Silver (1999) and Will Schutz (1979) we knew that, in the simplest of terms, all relationships have their points of attraction and connection, and all relationships have their potential derailers.

So how could we manage the challenge of growing together: recognising and building upon our points of connection and recognising and managing our potential derailers?

This is where The GC Index has proved helpful. It has given us a framework for thinking about our relationship, for stepping back when things feel fragile, for gaining understanding, learning and adapting to each other.

Here's the story so far

Here's a bit about Teresa

> *'I grew up as one of four daughters who were all quite close in age. We were encouraged by our mother to "get along", to "play nicely". I value collaboration, working with others to get things done. I will often, at home and work encourage people to find agreement rather than difference; I'm not good at conflict. So, I wasn't at all surprised by my GC Index profile. (See Fig. 1 below.)*

> *'My life has been quite eventful, and I feel that I have needed to be adaptable, to "fit in" and to be useful. So, when the situation requires it, I can "get the chores done" in an Implementer way that keeps life ticking over; I quite enjoy being busy in this way.*

And I also know that I can be the "picky Polisher". As a musician, at work and home, I value precision: taking care to hit the right notes!

'My turbulent early life also comes through in my need to think ahead (Strategist) and plan for the future (Strategist/Implementer). I'm at an age where I don't want to waste time.'

Fig. 1: Teresa's GC Index profile

Here's a bit about John

'My mother described me as a "dreamer". I've always felt comfortable in the world of ideas and possibilities and most comfortable when I was around people who also wanted to explore "what might be" rather than "what is".

'My comfort with dreaming, I'm sure, played a part in my being asked to leave school at the age of 17. Since then, my dreaming has been manifest as a life of entrepreneurial endeavours: I have been involved in eight start-up businesses and am just about to embark upon my ninth.

'As a clinical psychologist I worked with couples seeking to develop their relationships.

'My GC Index profile, presented below, captures my need to dream about possibilities – Game Changer – and, ideally, with others.'

Fig. 2: John's GC Index profile

Recognising and managing potential derailers

Echoes from the past

Maybe because of our past, our early preoccupations were with making the relationship work. There were so many positive points of connection we were concerned to avoid the 'banana skins'; the derailers.

Anyone who has had more than one serious relationship will recognise the potential for the past to influence the present. Sometimes we see it coming, we anticipate its impact upon us and try to manage it. Sometimes the past ambushes us, the 'throw-away' comment that we weren't expecting that can feel like a criticism that produces a visceral response in us and, often, an unhelpful emotional discharge.

These 'echoes from the past' can be bewildering for couples – 'where did that come from?' – and, potentially, derail a relationship before it really has time to establish itself.

Conflict is inevitable in all relationships and couples need to find a way through these conflicts if their relationship is to survive and thrive. If couples struggle with this then the relationship risks breaking down and ending in separation or in living 'parallel lives'.

John Gottman and Nan Silver (1999), experts in relationships and communication, have highlighted the importance, in successful relationships, of being open to each other's influence.

One example of their research shows that when men are not ready to accept influence from their partners, there is an 81% chance that the relationship won't last.

Consistent with this, Will Schutz (1979) took the view that a relationship cannot exist unless the individuals in it are open to each other's influence. In effect the view was that a relationship is defined by influence; the preparedness to be influenced by someone *is* the relationship.

If we are open to our partner's influence then we are *really* listening to them, taking them seriously and respecting their views.

Influence, of course, is the product of potential conflict or difference. So, managing conflict is a key skill for a successful relationship.

This becomes particularly difficult when conflict is produced by, or distorted by, the events of the past. If, for example, our experience of the past is that we haven't felt 'seen' or listened to, then we will be hypersensitive to similar events in the present, exaggerating the potential for conflict and potentially misinterpreting an innocent remark or action.

Understanding conflict with The GC Index

There are some couples who thrive on conflict, or so it would appear. Couples who seem to get 'closer' through conflict and robust exchanges that 'clear the air'.

We hate conflict. We are two Play Makers. We value harmony and cohesion in our relationships. We both fear that conflict is more likely to destroy than bring us together and we have both previously been on the receiving end of some very unhelpful behaviours. As such, neither of us have really developed that sophisticated skill set that we have seen in some Play Makers that leads to healthy negotiation of conflict; and all healthy relationships are a negotiation.

And, of course, our history reinforced the narrative that unresolved conflict destroys relationships and breeds resentment. Whether manifest as a 'shouting match' or withdrawal, we both felt that conflict could drain our energy.

For us then, we saw our lack of comfort with conflict as a potential derailer. Could we go through life together avoiding the arguments, the cross words, the irritations?

An exploration of our GC Index profiles helped us to anticipate conflict, to understand it and to step back from it in a more detached way that took some of the potential emotional heat and misunderstanding from our exchanges; it helped us to *recognise and manage the derailers.* It also helped us to *accentuate the positive.* Here's what we have learned so far:

Our Game Changer energy

Recognising and managing the potential derailers

Our Game Changer scores are similar and a point of connection as we'll note below. But we quickly recognised its potential as a derailer: as noted above, John can be a 'dreamer'; he can 'drift off' like a Banksy balloon, consumed by his own thoughts. For Teresa, the distance that this created triggered historic feelings to do with a loss of closeness and intimacy. John had to recognise this and learn new behaviours and Teresa had to understand that he was still 'with her' even when he seemed to her to have 'disappeared'. We have learned to recognise these moments, hold them if needed, not judge them and never let them fester.

Accentuate the positive

Consistent with our GC Index profiles, we can both get excited about ideas and possibilities and can generate a lot of energy together when we find something that gets our creative juices jointly flowing. John has learned that it is safe to have an idea that won't necessarily come to fruition; Teresa, naturally, embraces ideas without a fixed expectation that they must then happen. Sometimes when our ideas converge they take us on an adventure that energises us both; given her Game Changer/Implementer energy, Teresa enjoys turning ideas into a reality and John enjoys polishing those ideas, tweaking and fine tuning them.

Our Polisher energy

Recognising and managing the potential derailers

Polishers care about doing things properly, but not necessarily the same things. Thankfully, we both care about the tidiness of our physical environment and how we stack the dishwasher! But our moderate Polisher energy – scores of 6 – is consistent with the fact that we don't obsess over things in our relationship and that works well for us.

However, we can both be critical and this, typically, reflects the values we have as Play Makers: we care about courtesy and treating people with respect. For a couple that values harmony, these moments of discord, when we feel upset by other's behaviour, can be very unsettling and we both feel responsible for each other at those times wanting to return to some level of equanimity.

We have found the work of Eric Berne (1964) helpful at these times. Berne built upon Freud's Id, Ego and Superego structure of human psychology and gave us the ego states of Parent, Adult and Child. This model is the basis for Transactional Analysis, a way of understanding and developing the quality of human interactions. The view is that human beings spend their waking lives, to varying degrees, in one of these ego states.

A subset of 'Parent' is 'Critical Parent', that ego-state that, as the names suggests, is manifest as criticism, that our experience of the world does not map onto the ideals that we have in our heads: that people have let us down, have not lived up to our expectations in some way.

We've learned to recognise that this mismatch is usually associated with lots of 'shoulds' and 'shouldn'ts' in our conversation. We have learned to give each other space to offload at such times and, when done, try to gain some perspective by reviewing and challenging our expectations.

Any ongoing and distorted perspective is often at the heart of emotional distress and a fragile sense of well-being.

Accentuate the positive

Our physical surroundings are very important to both of us. Our Play Maker need for harmony also comes through in a need for a harmonious physical environment; we don't like clutter but we do like eclectic and beautiful things. We get great joy from finding little treasures together on our travels.

A decluttered home helps the two of us to have quality time together, time to connect without the distraction of jobs to do!

Our Implementer energy

Recognising and managing the potential derailers

Implementers have energy for getting things done. Teresa's energy in this regard is stronger than John's. Implementer energy lends itself, day to day, to doing the washing-up and putting out the rubbish; those tasks that must be done to make life bearable. Reinforced by her one-time life as a single mum, Teresa's Implementer energy would play out as getting the chores done with some impatience and before John. We both recognised that this imbalance about the seemingly little things, could, over time, prove corrosive; one feeling resentful, the other feeling guilty. With this understanding, it proved to be an easy fix.

Accentuate the positive

Teresa's need for a 'to do' list also includes planning events and filling the diary for some time ahead. This is consistent with her Strategist /Implementer energy and given John's more 'go with the flow' Strategist/Implementer profile, could have created some tensions for us but we have managed to find a happy and energising balance between being planful and spontaneous.

John recognises Teresa's difficulty with 'switching off', being busy to the point of exhaustion. Together they have worked on ways – 'let's go for a walk' – to get her to 'just stop' and 'smell the roses'.

Our Play Maker energy

Our Play Maker energy shapes all our interactions with each other and with our close friends. We worked at staying open to how this works positively for as well as how it could be a derailer.

Recognising and managing the potential derailers

As Play Makers we put a lot of energy into our relationships; we like to give. Within our families we are seen as people who are 'always there for people'.

In any social situation we can feel responsible to make everyone feel comfortable and involved: 'if you're okay, I'm okay'.

This giving out can be draining for both of us and lead to energy dips. Early on in our relationship we discovered the potential for a 'dip' in energy from one of us to negatively influence the other – a sort of 'energy-matching' effect. Teresa had a tendency to think that she must have done something wrong when John 'dipped' and consequently started to feel low and ineffective herself. As a consequence, John would feel responsible to make sure that Teresa was okay. This could quickly become a vicious circle with neither having the emotional 'bandwidth' to pull the other from the dip.

This came to a head during an extended holiday when a frank discussion and an examination of our profiles gave us a very big 'aha' moment.

We both realised that our accommodating natures could have an adverse effect upon our relationship: we would give so much to others that, on occasions, we would have nothing left to give to each other.

As you might guess, we're not very good at saying 'no' and looking after ourselves and our relationship. But we are trying and getting better, with each other's support, at more effectively managing those situations that could leave us feeling depleted.

Accentuate the positive

Not saying 'no' to people could aften leave us feeling compromised, that we were putting others before our own needs and our relationship. This pattern, at an extreme, can lead to feelings of resentment.

We have also worked on helping each other to say 'no', given that we both hate to feel that we are letting people down. We both enjoy the company of others and hosting events, but we need to make sure that we 'take care' of each other as well.

References

Berne, E., 1964, *Games People Play: The Psychology of Human Relationships*, Grove Press, New York, ISBN 0-14-002768-8

Freud, S., 1961, *Beyond the Pleasure Principle (The Standard Edition)*, Strachey, James (translator), Liveright Publishing Corporation, New York

Gottman, J. M., and Silver, N., 1999, *The Seven Principles for Making Marriage Work* (1st ed.), Crown Publishers, New York

Schutz, W., 1979, *Profound Simplicity,* Bantam, New York

Chapter 4

How Differences in Energy for Impact Shape Family Dynamics

Jon Crocker is an experienced GCologist and family coach. His chapter tells the inspiring story of a family struggling with difficult dynamics who found a way to cope with the help of The GC Index.

Family units, much like business units, come in a wide variety of formats. From small start-ups created in a bedroom to internationally recognised legacies and everywhere in between. There's no guarantee of success and much depends on the people and culture.

Both families and businesses operate at their best when they have shared goals and values, effective communication and great leadership. In difficult times, they need to draw on their adaptability and resilience, while always remaining mindful of opportunities for growth and development of each member. Talent acquisition and retention can be challenging too, but for those that stay the course and remain fresh and alert to the possibilities, the rewards are well worth the effort.

Every family is a microcosm of diverse personalities, aspirations, and challenges. These can include navigating the complexities of academic struggles, parental stress, financial challenges, and myriad decisions that shape their lives together.

Equipped with the knowledge gained from The GC Index and Young People Index (YPI), families can better chart a course towards their desired destination. This is not a one-size-fits-all approach; instead, it is a means to explore the unique DNA of a family, recognising that each one has potential. It's about self-awareness, collective understanding, and then using that information meaningfully.

To illustrate this approach, what follows is an example case study.

The family

The family is made up of three people: Emma (Mum), Tom (Dad) and Sam (Son).

Emma and Tom are separated but maintain a good relationship.

Emma works part-time as an office manager, while Tom is self-employed working in project management.

Sam did not fare well in education and is 'NEET' – not in education, employment or training. He lives with his mum, and they tend to argue frequently. Sam was 17, nearly 18 years old at the time of writing.

The context

Emma found out about the YPI through a friend and got in touch. She explained her concerns about her son and her worries that he had already ruined his chances because of his educational background and lack of qualifications.

The two of them were arguing constantly and Emma was frustrated that despite the fact she was giving him job vacancy details daily, Sam was showing no interest in applying for them.

Emma said she wanted Sam to take the YPI in the hope that it would help him to find employment.

I explained that this wasn't a career search tool but rather a means to gain self-awareness and the Energy for Impact Sam might have within the broader context of work. The importance of her profile along with Tom's was also discussed as part of the process as it was agreed that this would provide more meaningful insights into the existing situation and a greater chance of finding solutions.

The process

All family members were sent links to complete a set of questions that would generate their individual profiles. These would show their Energy for Impact using the five proclivities of Game Changer, Strategist, Implementer, Polisher and Play Maker.

Sam completed these questions for The Young People Index, while his parents did so for The GC Index and then individual online meetings were set up to walk them through the results.

The format for each of these one-to-one discussions was broadly the same, but it differed from the more traditional business focus. It was important to centre on the family and see the areas of leadership, teamwork, etc. in that context.

In all these meetings, Sam and his parents began by talking about their own experience with education, what that meant to them and then about their hopes and goals for the future.

Following on from this, each proclivity was explained in further detail with a particular focus on values and beliefs, plus what most and least energises each one. See table below:

	Values	+ Energy	- Energy
Game Changer	Rules are there to be questioned and challenged	Having the freedom to be creative People who give me the space to 'free associate' When others share my enthusiasm for possibilities	Desire for creative expression is thwarted Feeling constrained by arbitrary rules People don't see what I see

Strategist	It's possible to make sense of events	I can make sense of my world and see what to do Having freedom to bring structure to my work and life Having a clear sense of purpose and direction	Feeling bewildered and unable to make sense of things Not having time to think Having to do things for no purpose
Implementer	Hard work is rewarded	Having clear expectations and objectives Feeling they have the skills to deliver Having a reputation for getting things done	A lack of clarity about what is expected Too much talking and not enough action Feeling unable to get on with things
Polisher	If a job is worth doing, it's worth doing properly	A feeling of making progress, learning and developing Able to take pride in what they are achieving Know they are delivering to the standard they expect of themselves	Unable to do something properly Feeling that their standards are compromised Others don't share their high standards
Play Maker	Good relationships are the basis for getting needs met	Feeling a part of a cohesive team, working towards shared objectives When feeling part of something bigger than themselves	Not feeling heard and are not able to influence Others just want to do their own things or feel they can't express their own views and opinions

While digesting this information, each family member was asked to note down their predicted score between 1 and 10 for the five proclivities. This wasn't to test them but to keep Sam engaged and actively listening. It also provided an opportunity for them all to check their understanding of the proclivities and to see how well they felt they knew themselves.

At that point, there was the 'big reveal' allowing each person to see their profile proclivity scores and give their initial reaction. From there, each proclivity was looked at in more detail with Sam, Emma and Tom all given time to talk about their scores, how they felt about them and how accurate they judged them to be. They were asked to give real-life examples for each proclivity that backed up their views and/or scores.

Finally, they were asked what the 'so what' question in terms of how this new-found self-knowledge might be used by them and what the impact could be on themselves and the rest of the family. Only their personal profiles were discussed, without reference to the others, with an agreement to meet again together to consider the collective findings.

Only when they met together were the profiles revealed as a whole, and this prompted some lively discussions and further examples that supported the different proclivity scores. The session ended with the family agreeing some actions points that they felt were realistic and would improve their situation.

It was a positive experience for everyone that produced meaningful outcomes, and I will now look at each session in greater depth.

Individual profiles and discussions

Sam

Sam started by opening up about his time at school and it hadn't been a positive period in his life. Intelligent and articulate, he explained how he had struggled to stay silent and compliant in the classroom, which had resulted in clashes with his teachers. What he perceived as following petty rules wasn't something he had coped well with, and his questioning nature had been viewed as troublemaking.

Schools, in my experience, may pay lip service to individuality but, generally, seek compliance and take the view of 'this is how we do things'. They are certainly not looking for students to offer alternatives or challenge the wisdom of existing authority.

The relationship Sam had with his teachers was gradually eroded, starting with reprimands, then being sent out of class. The situation escalated from there to suspension, expulsion and a transfer to a local pupil referral unit.

Sam said he had, in a strange way, enjoyed his time at the PRU as at least the staff took time to listen to him and there was more opportunity to express himself. However, the lack of academic rigour and lower expectations had a significant impact, and he left with no qualifications.

It wasn't that he didn't want to learn, it was the environment and constraints that he struggled with, and he felt that given his time again, the outcome would still be the same. He didn't seem to regret what had happened as he felt it was largely out of his control to conform.

Sam then went on to talk about his plans and his parents. He was determined to work for himself and by himself. He mentioned having social anxiety which hadn't been diagnosed and the thought of meeting new people frequently made him physically ill beforehand.

He had a couple of friends that he played video games with and watched football, but his social circle was extremely limited.

He acknowledged that he often argued with his mum but only saw things from his own perspective. He complained that all she wanted him to do was get a job and any job would do. Every day she would put job vacancy details in front of him, telling him he should apply, and they didn't interest him.

He said he had loads of ideas for a business which he told her about, but she never listened to him, or if she did, it was only to point out the reasons why something wouldn't work and that made him angry.

When Sam listened to the characteristics of the different YPI (Young People Index) proclivities, he was highly engaged and commented on the fact that he really hoped he was a Game Changer and when he predicted his scores, he gave high scores for Game Changer and Polisher energy. He also awarded himself low marks for Implementer and Play Maker.

This is Sam's profile below.

It was then time to reveal his profile …

He was visibly delighted by his score of 10 for Game Changer and, in fact, his predictions had been very accurate, suggesting a high degree of self-awareness.

The initial focus was on this proclivity and that of the Polisher. Sam cited his ability to come up with new ideas and claimed that when he did something that interested him, he was obsessed with getting it absolutely perfect, to the point that it would even keep him awake at night.

He spoke about the fact that while his mum instantly rejected his ideas, his dad, meanwhile, was always receptive to them, offering his thoughts and suggestions. Sam felt that he had big dreams that he would make a reality, and nothing was going to force him down an unwanted route.

When considering his lower proclivity scores, Sam readily accepted them as an accurate reflection. He admitted that he wasn't the best at implementing and getting things done. He often found it hard to stick to a to-do list and admitted that many of his ideas never developed any further than the concept stage.

For the Play Maker, Sam said he found the thought of needing to work with other people draining, in particular, if they were needy and constantly needed support. He felt he could work with others who shared his sense of independence and were self-sufficient people.

However, as the discussions continued, Sam did express an understanding that even if he had his own business, he could benefit from having the support or expertise of others. He recognised that strong Implementers and Play Makers might help fill gaps and even improve his chances of success with a project. He wasn't totally convinced how easily he might work with these people, but he did see that there could be advantages.

On being asked what learning about his profile might mean for him and how he could use this information, his first reaction was that he felt his Game Changer vindicated his belief in being a successful entrepreneur and that would be enough to convince his mum. He said he knew his lower proclivity scores might need to be addressed but he felt that was something he could solve at a later date.

He was asked not to disclose his profile to either parent as there would be a group discussion in the near future which he agreed to, but confessed that he was eager to show his scores to his mum. This was expressed in a somewhat combative way, as if the goal was to prove her wrong in her attempts to find him a job. This seemed to come out of frustration more than anything else, with Sam determined to be financially independent on his terms.

The whole session was a positive experience, with Sam being eloquent and at times very witty. He held quite strong views about himself and about how he saw his life and work unfolding. His focus was very much on his high-energy proclivities, with relatively little importance attached to the lower ones.

It was then time to meet his mum.

Emma

Mum initially said she had enjoyed school and then changed that to: 'School wasn't there to be enjoyed. All you had to do was follow the rules, keep your head down, do the work and pass your exams.'

That was exactly what she had done, and it was beyond her comprehension that Sam had failed so spectacularly to do the same. She admitted that there was a mixture of anger, shame and concern.

Some of her anger was towards Sam in that she felt he could have been more flexible at school and 'bitten his tongue', but it was also directed at the education system that she perceived as letting him down, and there had been no support unless her son had been willing to comply which, after all, had been the root of the problem.

She said she was embarrassed to tell people that Sam had failed his exams and was now sitting at home every day without any signs of progress. Her main worry was that he had destroyed his life already.

The constant arguments were draining her energy and Emma explained that the constant bombardment of ideas from Sam exhausted her. She was tired of hearing yet another business plan that ended up going nowhere, plus she was taking the time to find him jobs to apply for that might not be ideal but would at least provide him with experience and some income.

When asked about Sam's relationship with his dad, Emma said that it was much better and they rarely if ever argued. She put this down to three main factors: the first being that Tom was happy to listen to Sam's ideas and plans much more than she was. The second was that her ex-husband was less confrontational, admitting that Sam and she were more volatile, and things often escalated quickly. The final point was that it was much easier for Tom as he lived some distance away from them and, therefore, didn't have to face the issues on a constant basis.

This is Emma's GC Index profile:

As Emma learned about the different proclivities, she was very clear that she saw herself as an Implementer and definitely not a Game Changer. However, she also gave herself a high score for Play Maker.

Upon seeing her profile, she wasn't surprised by her maximum score as an Implementer nor her very low Game Changer score. She commented that she had to implement, or nothing would ever get done, with little patience for sitting around talking when it was more important to get on with things.

The Play Maker score was a surprise though as Emma felt that she was good at bringing people together and making sure they did what they needed to.

She acknowledged the Game Changer score was probably accurate, saying that she didn't see herself as an 'ideas person', but rather as the one who could be relied on to make things happen.

Although not pleased by her Play Maker score, she suggested that perhaps she tended to lead through pushing in a certain direction, but she saw that as the only way to change the current situation.

When asked what she would take away from the session, Emma said that the data had reinforced her belief that nothing ever got done without her driving the agenda and that was a source of her frustration and exhaustion.

She wanted to know Sam's scores but agreed to wait until everyone met together. Her main desired outcome wasn't about her, but about Sam. Her priority was that this was going to help Sam understand the types of job that he would be good at, and this would result in him applying for them.

Tom

Tom recalled not enjoying school for many of the same reasons Sam had given. He hadn't appreciated the teacher-student relationship and the rules that often seemed to be applied without reason. While he had found learning easy, he had gradually grown more and more frustrated by the system, eventually being expelled.

The difference between Tom and his son though, was that he had taken his exams and had some qualifications, although, like the rest of the family he had not gone to university. However, he had over the years, and through numerous career pathways, established himself in project management and said he enjoyed the freedom self-employment provided him.

He touched on the tensions between Emma and Tom, saying they could both be as bad as each other at times, refusing to back down and determined to win every battle. He didn't like seeing it and it worried him that so much pressure was put on his ex-wife, saying he felt she coped much better than he felt he would if the roles were reversed.

As for Sam, he was clearly less concerned, believing that Sam needed time to work out what he wanted, and he actively enjoyed hearing about his business ideas. This was both because he found them interesting, but also because it ensured they maintained a relationship that Tom was anxious to keep given the geographical distance between them.

This is Tom's GC Index profile:

STRATEGIST MAPS THE FUTURE	POLISHER CREATES A FUTURE TO BE PROUD OF	PLAY MAKER ORCHESTRATES THE FUTURE	IMPLEMENTER BUILDS THE FUTURE	GAME CHANGER TRANSFORMS THE FUTURE
6		7		6
5				4

Tom predicted high scores for Game Changer and Play Maker, with a low score for Polisher. When his profile was revealed to him, he was clearly expecting a higher Game Changer score but felt that the overall scores were very accurate.

He also declared that Sam was a Game Changer and Emma an Implementer, but understood that he would find out in the imminent group meeting.

Tom was inclined to start relating the proclivities to his work environment, but in general the focus remained on his family unit.

He saw the Play Maker role as being that of a peacekeeper and commented on the fact that he should probably try and do this more.

His views on how this information might inform his next steps were that he felt it reflected his balanced approach to life and he also said that it was probably true that he was capable in many areas but not necessarily an expert in any of them. He saw this as both a strength and a weakness, saying that until he knew Emma and Sam's scores, he couldn't really comment further.

Like Emma, he was less interested in his own profile and more curious about his son's. For both parents the focus was on Sam and the clear desire to see him 'find his way'. They wanted him to be happy and they wanted him to find his career path. Emma and Tom also wanted the arguing to stop and a de-escalation of the tension that was becoming overwhelming for all of them.

Tom wasn't sure what part he could play in this beyond what he was already doing, but did repeatedly say that Emma was in a difficult position, which he felt was unsustainable. He did feel guilty that she bore the brunt of the pressure while he seemed to get all the 'good bits'.

The family meeting

When the family met together, this was the first time they would see each other's profiles and it was clear they were looking forward to that. The session began with a recap of the five proclivities and, without prompting, the family began to predict the other members' scores.

I have presented their profiles below.

STRATEGIST
MAPS
THE FUTURE

POLISHER
CREATES A FUTURE
TO BE PROUD OF

PLAY MAKER
ORCHESTRATES
THE FUTURE

IMPLEMENTER
BUILDS
THE FUTURE

GAME CHANGER
TRANSFORMS
THE FUTURE

MUM

DAD

SAM

The family was asked to take a couple of minutes to digest the information and then be ready to give their thoughts on what they saw.

All of them, quite understandably, honed-in on Sam and Emma's highest scores and an 'aha' moment of how these could be a source of their ongoing conflicts. It was immediately clear to all three that this was important, with two of them full of ideas and the other eager for action. This was a significant moment as they discussed the fact that this, in itself, might explain a great deal. Emma and her son acknowledged that they approached things from a different perspective and simply seeing that visually was illuminating for them.

The focus remained on them, with the identical Play Maker score, suggesting neither of them placed cohesion or collaboration high on their agendas, with both confessing that they liked things done their way or, as they saw it, the 'right' way. Sam and his mum agreed that they didn't back away from an argument and were always willing to 'fight their corner'.

Sam's Polisher score was a surprise to his mum at first but when scrutinised more thoroughly, everybody concurred that when something mattered to him (and it had to matter), then he was obsessed with getting things right and wouldn't rest until he was satisfied. In fact, Emma mentioned that when she thought about it, she was often impressed by his tenacity and eye for detail when she would have accepted 'good enough' long before.

The entire family felt that Tom's profile was accurate, picking out his Play Maker score in comparison to theirs. They all agreed that this was his main role and he was the one who tried to bring everyone together, although they also said that sometimes he was too quick to avoid any conflict when perhaps issues needed to be out in the open and dealt with.

The question was then posed that while seeing each other's profiles was interesting, what could they now do with this information and the suggestions were free-flowing and constructive.

Between them they agreed that things could not continue as they were, and changes needed to be made. The first step was to use Tom as a filter for Sam's ideas and relieve the pressure on Emma: Tom would be the 'sounding board' for Sam's creativity and together they would use their strategic proclivities to identify an idea that had the greatest probability of success.

This would be the one presented to Emma who avoided being bombarded with concepts and could instead focus on one idea with her son. For her part, Emma agreed to support Sam by helping him formulate an action plan with SMART objectives and provide him with a form of accountability so that he could keep on track and maintain his focus.

Sam needed to agree to this and also to the fact that his mum could still give him jobs to apply for, but she would consider the relevance more. There was a feeling that Sam's agreement to this was more symbolic than sincere, but it was at least something.

Tom's role was to take the pressure off Emma while allowing Sam to express himself and then continue to support both of them as needed.

Everyone agreed that this was a workable plan, as long as they all took a step back when their strong proclivities were 'kicking in' and threatening to destabilise the process. Emma said that while she was happy to try this, there had to be a deadline for Sam to either start a viable business or find a job. No deadline was agreed but a broad consensus that it was fair.

To sum up, everyone in the family found it fascinating and constructive to learn more about themselves and the others. They felt it was time, money and effort well invested and that it had helped them form a plan to improve relationships and give Sam some clarity.

Sam has started a website design business that is yet to be financially viable. Importantly though, he has enrolled on an evening course to boost his knowledge and skills which for him is a huge leap – choosing to join some formal education and with complete strangers.

Emma is supporting him and happy that he is gaining skills that might improve his future employability, while Tom is playing a more active role, reducing Emma's tasks and helping Sam with his venture.

Now we have looked at Sam, Emma and Tom, we can explore how The GC Index and Young People Index can be applied to different scenarios.

The initial step always involves discovering the unique profiles of each family member. Whether it be the introspective teenager or the busy parent, these indices offer a language and visually accessible framework to describe each person: how people are similar and how they are different. This awareness, when combined with the collective data showing family dynamics (as demonstrated with Sam and his parents), can influence daily decisions, communication, and the approach to challenges.

Topics to consider include

- Impact on daily Interactions and family culture.
- Flexibility, adaptability, and celebration of diversity.
- Navigating challenges and managing change and resilience.
- Academic struggles and educational pathways.
- Career decisions and transitions aligned with passion/energy.
- Financial stress and lifestyle planning.

- Relationship dynamics and communication styles.
- Clash of proclivities and conflict resolution.
- Embracing emotional and energy contagion.

Chapter 5

The Entrepreneurial Couple

Life changes always put us under pressure to adapt and they test the resilience of our relationships. This chapter follows John and Natalie Franklin-Hackett's inspirational journey from despair to joy as they went through a dramatic transition in their lives.

Do opposites attract? And what happens when a relationship is tested? How is energy lost during a period of challenge and regained from a major life change that can result? And how can couples work together as a successful team to navigate all this?

Relationships are interesting things. It's said that 'opposites attract', and my wife and I have always been opposites. While I enjoy setting 'big fat hairy goals' and making sense of how to achieve them, she enjoys getting tasks done. She lives for tangible achievement, I live for ideas and, dare I admit, more than a touch of 'navel-gazing'.

Were you to watch each of us work, isolate us from one another and see how we prefer to do things, I'd be willing to bet that you'd have little difficulty identifying that we go about our business in totally different ways.

This difference in the ways in which we channel our energy is reflected in our GC Index profiles (see Figs. 1 and 2 below).

Natalie has a high-energy Implementer profile, with a touch of Polisher energy in the mix. My profile features a healthy dose of Game Changer energy, followed by Strategist and Polisher energy. I share next to nothing of Natalie's Implementer energy, and she shares little of my Game Changer proclivity.

Fig. 1: Natalie's GC Index profile

Fig. 2: John's GC Index profile

In terms of our energy to make an impact, we are truly opposites.

At home, our differing energies play out clearly and in ways consistent with our GC Index profiles. I am often the one who comes up with ideas about projects we could carry out in the house, places to visit or life goals to achieve. Natalie is usually the one who takes the initiative to get things done. While I can regularly be found thinking, dreaming and analysing, she is usually found attending to tasks, ticking things off lists and working out what to do next.

You may think after reading this that I do the thinking and Natalie does the doing. And to some extent, this is true. In reality though, there is rather more nuance than that. There are times when Natalie comes up with interesting, albeit practical, ideas, or is more inclined to take a risk than I am. Conversely, there are occasions where I can be very task-focused. What seems to be true, though, is that we largely 'stay in our lanes' and we've learned over time to give each other the space to express our energies and stay true to what motivates us.

This is not to say that we don't clash. While we have been lucky to share a harmonious relationship, there are times when, inevitably, we become frustrated with each other. What's interesting is that conflict often arises when our differing energies are not aligned towards the same purpose or motivation. In these situations, we can become irritated with each other: Natalie may tire of my 'big picture' focus or tendency to over-analyse, while I may become intolerant of her relentless task focus. My willingness to hold back from doing something while I try to establish whether acting on it makes sense in the bigger picture can be highly frustrating to Natalie. Her whirlwind of implementing and dislike of standing back and considering the 'why', 'what' and 'how' can exhaust me when I don't see a strong 'why' behind the effort.

It would be tempting in these situations to point the finger at who is right and who is wrong. But it turns out that most of the time we're both right. In reality, the problem to be solved is usually whose energies will make the most useful impact at a specific time.

Fortunately, in most cases, our understanding of each other's energies allows us to identify the source of conflict and find a suitable resolution. Commonly, all it takes is for us to remind ourselves to give each other space and respect. I sometimes think that getting the best balance in this way is one of the ongoing challenges and successes of our relationship.

To illustrate how this energy dynamic has played out, I'd like to tell you about one of the biggest challenges in our relationship and how our GC Index profiles helped us to overcome it. And it's all about purpose and meaning in life, via a huge change in career and lifestyle.

As in most areas of life, our energies were strongly reflected in our earlier career choices, as well as our satisfaction with them. In fact, in this respect we were entirely different from each other.

Natalie knew what she wanted to do from her early teens. She wanted to be a teacher.

This she achieved immediately after leaving university, following which she 'climbed the ranks' to become an assistant head teacher in a very large and challenging inner-city primary school. Her career was a great match for her energies. Teaching is all about tasks: delivering learning, marking work, planning lessons. She loved the clarity of purpose that came from carrying out a clearly defined role. She was fortunate to work with head teachers who set clear priorities, which made it simple for her to understand what she had to achieve, what success looked like and when she'd achieved it.

She spent her entire career in one school, which she loved, as it gave her a clear sense of what she needed to do to make a difference. She knew the children, understood their needs and how best to help them learn. She could see the difference she made on a daily basis and this then fuelled her energies to keep going, keep implementing and stay energised.

I've met very few people who truly love their work and who get up each day full of enthusiasm for what they're about to spend the day doing. Natalie was one of these people. She truly loved her job. It's true to say that in some respects, her job was her life.

And for the best part of 18 years, the alignment between her Implementer/Polisher energies and her career couldn't have been better.

My career path was less straightforward and comparatively chaotic. On leaving university, I felt a desire to explore entrepreneurial ideas, do something creative, find a direction through experimentation. Perhaps, in keeping with many others, that's not what I ended up doing.

For one reason or another, I found myself working as a project administrator at a small charity and not having a particularly fulfilling time doing it. I had the skills required but I struggled to find the energy to stay on top of administrative tasks, often leaving things incomplete until the last moment and then being dissatisfied with the result. Sensing that this wasn't the recipe for a great life, I attempted to move up to more challenging roles, eventually finding myself as a business analyst in a local authority. This seemed to fit better, as I enjoyed the process of analysing a service, finding out the facts and coming up with recommendations for how things could be improved; the role, to some extent, fed my Polisher energy. However, when I began to notice that my recommendations were either not approved of or not implemented, the familiar loss of energy came to the surface once again. So, I tried my hand at corporate project management – too formulaic; then service management – too administrative, until I finally fell into the role of customer services development manager. This role required me to both manage customer services functions while also making changes and improvements. It seemed like a nice sandpit to play in. Except, once again, I found my creativity stifled by corporate processes and risk aversion.

I remember one such example: I had been reading about some fascinating science that had shown that smells in buildings could have a measurable effect on human behaviour. As I was in charge of a one-stop shop in a town hall where we were often visited by agitated and emotional customers, I saw an opportunity to use fragrances to create a more welcoming, relaxing mood that would help to calm customers down and create a more positive environment. After researching the required equipment and costs, I presented a proposal to management. Despite the very low costs involved, the proposal was rejected on the basis that an influential councillor thought it was 'mumbo-jumbo'.

And so, it was goodbye to yet another idea and hello to more swearing and shaking of fists on my part.

This inability to bring many of my ideas to reality became increasingly frustrating and I found myself sinking into apathy and cynicism.

So finally, and perhaps, inevitably, out into the land of self-employment I ventured, becoming an external consultant and adviser. I was free to work with lots of organisations, make recommendations and not have to worry about whether they would be implemented or not. I could move on to something else and gain new creative energy that way.

This proved to be a 'baptism of fire'. On one hand, I had lots of 'sandpits to play in', where I could make good use of my Game Changer energy and be paid for doing so. On the other, I had to find these sandpits in the first place and often convince people who didn't share my energies that they should let me play in them. It turned out that while I was good at the former, I wasn't so good at the latter. This was often due to the fact that the individuals who held the purse strings in potential client organisations were most likely more Implementer-biased and were, therefore, less receptive to my Game Changer-led sales pitch than I'd have liked.

The irony here was that I needed Natalie's energies to fill in my gaps; but more on that later.

So, after nearly 10 years of this, I was on the cusp of building my business into something more than a solo performance. My 'big picture thinking' looked to have paid off with the advent of two potentially game-changing partnership opportunities. Once these were live, lots of leads would be coming my way and, therefore, I needed a team of associates to help me deliver the work. Now this was a 'big fat hairy goal' that I could get excited about!

During this period, Natalie provided unwavering emotional support and a fair degree of patience as I landed a new role or project, became loudly dissatisfied and then moved on to something else. I've wondered if this was easier for her because she was so fulfilled in her own career. Because her own energies were recognised, rewarded and utilised, she had space to better support me as I struggled to find the same fulfilment for myself.

So, for the first 15 years of our relationship, Natalie was the satisfied Implementer who loved her career and managed our home, and I was the dissatisfied Game Changer, looking to express my creativity, land a big idea and struggling to find a fulfilling career.

As ever, opposites.

Which brings us neatly to the cataclysmic events of 2020.

At the start of 2020, as for many, we had hopes and aspirations for the year. Except this year was different. For one, both of us were approaching our forties, which certainly made us evaluate where we'd been in life and where we were going. But at the same time, both of us had career aspirations that were on their way to being realised during the year. Natalie was exploring a potential opportunity to move on from the school she'd worked at for 15 years into a new role under a previous head teacher, who'd moved on some years earlier.

For me, from a business perspective 2020 was 'the big one'. I had spent much of 2019 working tirelessly to set up two partnerships, one in the recruitment sector and one in the public sector. The master plan was this: by having partnerships with member organisations in two key industries, I would have access to thousands of potential clients and two influential organisations promoting and helping to sell my consulting services. It was probably in keeping with my Game Changer energies to find a left-field approach to expanding a consultancy business as opposed to growing organically. I'd always struggled with the process of securing individual projects and clients and felt that a 'top-down' systemic approach would deliver better results, more quickly. I suspect I was compensating for my weakness in the sales process by finding teams of individuals with a more task and relationship focused energy. But nonetheless, as we neared the start of the new financial year in April 2020, I was sufficiently confident in the potential of this to start recruiting associates. With all the leads coming in, I would need support. Lots of it.

It's hard to overstate how obsessed I was at seeing this vision become a reality. My career as a self-employed consultant had been less satisfactory than I'd have liked and I really felt as though I had finally found a way to make a big impact. It seemed I was about to unleash a system, through these partnerships, that would allow me to deliver game-changing results in two key industries. The website was in place, I was building a team and press releases were being prepared. I'd visualised what success was going to look like. I was hungry, even desperate perhaps, for seeing this success become a reality.

My achievement in getting these partnerships in place gave me a sense of pride, as well as confidence that I could make exciting things happen as an entrepreneur.

In hindsight, it was a classic example of my Game Changer/Strategist energy working overtime to drive me forward in pursuit of a big vision. It was a feeling of 'potency' – an ability to express one's energy freely in an effective manner.

During the second week of March 2020, I was in London training a team of 10 account managers at one of the member organisations to sell our services. We weren't sure whether to shake hands, as there was a flu virus of some sort featuring prominently in the media, but I paid little attention to that. Training these people, who were in regular contact with 11,000 professionals in their industry, to sell my services was the prelude to my 'big picture vision' becoming a reality. It was tremendously exciting and as far as I was concerned, nothing was getting in the way of making it happen.

At the same time, Natalie was navigating some changes in her work environment. During 2019, a new head teacher had taken over at her school. His style was very different from his predecessor's, with whom Natalie had enjoyed a healthy working relationship. He seemed less concerned about detail and process and had a lot of ideas about how the school could do things differently.

As 2020 rolled in, Natalie began to feel some dissatisfaction with her job, possibly for the first time in her career. The new head teacher was merrily tearing up processes and procedures in the school, some of which she'd implemented herself. It was becoming more difficult to understand the 'why', 'what' and 'how' in her role, as despite having thrown a 'wrecking ball' at these things, her new boss was unable to articulate exactly what would take priority in their place. As we came to the start of March, she was beginning to lose some confidence in what she was doing.

Nevertheless, the potential of an opportunity to move to a new role under her previous head teacher loomed on the horizon. It was just a matter of having a few conversations to firm things up which meant that the situation at her present school, while concerning, was not necessarily a serious issue for Natalie. She had a list of tasks to carry out that would create a path to continue her hitherto satisfying career somewhere else. So, from her perspective as an Implementer, all she had to do was implement them and everything would be fine.

So here we were in March 2020. I was seemingly 'on a roll' as my 'big business vision' began to come together, and Natalie was becoming less satisfied and less certain in her role as an assistant head teacher. After years of me being the frustrated individual looking for a more satisfying career and Natalie being the contented, dedicated professional, had we switched places?

As events would have it, it didn't matter. Because then everything went crazy.

On 23 March 2020, the then UK Prime Minister Boris Johnson announced lockdown in response to the Covid-19 pandemic. I can vividly recall watching my email inbox in the following hours, recoiling in horror as both of the partnerships I'd been working so hard to secure, both of which were on the cusp of going live, were immediately put on ice. Then, I saw my entire business diary wiped out for the foreseeable future. Everything withdrawn or cancelled. All my paid work and potential work, gone. I was suddenly in a position where I had no business, no income and no sense of when or if things would change.

As someone with a Game Changer-biased GC Index profile, this was a devastating blow. The great benefit of this energy is the enjoyment of developing original and creative ideas and the intense obsession with seeing them come to fruition. For me, watching my business and my goals being wiped out by such a dramatic set of external events was the equivalent of watching one's house burn down in front of their eyes. It was my ideas being 'shot down' in front of me. It was deeply distressing.

I had some history in this area which made this situation even more traumatic. When I was 23, I had attempted to buy a redundant building from my old school – a fantastic modern building with a drama studio, recording studio and great facilities. I was obsessed with it. After a long battle with the local authority I'd finally secured the money from a third party to buy the building and get going, only for political shenanigans to stop us from proceeding. I eventually saw the building destroyed in an arson attack after sitting derelict for several years.

So, because I was obsessed with getting these business partnerships 'over the line', because I saw them as the means of achieving my goal of creating a successful consultancy practice, I cared intensely about their success. Just as with the earlier project, failure was therefore an incredibly personal blow. It was my energies working against me once again. Losing all of my existing paid work as well meant that I felt my strategy for providing my share of the income into the household had failed. Therefore, I was a failure.

Conversely, for Natalie the start of lockdown was somewhat less problematic. Although, like me and many others she was concerned about the future and the effect on our financial and personal health, she reacted to the news by getting busy. She developed a schedule for our week so we'd have a sense of what to do each day. She enjoyed getting on with jobs in the house that she'd previously not had time to accomplish.

Her Implementer energy came to the fore helping her to feel potent in her world in contrast to my feelings of impotence.

As a teacher, she had to navigate considerable change as lessons initially switched to remote learning and then, arrangements for in-school provision chopped and changed as the government lurched from one set of rules to another. She found each change was initially jarring, but once she knew the parameters for working, she would quickly internalise them and get on with the business of delivery. This again, showed her strong Implementer energy working at its best. So long as she knew what she had to do and what outcomes were expected, she was 'good to go'.

The concern she had felt about her new head teacher's style temporarily abated, as the school focused on delivering the government's guidelines, leaving no room for anything but operational delivery. In hindsight, she effectively built a protective environment for herself, concentrating on implementing what was possible in the here-and-now, without worrying about the future.

My first reaction to lockdown, once the initial shock had lessened, and in keeping with my GC Index energies, was to come up with ideas for how to adapt my business to suit the situation. Maybe I could sell my services in a different way? Perhaps companies needed more help than ever now their staff were furloughed and working practices had changed so dramatically? Could this be a spur to even greater success? It was a classic example of what Kübler-Ross described as the 'bargaining' stage of the grief cycle[2] (see Fig 3 below). I was kidding myself, trying to use my Game Changer energy to find a way through. And, in keeping with her model, I slowly began to realise that there was no room for bargaining. I was on the bench at the side of the field and I wasn't going to be getting back on the pitch for some time, if ever.

KÜBLER-ROSS GRIEF CYCLE

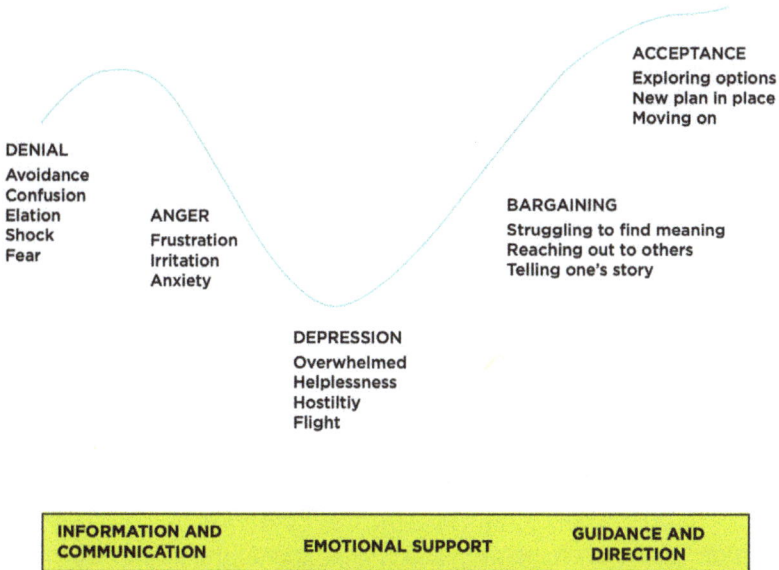

DENIAL
Avoidance
Confusion
Elation
Shock
Fear

ANGER
Frustration
Irritation
Anxiety

DEPRESSION
Overwhelmed
Helplessness
Hostiltiy
Flight

BARGAINING
Struggling to find meaning
Reaching out to others
Telling one's story

ACCEPTANCE
Exploring options
New plan in place
Moving on

| INFORMATION AND COMMUNICATION | EMOTIONAL SUPPORT | GUIDANCE AND DIRECTION |

Fig. 3: Kübler-Ross Grief Cycle

So, as the months in lockdown rolled by, the impact of the loss of my business began to affect my health, both physical and mental. I lost a large

---

[2] E. Kübler-Ross and D. Kessler, *On Grief and Grieving: Finding the Meaning of Grief Through the Five Stages of Loss,* Scribner, New York, 2014.

amount of weight, experienced fatigue, skin issues and digestive problems. In terms of mental health, I found my creativity stifled, my self-confidence collapsed, and I began to sink into depression. Forgive me for saying it, but on the worst days I became interested in the height of bridges!

From a GC Index perspective, all of this was predictable. My strongest proclivity is Game Changer, which means I thrive on original thinking, setting big goals and nurturing them to fruition with considerable obsession and emotional investment. The shock of lockdown was telling me that my ideas were now unrealistic, my goals unachievable and my emotional investment was wasted. Lockdown and the uncertainty around the future at the time was telling me that I had no means of understanding the situation, no way of forming a plan to get out of it and no certainty about what may happen in the future. This was also depleting my Strategist energy. The feeling that my energies were wholly unsuited to the situation at the time was a key cause of my emotional and physical ill health.

So, it took Natalie, still in a relatively good energy space, to fill in my gaps. This she did in the form of a distraction. In order to get me out of my head and into an environment that might be therapeutic, she hit on the idea of taking me to an alpaca farm. As ridiculous as it may sound, this small act would prove to be life-changing.

Natalie had visited the alpaca farm once before with our niece, so she knew what to expect, what activities would take place and how enjoyable the outing could be. It was classic Implementer energy – 'here's something we can do right now, and I know it will work because I know how to do it and have done it before. So let's go.'

What she was doing was taking me away from my natural energy space, obsessive imagination, and putting me in a task space. This simple, pragmatic and task-based approach is typical of the way in which Natalie 'grounds' me when my energies are working against me.

And so it was that in July 2020, I came face to face with an alpaca for the first time. Initially, I didn't know what to make of them. A bizarre mix of deer, camel, sheep and goodness knows what else. I found them fascinating.

So, after an hour in the sun walking alpacas around a small, ramshackle farm in Warwickshire, both of us had fallen in love with these cute camelids. And I felt better than I had in months.

For the rest of the year then, every time Natalie felt I was sinking into the pits of despair, she would book a visit to the alpaca farm. Strangely, this usually seemed to be in keeping with the Covid restrictions. But no matter, it was a great way of getting out and distracting ourselves from the worries at home.

By December, I'd seen barely a sniff of any consultancy work since lockdown was announced. Attempts to rescue the two partnerships had failed and it was increasingly obvious that when the pandemic was over, it was unlikely that I would be able to put my business back to where it was. The thought that this may be true filled me with horror and as Christmas approached, I sank further into depression. This was exacerbated by the fact that as a Game Changer I had no other goal or vision to re-energise me. I was still emotionally attached to what I'd lost. To reference the Kübler-Ross Grief Cycle again, I was a million miles from acceptance, let alone integration.

At Christmas 2020, government guidance once again dealt many people another bitter blow as they found themselves unable to legally see their families. This included us, as a planned visit to meet up with my parents and siblings in the Black Country was cancelled; particularly sad as we hadn't seen some of them since January. Natalie once again booked us in for an alpaca experience and on Boxing Day 2020, we found ourselves back at the little farm in Warwickshire.

As we left after another lovely experience, I lingered at the entrance to the farm, watching people happily walking their alpacas around this tumbledown, slightly shabby but charming place. I thought about the events of the past few months, still in disbelief that it had happened at all. I noted that I wasn't particularly keen to go home, as I'd had such a relaxing time plodding around with the alpacas.

Then, the Game Changer/Strategist energy kicked in. I thought about what we'd paid for our experience, counted how many people were there and how many more were arriving and did the sums in my head. This was a neat little business, but not only that, it was the easiest sales pitch since bread came sliced. Who doesn't want to get out and do something fun in a beautiful countryside setting? It was certainly a world away from the corporate world where I'd been doing business before Covid-19 came on the scene. Consultancy is not the easiest service to sell at the best of times, but this was very different. I could see how this shabby little farm was making money; and making a lot of people very happy too. For the first time in months, the Game Changer/Strategist energies were working again. I was making sense of the place from a business perspective, and that was sparking some exciting ideas.

That little spark of excitement at a new possibility shot through me.

As we got into the car, I turned to Natalie and said, 'Do you think we could run an alpaca farm like this?' She thought for a moment and replied, 'Yes, I think we could. We have the skills and we're both good with animals.' Hearing this, I then said, somewhat nervously, 'Would you like to?' Natalie immediately replied, 'Yes. Yes, I think I would.'

As 2020 rolled into 2021, the government eased restrictions and started rolling out the vaccination programme. Things were a long way from 'normal' and would remain so for some time to come, but the lifting of restrictions allowed schools to return to something approaching business as usual. Natalie therefore found herself back at school full-time, in her role as assistant head teacher, much to her delight. This, she thought, would be relatively easy. She loved her job, she enjoyed being a busy Implementer in a challenging environment and it was good to be properly back in the driving seat. All she needed was a little direction from the head teacher so she could get on with leading her teams to deliver for the children. Easy Implementer comfort zone stuff – 'show me what I need to do, and I'll get on with it'.

And this is where the wheels fell off for Natalie. The new head teacher, as I explained earlier, was in the business of change and disruption. Having been prevented from getting his hands excessively dirty by the onset of the pandemic and lockdown restrictions, he now decided that this was the perfect time to put his 'stamp' on the school. I liken this stamp to the giant foot that appears at the end of the opening titles to the UK's *Monty Python's*

Flying Circus television series from the 1970s, squashing everything below it with a resounding 'splat!' He thus began a ruthless process of ripping out process and procedure across the school, while providing no coherent direction as to what the alternative approach might be. He also preferred an autocratic, manipulative leadership style. He disliked giving feedback and would only do so if he had something negative to say. And he was certainly not prepared to receive any feedback whatsoever.

Within months, the mood among staff at the school had sunk as they realised that they lacked strong leadership and that standards were slipping. Morale was dreadful and staff began to leave.

The head teacher's behaviour deprived Natalie of the two things she needed to fully express her Implementer energies: clear direction and positive validation for the outcomes she achieves. Suddenly, for the first time in 18 years, she found herself getting in the car to head home at the end of the day not knowing what she'd achieved, whether it was any good, and what she needed to do tomorrow. She was deeply concerned that the school was not delivering for the children and as someone who was emotionally attached to their workplace and their role, she took it very personally. She was an Implementer without purpose, who had no gauge from which to determine whether she'd achieved anything. Effectively, she was becoming an Implementer who wasn't being allowed to implement.

This was totally alien to a person who had always enjoyed a seamless match between their job and their energies. And as a result, coming as it did after many years of a happy career, this was an enormous shock for Natalie. She'd entered the first stage of the Kübler-Ross Grief Cycle and was about to take a trip through its various stages, just as I was doing.

She initially found herself becoming incredibly angry at the head teacher for stopping her doing what she loved in the way she preferred to do it. She began to believe that she was a 'failure', that she was not competent in her role. Her inability to maintain the high pace of delivery that she'd become accustomed to was deeply de-energising for her. She felt blocked at every turn by the head teacher.

From a GC Index perspective, two of Natalie's energies were being suppressed. Clearly, she could no longer express her Implementer energy with the same enthusiasm and freedom she had before. Her score of 10 here, the highest possible, only magnified the resulting trauma. A situation that would have been merely problematic for individuals with a lower scoring Implementer-led profile was completely disabling for Natalie, the strength of her proclivity making the negative expression of it far more extreme. Her secondary Polisher proclivity seemed to worsen the negative effects of the situation. Her need to do things well, to hit high standards as well as 'getting the job done' emerged as a tendency to self-punish. Not only was she de-energised from being unable to fully implement, but she was disabled by a belief that, as a result, she wasn't 'good enough'.

In short, she couldn't fully implement and when she could, she couldn't do so to her own self-imposed high standards. Depression inevitably set in.

This situation was the same as my own, just 12 months earlier, albeit resulting from the suppression of a different set of energies. The GC Index science was incredibly helpful in understanding what was going on for each of us when we found ourselves struggling. We can think of proclivities in two ways. In situations where a proclivity is utilised, recognised and rewarded and appropriate, it can emerge as a 'superpower': individuals feel potent, they have higher self-esteem, and they make a positive impact. But in situations where a proclivity is suppressed, undermined, disabled or simply inappropriate, it can emerge as a 'disabler'. Individuals feel impotent, they lose self-esteem and they become less ineffective. They may shut down altogether or even become disruptive and/or destructive.

For Natalie, things finally came to a head in early 2022 when an Ofsted inspection heavily criticised her school, in particular, areas she had personally managed. In keeping with the manner in which her proclivities were working against her, she once again took the criticism personally. We've seen some high profile and very distressing case studies in the media of senior education leaders experiencing catastrophic mental health issues as a result of the very same set of circumstances. And in much the same way, it was clear how severely Natalie's self-confidence had declined when, one morning on the way to work, she was tempted to steer her car into the central barrier on the motorway.

At this time, our roles reversed once again, as I took it upon myself to help and support Natalie. I did this by encouraging her to see the 'bigger picture' behind the situation. I helped her to understand that she wasn't to blame for the problems at her school, encouraging her to reflect on all the things she'd achieved over the years. I also encouraged her to think about the opportunities that the situation offered, even though it was challenging, it could be a springboard to move on to newer, better things.

You will no doubt have realised that I was using my Game Changer/ Strategist proclivities to 'fill in the gaps' for Natalie, in the same way she used her Implementer proclivity to do so for me when I struggled. By taking her away from her natural task focus and providing context and meaning, I was able to help her appreciate how she might regain her energy in a new environment in the future. From here, she could work out the steps towards achieving that herself, thus reasserting and redirecting her Implementer energy in a more positive direction.

So, by this point, both of us had experienced a physical and mental health collapse due to a traumatic experience that had suppressed our energies. And we'd both used our energies to support the other in moving forward positively by regaining their energy.

So, what did we do next?

In early 2021, as things were becoming more difficult in Natalie's role, we discussed the possibility of a new direction. We were in our early forties and there was a sense of time marching on. I was still uncertain as to whether I would be able to rebuild my consultancy business and was feeling utterly burned out with the whole thing. With Natalie feeling disenfranchised with teaching for the first time, we were both in a bad place. Would it be easier to plan a new path, leave our old life behind and do something different?

After all, at this point, with everything going on in the world, what did we have to lose?

The potential new direction was obvious to both of us. Following the inspiration we'd felt at the alpaca farm we visited, we wanted to move to the countryside and set up our own farm-based visitor attraction. This was a big ask. Firstly, neither of us was from a farming background, nor had we ever lived in the countryside. Secondly, we didn't have any money to start anything. We'd been operating without 50% of our household income for the best part of 12 months and, like many, were amassing debt trying to stay afloat during the pandemic. And finally, could we actually work together? Being life partners was one thing, but business partners as well?

However, this new life held appeal for both of us from an energy perspective. For Natalie, the idea of a life spent performing husbandry tasks on a farm, looking after animals, teaching groups of people facts about them, appealed to her Implementer energies. She would have plenty of tasks to get stuck into, but she would also have control over how and when they were completed. For me, the opportunity to start again with a new business idea and build something unique with wide appeal got the creative Game Changer juices flowing. The need to understand how best to do it and under what structure was ideal Strategist territory.

This set the template early on – I would focus my energies on vision, direction and marketing, while Natalie would focus her energies on delivery, administration and husbandry.

It took me then, with my Game Changer and Strategist energies to start the process. I began thinking about what we needed to do to get underway. I felt it would be a five-year undertaking to gain knowledge, build a credible business plan, establish networks, improve our financial position after the impact of the pandemic and finally approach a bank for a commercial mortgage to buy a farm.

Firstly, we both agreed to target Shropshire, as the county was an ideal place to base a visitor attraction due to its proximity to the West Midlands conurbation. A bit of research had established there was a gap in the market for an alpaca-based attraction in the south-east of the county. Because my confidence in my ability to run and grow a business was completely gone following the events of 2020, I suggested we enrolled in some business start-up mentoring. Natalie was strongly in favour, as she felt this would help her understand how to run and manage a business from a task-based perspective, something that would be important to giving her confidence to fully engage her Implementer energies. For my part, I was looking for guidance on strategy, primarily to re-engage my Strategist energies, which had been suppressed by the uncertainty of the previous 12 months.

So, with this in mind, I signed us up with an organisation called Good2Great, based in Bridgnorth, Shropshire. In summer 2021, we began attending their start-up course and were assigned a mentor.

While following the start-up course we spent a lot of time carrying out research. I tended to focus my attention on identifying successful farm-based tourist attractions and looking at their branding, marketing, product offer and pricing. Classic 'high-level' Strategist territory. Natalie focused on the details of animal care, farm operations and accounting. Excellent topics to direct Implementer energy towards. We would often compare notes, although we found that if one of us spent too long talking from their energy perspective, the other would lose interest. We quickly realised there was a sweet spot where our energies met in the middle and if we focused our time there, we came up with solutions to problems incredibly quickly. This helped to prevent arguments! In essence, I would 'set the scene', Natalie would identify what tasks needed to be completed in the short and medium term and I would then contextualise what was more or less important in achieving the plan and long-term vision. We usually found ourselves agreeing with each other by the time the conversation was over.

In the first couple of months, I received an education in how to manage my own energies better to help Natalie engage in the process. One afternoon, I sat in our old garden with her, daydreaming about our mythical farm and what an amazing place it would be. I imagined it filled with animals and people, all having a great time. I imagined a cafe, a gift shop, a function room. I pictured the money coming in from all the bookings. It was going to be the best farm in the world ... in my head anyway. I turned to Natalie and played back my daydream, asking her, 'Isn't it going to be amazing?' Her reply consisted of little more than a muted, 'Yes, I suppose.' Getting anxious, I asked her, 'Aren't you up for this any more?' Her reply, 'Of course I am. It's just that I can't share in your daydream because I don't know what it is I need to do right now to get us there.'

I then realised that I needed to use more task-focused language to appeal to Natalie's Implementer energies. This was confirmed when, the following day after reflecting, I asked her if she'd like to look into what merchandise we could sell in a gift shop. She was so enthusiastic about this that she appeared a couple of hours later with a comprehensive list of products and prices to talk over.

When we set out on our journey, I was adamant that we would have to raise a lot of money to acquire a farm via a mortgage. I suspect Natalie was more open-minded than I was, although we would both admit to a complete lack of understanding of how things work in the countryside at that point! No matter, the perceived need to own a site was a major headache. We could see how we could run an attraction, how we'd market it and how we'd make it a success. But we were very concerned that we'd never raise the money to actually have a farm from which to run a business in the first place.

Our mentor on the start-up course was skilled at coaching us through issues like this. I noted that he changed his style depending upon whether he was talking to Natalie or me. Good coaching technique! I suspect he was matching our energies as he'd talk operationally with Natalie but indulge me in the big picture stuff. One day in late summer 2021, he suggested that we talk to an important figure in Shropshire who happened to be a partner in a large firm of estate agents, on the basis that he'd help us understand how best to acquire a farm. As this was a big picture conversation, it fell to me to talk to him.

He started our conversation with an existential question 'Why do you want to buy a farm?' I found myself slightly irritated by this – most likely because as a Game Changer, I was now obsessed with the idea of owning a farm and as a Strategist, I'd spent a lot of time thinking through the pros and cons. Why was he challenging me? After what was probably a lengthy and overly detailed reply, he said to me, 'You don't want to do that.' Now I was definitely annoyed! I asked him why not. He replied, 'Because you don't need to. You can rent one.'

What neither Natalie nor I understood is that much of rural Shropshire is owned by large family estates and the National Trust. This means that farms rarely come onto the market for sale and when they do, they often have eye-watering price tags. The estates have lots of farms on them and many of them are at risk of becoming void properties as the tenants die off and hand them back to the estate. This means there are opportunities for new tenants to come in and breathe life back into the properties.

Such an arrangement was exactly what this gentleman was proposing to me, but I didn't want to hear it. It was a case of 'not my idea', an example of my Game Changer energies working against me, and 'not in my plan', which was the shadow side of my Strategist energies.

I took the idea back to Natalie, who shared some of my scepticism, but was keener to consider it. She could see, from a pragmatic perspective, how it might be achieved. However, I pooh-poohed it completely and went back to writing the most robust business plan the world has seen so we could raise the money from a bank to buy somewhere as planned. I've wondered since if this is the same impulse that led me to spend so much time building two partnerships to enable the growth of my consultancy business. I suspect that my Game Changer energy sometimes blinds me to the obvious, as I go for the more audacious big fat hairy goals instead of seeking a more pragmatic route. When I worked by myself in the consultancy business, I had no one to restrain me from this overindulgence of energy. However, with the new business we were planning, I had Natalie to bring me back to Earth. She suggested I speak to a few more people for a second opinion. Very pragmatic, very task based.

Thus, as summer led into autumn, I spoke with a financial adviser and another local estate agent. Both advised us to find a family estate and to rent a farm from them. I ignored both.

Finally, the owner of Good2Great, the start-up mentoring organisation, asked to speak with us. He repeated the advice about renting and told us that he knew the person who ran an estate in South Shropshire and that if we wanted, he could put us in touch with her. At this point, not even I could afford to continue to be stubborn. Both of us agreed; we had to meet this person and find out what opportunities might lie in wait.

It was a windy, cold autumnal evening in October 2021 when we made the long journey to a rambling old rectory in a tiny village, a few miles up the road from Ironbridge, to meet the chief executive and co-owner of the estate in Shropshire. After a very convivial chat over tea and biscuits, she suggested that she could find somewhere on the estate for us, but that an existing tenant kept alpacas and, on account of decency, she wouldn't want to put us in competition with him or him in competition with us. Feeling slightly deflated by this news we were reassured by her offer to put us in touch with him as 'he might be able to give you some advice about the alpacas'. Her parting words were 'If it's meant to be we'll hopefully speak again some time.'

We were still a long way from making our idea a reality but at least we now had another contact for the future and the possibility of another research opportunity with the alpaca-owning tenant. So, on an even colder and very gloomy December evening we made our way to Caughley Farm in Broseley, Shropshire, to meet him.

Once again, Natalie went into this meeting with a pragmatic approach. From her perspective, we were there to fact-find and things would pan out however they were meant to. I, of course, was looking to confirm my vision of what a farm might look like. I had a fixed picture in my head, so it was something of a shock when we arrived at Caughley Farm (pronounced 'Carf-lee') for the first time.

Firstly, the farm is accessed via 1½ miles of rough track. On the day we visited, this track was in a deplorable condition, with some sections being more in keeping with a highly challenging off-road driving course. This created many 'squeaky bottom' moments as our Lexus, entirely unsuited to such terrain, navigated the ruts and bumps. I was less than impressed.

Secondly, as we pulled into the farmyard we were taken aback by the state of the place. It looked like somewhere you might visit and never return from. The entire farmyard was strewn with litter, discarded pieces of equipment and various forms of the nasty brown stuff. A fire burned in front of the farmhouse and there was evidence of multiple other previous fires in several places. A primitive washing line had been fashioned from bailer twine, strung from a bracket on the farmhouse and tied at the other end to a telegraph pole. The various undergarments that had previously escaped this feeble construction were hanging from the branches of the trees that ran along the entrance to the courtyard. Two fearsome looking dogs stared at us from behind a gate under an archway between a pair of barns.

And finally, there was the pièce de résistance: a steel funnel on legs that was dripping with blood, the result of it having been used to 'dispatch' many turkeys which the farm's occupant was rearing to sell to people for their Christmas dinners.

It's fair to say we were both a little uneasy about our visit.

However, our host was affable enough and on meeting his alpacas, we found they were surprisingly attractive and seemed to be well natured. After a conversation about the 'whys' and 'wherefores' of alpaca farming, we asked him what his future plans for the farm were.

To our surprise, he revealed that his plan was to leave and move to a remote island near Scotland. Not really what we expected to hear. Furthermore, if we liked, we could buy some or all of his alpacas and maybe talk to the estate about taking over the farm when he left.

As a Game Changer, my energy was immediately piqued by this revelation. One of the strengths of the energy is a high appetite for risk and opportunity. And I could clearly see the door of opportunity opening in front of us. My Strategist energy was less convinced. This ramshackle place, which at the time seemed to be in the middle of nowhere, did not in any way represent a successful visitor attraction. From a pragmatic perspective, it was nothing like what we thought we had planned.

Natalie's Implementer energy kicked into gear straight away. From her perspective, here was a tangible opportunity to get the task of moving to the countryside underway. She could see what we needed to do and how it could be done. Even though it was a leap of faith from our present lifestyle, she knew that this was an easy way of getting hold of a property suitable for alpaca farming. The tenant had shared with us the value of the rent he was paying, and while this had me yodeling with nerves, Natalie had already worked out that the amount was the equivalent of our mortgage payment, one car loan that we were already paying and a few little indulgences. If we could sell our house and make some cutbacks, we could just about get away with it.

So, with night falling we set off back to Warwickshire. On the journey home, Natalie was full of energy, making verbal lists of tasks we needed to undertake in the next couple of days. I was a bundle of nerves, wrestling between the two extremes of my Game Changer and Strategist energy. The creative energy in me said 'this is the one'. The pragmatic side said 'this place needs a lot of work, and it may be quite a challenge'. The shadow side of both said 'what if it all goes hideously wrong?' It was a strange feeling. I felt very conflicted.

Natalie and I spoke extensively about Caughley Farm for several days after our visit, weighing up the pros and cons of taking it over when the existing tenant left and trying to visualise ourselves living at the farm. It was such a stark contrast to the neat new-build estate on which we lived. Could we make it work?

Our eventual conclusion was simple; this was too good an opportunity to turn down. And anyway, we were both pretty unhappy with our life at that time. It had been a tempestuous 18 months, and we'd come close to losing everything. So, what was left to lose? We had to try.

The deal was sweetened further for us when the estate, having learned of the tenant's island escape plan and our interest in buying his alpacas, offered us the use of a 14-acre field for six months, rent free if we bought them, so 'you can see if you think you can make it work'.

So, in February 2022, Natalie and I signed some paperwork and became alpaca owners for the first time. We put our house on the market shortly afterwards and after one week it was sold subject to contract. Things were suddenly getting VERY interesting ...

Here we were with a 14-acre field that we didn't own, that we weren't paying any rent for and which we only had the use of for six months, plus nine alpacas and absolutely no experience of owning livestock or running a tourist attraction. We didn't even have running water, electricity or any facilities at the site, which was around a quarter of a mile down the lane from the main body of Caughley Farm. We were still living over 1½ hours away, in a house that was sold subject to contract and with, as yet, nowhere to go once it came time to move out. I was still struggling to revive my consultancy business, so we continued to exist on Natalie's income alone, which came from a job that was progressively ruining her health. We were unfit, tired and feeling very middle aged.

It was from this point on that the combination of our individual energies became a recipe for success. Realising that we had to double down and make this situation work, we set about creating a business that could grow into the farm attraction we wanted to develop. Firstly, the name, which came about in a brainstorming conversation with my dad, who to his credit suggested a pun on our surname 'Franklin-Hackett'. So, our new business was quickly christened 'Frankly Alpacas'.

Next, we had to develop a website, a social media presence and set up a booking system and means of taking money. As these tasks seemed to fit naturally with our energies, I took the first two – website and social media – and Natalie took the last two – booking system and payment system. Within a month, both were ready to go.

Getting the site ready for visitors was another example of our energies working in harmony. While I thought about the layout and the signage, Natalie sorted out the practicalities, such as animal housing, hand washing for visitors and parking.

Finally, albeit in an extremely basic and rough-around-the-edges manner, Frankly Alpacas opened for business on 1 April 2022.

In those early days, we offered just two tours. The first was a simple guided meet and greet with the alpacas, which allowed visitors to get hands-on and personal with them in a beautiful setting. The second was the same offer but followed by a picnic in the company of the herd.

We knew within a month that we had a potential success on our hands. Despite our clunky set-up, visitors loved the alpacas and were full of praise for the tours we led. We began to notice that Natalie and I had slightly different styles when running experiences. I would be more humorous and quirky in my delivery, while Natalie would be more factual and educational. Once again, this was a clear reflection of our energies. My Game Changer bias meant that I preferred a creative approach, while her Implementer focus meant that she would lean towards a task-based delivery style. Both, of course, worked equally well.

After three months, we had taken a few thousand pounds in bookings. Hardly retirement money, but it was a tantalising glimpse of the potential revenues that may be possible if we could scale up.

July came around and with it, another unexpected twist. The tenant at Caughley Farm was leaving earlier than expected and, as a result, this meant that we would need to sign the tenancy for the entire farm by the end of August. Our house sale was progressing very slowly and there were no guarantees that it would go through in time, which would leave us paying a mortgage and a significant amount in rent at the same time. We simply couldn't afford it.

In the end, we realised that we had no real choice. We had to make it work, there was simply no other option. Bailing out of the deal would leave us worse off financially than we started. So, we did everything we could to progress the house sale and called in a few favours to help us if we couldn't manage financially while everything went through.

As it turned out, our house sale went through in the nick of time and at the start of September 2022, we became the new tenants of Caughley Farm in Broseley, Shropshire.

Our life since then has been a real roller-coaster ride and we can scarcely believe it all happened. In the two and a half years since we started Frankly Alpacas in April 2022, we have had over 4000 visitors to the farm. We've expanded our range of animals to include the smallest sheep in the world; the smallest cows in Europe; ducks and chickens; other rare breed sheep and small animals, which is why we changed our name to Frankly Farm Tours at the start of 2024. We've launched a programme of animal education for schools and visited over 25 schools in our first year of running it. We've attended parties, village fetes, festivals and corporate events with our animals. We've seen births and deaths and watched the seasons come and go. We've built a huge wedding-spec marquee and watched it be destroyed two days after Boxing Day having been battered by six named storms. We've transformed the previously ramshackle and dirty farmyard and turned it into a welcoming and attractive destination to visit. In early 2024 we created a function room space out of a barn where the previous tenant kept his turkeys and started building a cafe in another former barn. Tripadvisor presented us with their Traveler's Choice award for 2023 and 2024 on the strength of reviews left by over 150 of our visitors.

It's been remarkable. If you'd have told me that all of this would happen on the evening of 23 March 2020, as I was watching my business burn down in front of my eyes, I would never have believed you.

Throughout the journey, Natalie and I have been sustained by our individual energies and the sheer joy of combining them to solve problems. While we do have moments of tension where one or both of us overplay our strengths, we both agree that our success in making this enormous change in our lives has come about as a result of our ability to be potent in making the impact that comes naturally to us.

As well as friends and partners in life, we've become successful business partners.

Life continues to have its 'ups and downs' and I would be lying if I didn't admit that we've had some very challenging days since we started our new life in the country. But the feeling of potency, the sense of being able to fully exploit our individual energies and the joy of working together to make an impact continues to be joyous. It has highlighted how much latent potential we both had, which was not fully utilised in our old lives. We've found ourselves wondering 'why didn't we work together before?'

It turns out that to be truly potent in our work lives, we needed each other.

Chapter 6

Keeping the Band Together

John Frost picks up this theme of energy in relationships in this chapter, which tells the story of a rock band and the ways in which they work to maintain their cohesion and creativity, making their collective energy work for them. At the heart of this exploration is the view that great art 'connects' with people and to do so, those making that art must feel connected to each other.

The arts definitely have something important to say to the world at this moment in our history. I am happy to make this bold statement because I believe it to be true.

In his book *21 Lessons for the 21st Century* Yuval Noah Harari said:

> *'We (humans) are left with the task of creating an updated story for the world.'*

I am attracted to the notion of reimaging contained in this statement. And, if we are to reimagine our future, then I believe that, together, the arts, The GC Index and leadership, connecting people on so many levels as they do, will have a critical role to play in how that updated story unfolds.

But what's that got to do with rock bands?

When I thought about the title of this chapter, 'Keeping the Band Together', it provoked a number of thoughts and feelings; and, as usual, for me at least, this led to a question.

What do I mean by band?

At one level, of course, I mean rock bands generically as well as my experience of the band that I play in: Rebel and the Banned. So, the band in this sense can be looked at from a team perspective. However, we might also think of the GCI proclivities themselves as a band of different energies; the interest there might be how does that (GCI) band work and interact within the individual as a leader or as a team member. And we can also think of a system, either local or global, as a band with different energies impacting on the look, feel and perhaps focus of that system.

So, however we define the band, the GCI proclivities interact with each other and provide one of the lenses through which we can understand what is happening and importantly why it is happening in that way. The band is, of course, more than just its energies and raw abilities. Thriving as an individual, as a musical group or even as a global system is also dependent on the skills and leadership with which we deploy our energies.

So, the focus of this chapter using the context of the arts, is how we create bands and teams that make beautiful music by understanding how The GC Index and leadership work together to create the platform for success.

So, let's turn first to bands and specifically the elements of a successful rock band. What might we observe? Perhaps unsurprisingly it looks quite similar to any team in any organisation.

The vocalist, guitarist, bassist and drummer all have defined roles and responsibilities on stage. For example, the lead vocalist is responsible for delivering the lyrics and engaging with the audience. The guitarists provide the band's melodic and harmonic foundation. Bass and drum drive the timing and rhythm that really anchor the band. The roles are critical and interdependent.

However, there is more to a band's roles and responsibility than just those attached to performance. The performance could be defined as the expression of the art but that is the culmination of a lot of other elements critical to the success of the band; essentially how they work together and the culture that they create within the band.

Collaboration is critical. For example, in the songwriting process which is often a collaborative effort of melodies, lyrics and arrangements.

This is, of course, supported by safe spaces for **communication** and enriching conversations. Making space for creative input and **feedback** is often based on the quality of the communication. Ensuring that each band member feels psychologically safe, empowered and trusted to bring their unique perspective and influences, contributing to the band's overall sound. This ensures that everyone feels valued, and that the music reflects the band's collective vision.

Leadership and how decisions are made is also key to a band's success. Bands sometimes have charismatic front people, for example Jagger and Mercury. However, in many successful bands, leadership is shared, with different members taking charge in areas where they excel, whether it's songwriting, production, or managing the band's business affairs.

Like any team, rock bands have conflicts, whether it's creative differences or personal issues. How these **conflicts are managed and resolved** can determine the band's longevity and success. So, compromise and negotiation have to be a part of the creative process, and successful bands will generally have the skills and mindset to appreciate what everyone brings and find a middle ground where all members feel valued and satisfied with the decisions made.

A sense of **shared purpose** will often be the hallmark of a great rock band. It could be creating groundbreaking music, achieving commercial success, or impacting on social justice issues. Whatever it is, a unified purpose drives their efforts and often supports the consistency of their artistic direction.

Mutual trust and support are found in all great teams. Band members often support each other in their personal and professional growth. Whether it's encouraging a fellow member through a tough time or pushing each other to improve musically, mutual trust and support is crucial.

The music industry is a crowded space and it's forever changing. So, bands that survive and thrive over the years often do so by **adapting to changes** in the industry, shifting trends, and personal circumstances

Collective achievement and accountability happen when bands feel connected to each other. Everyone contributes to the band's triumphs and deals with setbacks together. In the same way each member is accountable to the group, ensuring that they perform their best and contribute positively to the band's team dynamics and the quality of the **interpersonal relationships.**

So, this chapter is at one level a story about music and musicians. And it is also my story as a member of a band; someone who was only comfortable to refer to themselves a musician relatively recently. It's a story of how I have opened up a new chapter in my life, how I got here; and how I nearly didn't get here! And some of the stuff in between, including nearly losing it all.

However, it is also story of leadership, my leadership, the band's leadership and how leadership facilitates the power of The GC Index for bands and other teams.

The story includes my learning and observations; it will pose questions based on those observations not all of which I will attempt to answer. Some questions are best left for reflection and further thought as you draw your own conclusions.

I hope it also provokes further questions that may be a catalyst for your own curiosity whether or not you are familiar with the arts. And, of course, the chapter will also draw on my knowledge of The GC Index as a way of framing some of my learning and observations. This is my profile:

My strongest proclivities are Strategist and Implementer.

In this way I hope that this chapter will, in some way, also enhance my understanding of The GC Index and hopefully your own.

So, what about the music?

I haven't always been in a band, albeit I loved music from a very early age. I was born in 1961 when the Beatles were still primarily a covers band. As I grew up, I became aware of my parents' record collection including Beatles 45s as they became known for their own music. My parents were not musicians, but music was a noticeable part of their life, so I was very aware of music in my surroundings.

A brief flirtation with the guitar at a young age gained me some music school grades but not what I would call a devotion to the instrument! My love of music on the other hand continued to grow as I attended many gigs in my hometown of Wolverhampton.

These were the days when tours were long, and bands played smaller venues than the stadiums of today. It was therefore a much more intimate experience to see a band. This love of music was enhanced at Lancaster University, which also attracted significant names at the time; back in the early 1980s universities were very much on the tour list of bands such as U2 and Dire Straits.

Many of my friends at school and university were either into music, or formed their own bands. One friend even progressed in to a senior role in the music industry which he still holds as I write this. And yet, even with all that enthusiasm, I wasn't a musician, except in my dreams! That said, I know that I was always conscious of holding the question – could I do that? That never left me. Some of my friends took that further and made their dreams a reality – but, at that time, not me.

My interest in music has continued throughout my life and I am now also a trustee of the Bewdley Arts Festival a multi-arts festival based in my town on the river Severn in Worcestershire. The activity of the festival also offers young musicians a chance to develop their skills through performances supported by the event. It is amazing to see their confidence grow through this opportunity, not just as musicians but as people.

So, why did I sit on the sidelines and not take the plunge as some of my friends did? I can make excuses about other distractions and there were some, but, in the end, I think that it came down to a lack of self-belief fuelled by my personal fears.

Research shows that some of the reasons cited for not realising an ambition to play on stage are:

Fear of judgement: being worried about being judged by the audience or fear that you will make mistakes and not meet their expectations.

Lack of experience: a lack of experience performing in front of others, the unfamiliarity of the situation can lead to anxiety.

Perfectionism: the desire to perform perfectly which can create immense pressure and lead to fear of making even minor mistakes.

Self-doubt: doubts about abilities or feeling that you are not good enough to perform in front of an audience.

Physical symptoms: stage fright can manifest as physical symptoms such as shaking, sweating, or a racing heart, which can be distressing and make you feel even more anxious.

I can certainly associate with a number of these!

For me there was a lot of negative self-talk going on. 'What if I make a mistake or freeze?' and 'what if people laugh at me?' are two that were often present.

It is said that one of the strategies that we can adopt to handle fear is to embrace it. Understand where it is coming from and try small changes; breaking the fear down into smaller parts and dealing with those small parts in the first instance.

If I think about my own journey from the dream of playing in a band to actually doing it, I can relate to this idea. It started with a jam! Most music does, but in my case that jamming session with friends was a safe space to make mistakes and learn from other more experienced players not just technique but also the reality of playing music.

Musically, everyone starts in the same place and everyone, even the most experienced players, make mistakes. Mistakes are a part of the learning process. I have a low Polisher score in my GC Index profile. So, for me in GC Index terms the idea of making a mistake was not an obsession with perfection that was driving the fear of failure; it was more the insecurity that I felt from a fear of being embarrassed. I was, if anything, overthinking it; trying to understand the process and working out how to unfreeze the fear, to counter the negative self-talk rather than just play. But then again, as a Strategist/Implementer perhaps they were the lenses through which I was processing the problem! In hindsight, there were perhaps less dots to join up than I thought there were.

Our fears often exaggerate. As I built up the picture of what was possible (and good enough), I could literally feel my confidence growing. Susan Jeffers is right, sometimes we just need to feel the fear and do it anyway![3]

And when I was able to connect to my fear in this way then it was easier for me to address where my lack of confidence was coming from.

> 'Left unrecognized and unaddressed … self-limiting belief patterns can confine a potentially confident and self-actualized person to a lifetime of insecurity.'
> Thomas Rutledge, Psychology Today, US edition, July 2023

In the same article Rutledge talks about the core beliefs of confidence as:

- Knowing that outcomes cannot be controlled and that what matters is effort, persistence, preparation, and goals.
- Seeing success as an ongoing process and appreciating that setbacks are a necessary part of the process.
- Believing that success is inevitable if we can stick with it and adapt.
- Seeing failure as temporary, a source of feedback and a learning opportunity.

---

[3] Susan Jeffers, *Feel the Fear and Do It Anyway,* Harvest Publications, 2003.

- Seeing anxiety, fear and doubts as a healthy sign that we are testing ourselves rather than as a sign of impending failure.
- Not taking rejection of failure personally.

Pretty much all of the musicians that I have met would be able to relate to some or all of the above. For me personally, I really connect to the notion of 'seeing anxiety, fear and doubts as a healthy sign that we are testing ourselves'. And the belief that 'failure is both temporary and a positive source of feedback'. I see this all the time in the way that bands, like mine and others, work together in the creative process of making music.

So, what if we could connect to our fears in a different and empowering way? What else might be available to us? What might we be able to reach for? Who else might also benefit if we handle our fears in a more empowering way?

Another characteristic of the Strategist/Implementer is pragmatism. And it feels as if that pragmatic energy has underpinned my journey of growing my confidence and capability as a musician. A good example of this was the liberation, and it did feel like a sense of freedom, that came with the knowledge that all musicians, new and experienced, make mistakes whether in rehearsal or live.

This really helped me to connect with the process of creating and making music and the possibility of collaborating with others to do this. Imperfection is literally part of the creative process in this context. Easier said than done perhaps. Embracing imperfection can be a challenge! But having an amazing group of supportive people around you always helps! And, as a musician, I have always been fortunate enough to have such people around me.

Of course, sometimes life throws a curved ball at you. And this part of the story is where my self-leadership crosses over with my ambition to be a musician.

On 15 November 2022, I had a cardiac arrest.

I was fortunate enough to be in a place that had both a defibrillator and trained first responders. They saved my life before the emergency services arrived. I am one of only 7% who survive cardiac arrests. Most people are in the wrong place when it happens, a place where those two essential ingredients are not available. And so, by the time the paramedics arrive, it is often too late.

I believe that this is relevant to this story because of the connection that it gave me to myself and what was important to me. I remember quite soon after the cardiac arrest asking myself, 'what might emerge from this?' Of the many things that did emerge, my connection to the desire to play music became stronger and the fear (that was stopping me) was certainly put into perspective. I remember asking myself, 'what are you waiting for?' Had things turned out differently, I might never have played in a band, never had the opportunity to reframe those fears, anxieties and doubts, and do something that has been transformative for me and my life in many ways. The band in many ways is a metaphor for how I now want to live my life.

So, my question falling out of this experience was this: if we believe in the idea of creating 'an updated story' for ourselves and others, how can we possibly do this without embracing the unknown and the inevitable imperfection that sits in the space of not knowing as we learn and grow? And also, what might be the cost to us and those around us of being led by our fears?

I think that these questions highlight the role of leadership in navigating not just life but also the lenses through which we look at life and how we show up as people. And one of those lenses, of course, is The GC Index.

In GC Index terms I believe that leadership is a catalyst that really helps to bring the dynamic nature of The GC Index and its power to life. It is in that sense a factor that can really ignite the energies that are available within yourself and within your team. I would further argue that without leadership we, and the teams we work in, are limiting the scope of our potential.

Leadership has many definitions but central to many of these is a focus of leadership being about people, winning the 'hearts and minds' of people in pursuit of a defined common purpose.

I see The GC Index proclivities as a band of energies and just like a musical band the different energies can both support or conflict with each other and, of course, obviously do! But it is in the exploration of the diversity of The GC Index energies with an open and curious mind that we can ignite its possibilities and create extraordinary cultures in which teams and individuals thrive.

I have been working in leadership development since 1994 as a facilitator and professional executive coach. I came to the conclusion quite recently that what I have done for most, if not all, of that time is help others to curate their conversations; conversations with themselves (their internal dialogue), conversations in the team and sometimes conversations within the larger organisation and system. The quality of the conversations that we have I believe has a significant impact of the possibilities that we can imagine in any situation. And leadership tends to be a lens that I use a lot when looking at situations and how people are interacting with the situation; the conversations that they are having. It is an occupational hazard in that sense! And this was the case with The GC Index. I am interested in the energies and how they manifest themselves of course, but also the context in which the energies are working, and the impact of leadership on the energies in that context.

I think it's helpful to think about leadership in a number of dimensions:

Self-leadership: how we lead ourselves in any situation and stay empowered psychologically. This implies a degree of self-awareness and self-management that is often associated with our emotional intelligence and how we maintain an empowered mindset through the ups and downs of leadership.

Team leadership: the impact of our leadership on the team; maybe the team we are leading or in a team that we are a member of. Leadership in a high-performing team can come from any team member and not necessarily always from the nominal leader.

Organisational and systemic leadership: how we are leading within the context of the organisation or system in which our leadership is taking place and the impact that they have on our leadership.

If these different dimensions of leadership are relevant and pertinent to any given situation, then the skills that leaders have to work within these dimensions, alongside The GC Index, will be key factors in their impact and the outcomes they achieve.

Exploring this further, the inspiration for my beliefs about leadership came from a belief that at this time we also need to be reimagining leadership. The need for global change has never been more urgent whether you look at this from a political, organisational or social perspective; at the same time, we also need to hold what the great scientist Richard Feynman referred to as the 'satisfactory philosophy of not knowing'.

And yet, this notion of embracing doubt as he articulated it as something to be welcomed rather than feared, seems to pose a significant challenge to leadership. Perhaps this is because it is counter-intuitive to leaders who are part of a system that values certainty. Nevertheless, that is where we are; a place of not knowing. A place where we must reimagine our future and our response to the challenges that we face, rather than relying on the thinking and the ways of being that created the challenges in the first place.

Reimagining requires us to have conversations in which we can enter a space of not knowing in a creative and open way. One path that we might follow is to explore reimagination by looking at situations through what I call leadership lenses; this can help us to question and explore our perception of reality and find new possibilities.

So, what if we looked at situations using these five lenses?

- Consciousness
- Connection
- Curiosity
- Collaboration
- Compassion

What additional impact might we have from using these lenses in conjunction with The GC Index energies?

I believe leadership starts with leading ourselves. Our ability to lead other people is based upon our ability to understand and lead ourselves first. Therefore, the quality of the conversation that we have with ourselves and with those around us is significant in terms of our leadership impact. That also means understanding how we can work with The GC Index as a leadership development tool, understanding the proclivities to positively impact on our conversations. So, let's look at the lenses in more detail.

Consciousness

Consciousness gives us the potential at least to access our skills. Consciousness creates awareness of what we are experiencing in the moment; it is being present and aware of how we are feeling, our focus. It creates an understanding of the questions that make up our internal dialogue and the choices we are making as a result; those that are empowering and those that are disempowering.

Knowing our GC Index profile helps us to become conscious of how we are processing what is happening and from that we might ask, what are the assumptions and beliefs that I am holding about this situation? How are other people with different GC Index profiles seeing the situation? How might their beliefs and assumptions be influenced by their profile?

In my band consciousness is critical. Being aware of what underpins creative differences and how we might approach them, as well as how we are individually behaving in the situation is important, as is the ability to give each other feedback.

Connection

Connection enables us to find a sense of meaning in our lives; where our values are aligned with the contribution and the service we are providing to society. Connecting with ourselves creates the possibility at least of connecting with others. In a band this may manifest itself in discussions about creative direction or why we are choosing to be in a band at this time. In my band we, and therefore the music, are inspired by issues of social and climate justice. It is a factor that connects us all.

So, the action to use music to highlight these issues was a connecting factor as much as the playing of the music itself, which of course we also love.

Connection is critical in The GC Index when we look at how the different proclivities are interdependent and support each other to achieve the goal. From a leadership perspective using the lens of what connects us can help us to really explore the diverse knowledge and perspective that each of the proclivities offers.

Curiosity

> 'Two roads diverged in a wood, and I –
> I took the one less travelled by,
> And that has made all the difference.'
>
> Robert Frost, 'The Road Not Taken'

Curiosity is where we challenge what is, by asking, 'what if?' Curiosity is the catalyst for reimagining; the foundation of our innovation, creativity and our ability to manage differences. It is our motivation to take the road less travelled. Creating the 'updated story' will require a consciousness, that questions from a place of curiosity not judgement; one that can be present with uncertainty and tension while a solution is emerging; one that embraces and explores new options to find a just and equitable solution.

In our band curiosity informs our lyrics and the melody, but also the process of composing. The process often starts with a riff a musical version of the 'what if' question. The riff asks a creative question of the band members even while the future is just an empty space at this point. What can you add to this as the bass player, drummer, singer or guitarist?

An example of this was our guitarist in rehearsal saying, 'Let's just have some fun,' and we started a jam based on a few chords. It was mid-December and the riff led to the idea, what if we wrote a Christmas song based on the themes of sustainability and climate change. To cut a long story short, we had the basis of the song in 20 minutes. And the foundation of that was being able to hold the lens of curiosity to the suggestion and let this challenge our existing processes and ways of working. Curiosity helps our band of proclivities to get the best out of each other.

In GC Index terms curiosity supports connection and possibility. Genuinely being present to listen to the perspective of other energies is not always easy. It can challenge beliefs and assumptions and even highlight biases. But it is perhaps from the consciousness of this discomfort that we can find new solutions and routes; open the possibility for ourselves of taking the road 'less travelled'.

Collaboration

Collaboration is where we co-create. When we collaborate effectively it produces innovative and beautiful options, that embrace cognitive diversity and bring different ideas and perspectives together to, as Matthew Syed has said, 'recombine ideas'.

Collaboration happens when we are present for each other in psychologically safe spaces, where we can ask and explore the question 'what's the conversation that needs to happen here?' When we explore this question with authenticity, curiosity, and most importantly without fear, we thrive and grow. For my band collaboration in safe spaces is critical part of the creative process and the release of energies. So being aware of, and letting go of, our natural energies can be important particularly if they are dominating the creative process.

For example, in a band the imagination and obsession of the Game Changer can be really powerful in the development of original ideas for new songs. And in the case of my own band, our songwriter is incredibly imaginative with his lyrics. The rest of the band supports this by feeding him lyrics, usually just one line will fire his imagination and start the process.

A collaborative mindset perhaps starts with curiosity and is an essential component of creating great music by using all the collective strengths brought by The GC index proclivities. It is perhaps how we make our individual talents dance. This will, of course, mean that we have to manage conflict well, perhaps using our curiosity to let go of an assumption or even a belief about the best way forward; maybe managing the fear within ourselves of the uncertainty that this course might invoke. It will almost certainly involve compromise and a belief in the idea that we create, can create, something extraordinary by really leaning into the lens of collaboration.

Compassion

Compassion supports and enables and facilitates the other lenses. The Dalai Lama has said, 'Love and compassion are necessities, not luxuries. Without them humanity cannot survive.' Compassion enables us to find the resources within ourselves to collaborate with others to create together and to navigate through our own biases and the complexities of division and judgement. In a band context this is important.

Knowing each other from a GC Index perspective as well as just spending time with each other and getting to know the person that sits behind the musician is incredibly powerful. Compassion in that sense could be called the glue that helps to bind our energies and potential together.

When as a band we are preparing for gigs all the proclivities come to the fore. For some members of the band a gig is fun and while preparation in terms of rehearsal is critical, they love the fun of playing and so will take the pragmatic view of the Implementer. For others, the gig is a work of art so we can never do too much rehearsal in preparation. Shades of the Polisher perhaps! For others still the gig is also part of the ongoing development of the band's brand, a marketing channel to our help us create our audience.

The point is there are many different proclivities and energies at play in the different aspects of playing in a band and the understanding that comes from compassion is a lens that really helps us to navigate through this and, from our perspective at least, make great music.

The leadership lenses together with The GC Index proclivities can be a powerful cocktail of possibilities for bands and other teams. But how does that work in reality?

To start answering that question I want to talk about David Bowie. I have always been attracted to Bowie as a musician. There was something about his ability to lead musically and socially, standing up for his values, that has always stood out to me. I am instinctively drawn to curious people, people whose life appears to be founded on exploration and pushing at boundaries. And for me, Bowie was one of those people in life and even after his passing. I am still learning from him.

The language and structure of The GC Index provides a framework to help me unpick this fascination and it's also a great insight into the way that Bowie led his life and created amazing musical bands.

So, how does David Bowie, one of the most influential musicians and cultural figures of the 20th and early 21st century, exemplify the roles identified in The GC Index? I believe that his impact can be seen through all The GC Index roles. These are my thoughts:

Game Changer

- Innovation and visionary ideas: Bowie was a quintessential Game Changer. Throughout his career, he consistently pushed the boundaries of music, fashion, and performance art. His ability to reinvent himself — whether as Ziggy Stardust, the Thin White Duke, or other personas — demonstrates a relentless drive for innovation. He often introduced groundbreaking concepts and challenged the status quo, making him a visionary in multiple artistic fields.
- Influence on culture: Bowie's work didn't just reflect the times; it often shaped them. Bowie's influence extended beyond music, impacting fashion, visual art, and even social norms. This transformative effect on culture aligns perfectly with the Game Changer role.

Strategist

- Long-term vision: while Bowie was primarily a Game Changer, he also displayed traits of a Strategist. He had a keen sense of where he wanted his career to go and how to navigate the music industry's changing landscape. His ability to foresee trends and adapt his style accordingly (e.g. shifting from glam rock to soul, electronic, and industrial sounds) suggests a strategic approach to maintaining relevance.
- Cohesive themes: albums often had overarching themes or concepts (e.g. *The Rise and Fall of Ziggy Stardust, Heroes*), showing his ability to structure his creative output within a larger framework, which is a key characteristic of a Strategist.

Polisher

- Attention to detail: Bowie was known for his meticulous attention to detail in both his music and visual presentations. Whether it was the sonic texture of an album or the intricate design of a stage costume, he demonstrated the traits of a Polisher — someone who refines and perfects work to a high standard.
- Craftsmanship: his collaboration with producers like Tony Visconti and Brian Eno highlighted his commitment to crafting a polished, high-quality product. Albums like *Low* and *Station to Station* are testaments to this dedication to excellence.

Play Maker

- Collaboration and teamwork: while Bowie often took centre stage, he was also a skilled collaborator, working with artists like Iggy Pop, Lou Reed, and Queen. As a Play Maker, he facilitated creative collaborations that brought out the best in those he worked with. His ability to bring together diverse talents and create something greater than the sum of its parts is a hallmark of the Play Maker role.
- Band leadership: even as a solo artist, Bowie led various bands and projects, coordinating the efforts of others to achieve his artistic vision. His leadership in these collaborations often ensured that everyone's contributions were harmonised into a cohesive whole. This extended beyond the musician's team. In a recent webinar I listened to someone, who worked with Bowie as part of the backstage crew, talk with equal fondness of connection to everyone in the team in terms of putting on the show, musicians and road crew alike. He intuitively understood the role that every member of the team needed to play in a show and was appreciative of all. From the experience of the person leading the podcast who had worked with many musicians, Bowie's approach was not always replicated in other bands.

Implementer

- Executing ideas: while Bowie was more often the visionary, he also had the ability to bring ideas to life, a trait of the Implementer. His ability to take abstract concepts and turn them into finished albums, tours, and performances demonstrates an understanding of how to execute ideas effectively.

- Discipline and work ethic: Bowie's prolific output over his career, especially his ability to work across multiple mediums (music, film, fashion), shows the discipline and work ethic typical of an Implementer.

David Bowie's career can be viewed as a blend of GC Index roles, with a strong emphasis on the Game Changer due to his relentless innovation and impact on culture. However, his success also depended on strategic thinking, meticulous craftsmanship, collaborative skills, and the ability to execute his visionary ideas. Understanding Bowie through The GC Index framework highlights how his diverse strengths contributed to his legendary status as a musician and leader in the music industry and beyond.

For me, Bowie was also a great example of the how the leadership lenses I described earlier in this chapter can really catalyse The GC Index proclivities.

Bowie showed a level of consciousness about his role as a leader in the music industry as well as a musician. His focus was beyond himself extending to a consciousness about who he was as a person and also his opportunity to lead in the world of music and the arts. He also had a strong connection to his values and to the possibility to impact the system in terms of the leadership influence that he had in his position. He was incredibly *curious* and experimental, embracing the unknown, even finding a way in his last album, *Blackstar*, to explore his art right up to the end of his life (*Blackstar* was released two days before Bowie passed). His valuing of *collaboration* was, as we have seen, legendary and his *compassion* for others both within and beyond music was shown in his campaigning, as well as in other aspects of his life.

Two examples stand out for me

Bowie was very aware of the potential of his position to influence, and his values displayed that regularly. There are many examples of Bowie talking about his values and what was important to him on social media. Two examples stand out for me. The first was hearing him address young musicians encouraging them to get out there and play their own music, the music that's in their heart and not to be a copy of others. In the second example, I saw footage of Bowie taking an MTV presenter to task about the lack of black music and musicians on MTV: at the time the leading channel for music globally. This was Bowie literally calling out racism in his industry irrespective of the impact that this might have had on his own career, and at a time when many other white musicians were 'burying their head in the sand' about the situation. Both of these examples are, for me, acts of compassionate leadership aimed at changing the system and supporting his fellow musicians to connect the dots on what was possible for them.

The point for me here is that Bowie showed, in the way that he lived his life, how our self-leadership, how we appear in different situations, can really bring The GC Index energies to life for ourselves and for other people around us.

Looking at my own band, Rebel and the Banned, I want to highlight some key aspects of how we work together to create music and how we manage both our GCI profiles and leadership to get the best out of each other.

So, it may be helpful to start with the context and the profile of The GC Index band profile.

This is Rebel and the Banned's aggregate GC Index profile (see Fig. 1). As you can see, based on highest individual profile scores, there is a heavy leaning towards Game Changer and three of the five band members scored Game Changer as their highest proclivity (see Fig. 2 for individual GC Index profiles). We can hypothesise that in a creative group we might expect to see a disproportionate amount of Game Changer energy.

REBEL AND THE BANNED - AGGREGATE PROFILE*

* INCLUSIVE IMPACT: PERCENTAGES ARE BASED UPON HIGHEST SCORES

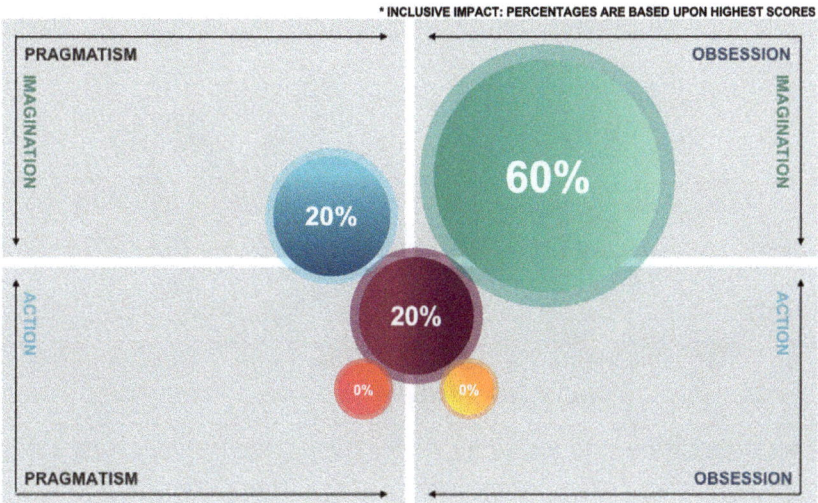

Fig. 1: Rebel and the Banned's aggregate GC Index profile based upon individuals' highest proclivity scores

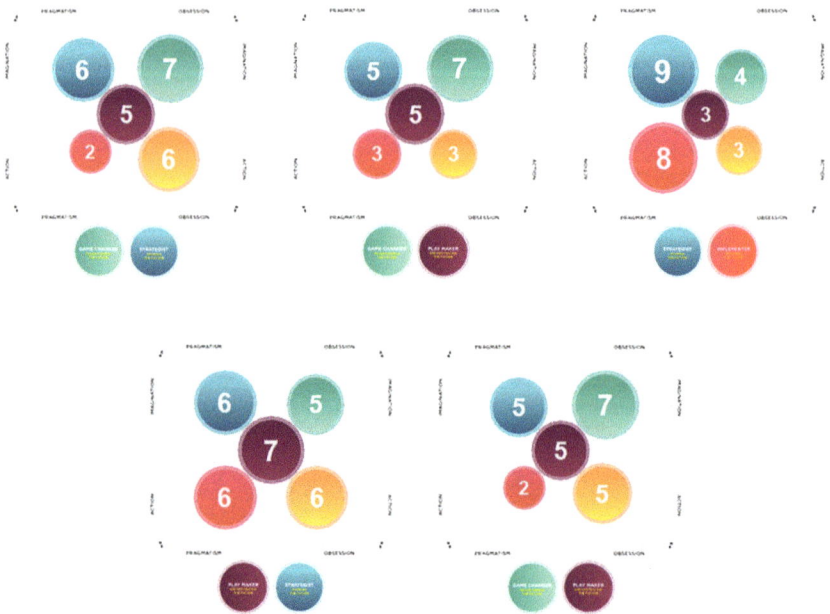

Fig. 2: Individual band members' GC Index profiles

If we look at this aggregate picture of the band alone then the other energies seem unrepresented by comparison, in particular Implementer and Polisher.

However, if we look at the individual profiles, we can see something of a more balanced picture of the band with all the proclivities represented to a reasonable degree across the five-person group.

For example, what becomes more evident here is the energy for collective endeavour and collaboration as represented in the Play Maker scores. I would suggest that this Play Maker energy supports the Implementer energy by acting as a good counterbalance or moderation to the energy of the high Game Changer scores.

So, when we look at a 'potential impact' aggregate profile (see Fig. 3) we can see again that the risk of dominance from the Game Changer energy is toned down considerably and the team looks more balanced. And this is certainly my lived experience as a member of the band.

REBEL AND THE BANNED - AGGREGATE PROFILE*

*POTENTIAL IMPACT: PERCENTAGES ARE BASED UPON SCORES 6 AND ABOVE

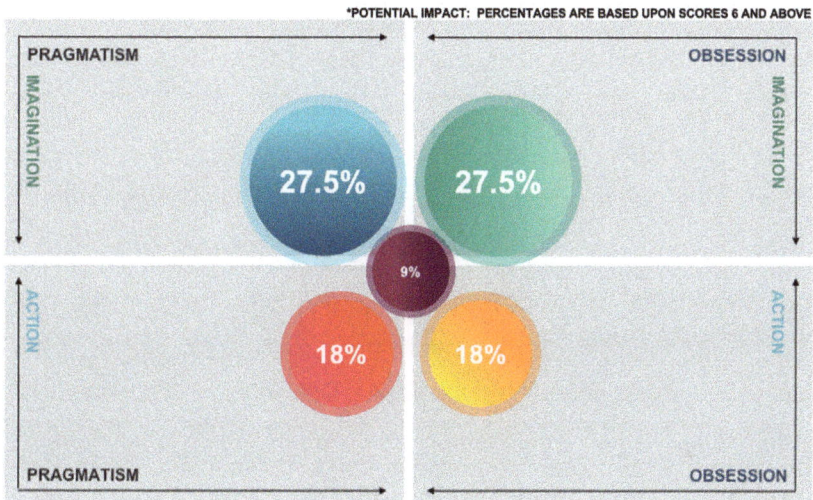

Fig. 3: The band's 'potential impact' aggregate profile. (Potential impact profiles take account of all proclivities with a score of 6+.)

Of course, the reality is more complicated and nuanced than a picture of these profiles on their own can reveal. So, it's useful to look at how both the profiles and the leadership lenses also impact on the reality of our team working.

In terms of a shared purpose and vision, the band is quite purposeful about this aspect of ways of working. At the start of each year we spend time thinking about what we want to achieve in the year musically, but also check in with each other on why the band is important to us and what we have taken from the previous year both personally and collectively. It's also a time to celebrate what we have achieved in the previous 12 months.

So, a look backwards and a look forwards in terms of our intentions for the year ahead. The different energies in the band mean that the discussion can be very broad, the Game Changer energy in this situation can really play! But we can also come back to the pragmatism inherent in the Strategist and Implementer energy and agree on what we are actually going to do. Because we came together around a common purpose, using our art to highlight and raise awareness about key issues of social and climate justice, we also take time to review and reflect on how we have connected to that over the year in the music we have created, the gigs that we have played, and the collaborations that we have started with other like-minded groups.

The GC Index provides a way of highlighting our different working styles and strengths, and, combined with the leadership lenses helps us to anticipate and manage the way that we collaborate and manage conflict effectively. Being conscious of the fact that there are differences while also appreciating that these arise from our different strengths rather than personal disagreements helps us to resolve conflicts constructively.

I can't say we always get it right; we don't! Conflict when it happens can be challenging and not all the band members are comfortable in that situation. For example, the recording process in the band attracts different energies and, therefore, different creative tensions. The energy to produce a new track and to make it brilliant (Game Changer and Polisher) does, at times, butt up against the energy to create something that is good enough and get it on a streaming platform to build the band's brand (Implementer and Strategist). So, being conscious of that tension, being able to articulate it as well as leaning into the Play Maker energy, which looks for collaboration, is a key part of our creative process. Not to do so would lead to resentment and potentially under-performance in both the studio and on stage.

This is where strong interpersonal relationships and focusing on what connects us rather than what might divide us in that moment, helps. When we get it right it is also a moment where we all lean into our leadership in the sense of being curious about the divergence of ideas and compassionate for other band members' points of view; suspending judgement and believing that we are safe to have an open and frank discussion that will combine ideas, build trust and create great music.

The quality of our communication and conversation is really important. Great conversations facilitate great performance. Just as we need to stay in sync on stage, so we need to, as much as possible, stay in sync off stage. We talk and share a lot of ideas. And the Game Changer energy in the band means that there are a lot of ideas and sometimes those ideas can be fiercely defended! Great conversations happen when bands feel safe with each other; safe to say what is in their heart and their head. They literally create the space for the Play Maker energy to do its job of facilitating collaboration.

A successful rock band, like a team, is built on mutual trust and respect. Each member must trust that the others will perform their parts well and respect each other's contributions to the group's success. Trust is the rock on which most high-performing teams are built. And a rock band is no different.

Trust can be delicate. And, as band members, being aware of what contributes to and withdraws from each other's trust accounts is critical. For example, in my band, I have noticed that we collectively need to be conscious of the power and impact that a strong creative vision, inspired by Game Changer energy can have on the band. It is critical to ensure that it does not overpower by creating a supportive space in which everyone has a sense of ownership of what we are working on and feels empowered to make their individual creative musical contribution.

Our band, like any other team, is a collection of amazing people with many different talents and energies to offer. The trick is to create a culture which enables all of that diversity and the confidence to breath and grow while having great fun along the way. It's easy to just focus on what we do, creating music; and yet it is so much more satisfying to also connect on how we do it and why it's important to us. We can do that more effectively if we really understand the energies we have in the band and how we can use our leadership to really make those energies dance.

So, what might we take from this story?

The title of the chapter is 'Keeping the Band Together', and I suggested at the start that the band can be within ourselves, within a team or within a system. I believe what ultimately keeps any band together and enables them to thrive is their purpose and what's important to them: the culture they create in the band and how they work and interact with each other in pursuit of that purpose. And this is facilitated by creating the space to explore the diversity in a team using tools like The GC Index and the leadership lenses.

Perhaps, therefore, using the metaphor of music I can pose a final question for reflection. 'How is your band at the moment, and what kind of music are you creating?'

Bibliography and references

Dalai Lama, *The Art of Happiness,* Hodder Paperbacks, 1999

Feynman, Richard P., 'The Value of Science', A public address given at the 1955 autumn meeting of the National Academy of Sciences

Frost, R., 'The Road Not Taken', *Atlantic Monthly*, August 1915

Harari, Yuval Noah, *21 Lessons for the 21st Century,* Vintage, 2019

Syed, M., *Rebel Ideas: The Power of Thinking Differently,* John Murray, 2019

Chapter 7

Leading People Through Change: 'What's *Love* got to do with It?'

If you lead people in any sphere of life, from CEO to parent, you will find this chapter a compelling read. Simon Phillips and Renée Smith give us a very practical approach to the otherwise complex challenge of leading others through periods of change.

Change is a natural and continuous part of the human experience. We are born, develop, learn, grow, and decline too, continually changing physically, mentally, and emotionally. We may embrace or bemoan these changes, but these shifts are the reality of being human. Both authors, Simon and Renée, for example, had dark brown hair, but now we are both silver. (Notice we didn't say grey? That reframe is a subject for another article!) But all jesting aside, change is a normal part of life.

Change is evident in the natural world and its seasonal cycles. Even within that anticipated rhythm, driven by planetary orbits and lunar gravity, these cycles have unpredictable variations that surprise us and require us to adapt and shift. Society too is constantly in flux, with elections, new technology, media innovations, and creative content offering us a new world each day. In short, we are constantly immersed in change.

This continuous change is a normal part of the workplace too. Every team experiences ongoing shifts whether driven by external factors such as market changes or internal developments like new team members; change is inevitable. Some changes feel like seismic upheaval and others feel like joyful breakthroughs. Some are minor, requiring slight adjustments, while others are comprehensive, necessitating a complete reinvention of how work gets done. Whether a change is considered positive or not can depend on preferences, perspectives, and impacts. But ultimately, many changes just are, they are neither good nor bad.

Consider these examples from the workplace:

> 'Our team was merged with another department, so I now report to a new manager and work with colleagues from different areas.'

> 'Our project management is now fully online, and we're using new software to track tasks and collaborate across teams.'

> 'A new CEO was appointed, and they've brought in fresh ideas that are completely reshaping our strategic priorities.'

> 'The company has redefined its mission to prioritise community impact, and now my work includes partnering with local organisations on projects.'

> 'With the new focus on digital products, I'm now helping to develop features for an app instead of our previous physical product.'

In any case, change can be unsettling for many people at work bringing uncertainty, anxiety, and resistance.

This is where the power of loving leadership becomes evident. Effective leaders understand that change is not just about processes or systems; it's about people.

When leaders approach change with empathy, compassion, and support, they are better equipped to guide their teams through transitions in a way that minimises disruption and maximises engagement. As we will see, loving leadership empowers individuals to embrace change rather than fear it. A compassionate approach to change reassures them that their leaders have their best interests at heart and that they will be supported throughout the transition.

Fostering love instead of fear in change can be supported in three key ways. It begins with leaders realising how people experience change and guiding them through the psychological journey, represented by William Bridges' Transitions Model (Bridges, 2009). Love expands with the leader engaging people in change utilising Simon Phillip's Delta Model of Change (Phillips, 2007). Love instead of fear in change is accelerated when leaders encourage team members to contribute to change in ways that energise them and unleash their greatest impact as measured by The GC Index.

Transitions

It is essential to understand the human experience of change as not a one-time event but a psychological transition. This is made most clear by the insights and framework offered by William Bridges in his seminal and enduring work, *Managing Transitions.* He reminds us that a change sets in motion a human process of transition that needs to be understood, respected, and guided for the change to be humane and successful.

Bridges reminds us that a transition begins with an ending, moves through a neutral zone, and ends with a new beginning. In the ending phase, the psychological response of team members may include shock, denial, and clinging to former practices. Emotions may run high with anger flaring up or sorrow spilling out. Resistance to the idea of change may be common here as people face the fear of not knowing what the change will mean for them and if they will be able to adapt and perform.

As the transition moves to the neutral zone phase, team members may express feeling untethered and bewildered. The old norms are no longer valid, but the new reality has not fully taken hold yet. This heightened uncertainty creates stress and anxiety, but it also opens space for creativity and exploration of new possibilities that former certainties did not allow.

Eventually, the team moves to the phase of new beginnings. Updated ways of working are integrated and taking hold. New habits feel more comfortable, and the gaps of uncertainty fill in with consistent new experiences. Confidence grows as team members establish their comfort and identities in the new reality.

It is helpful to note that this experience roughly parallels the grief process described by Elisabeth Kübler-Ross (Kübler-Ross, 1969). We have seen this grief play out in teams we've led and to which we've provided consultation. It strikes us just how attached we humans can be to the simplest aspects of our work life. Changes that seem innocuous – a change in space or process steps, for example, even changes for the better, can still trigger the full psychological process of transition.

The Delta Model of Change

Wise leaders understand that such changes must be led, not left to happenstance. Simon's Delta Model of Change emphasises a dynamic, human-centred approach to such organisational shifts, whether that change is simple and limited or a large-scale transformation. It has long been understood that the most effective way to lead people through change is to engage them in the process meaningfully. The Delta Model identifies five key elements, each represented by a letter in 'DELTA', to guide leaders in co-creating sustainable, impactful change:

D – Diagnose: Start by clearly defining the vision, goals, and purpose of the change, ensuring alignment with the organisation's values and mission. Test and refine the parameters of change with all key stakeholders. This clarity sets the foundation for successful transformation.

E – Engage: Engage all stakeholders, especially employees, by fostering open communication, active listening, and involvement in the change process. Engagement builds trust and commitment.

L – Lead: Effective change requires strong, compassionate leadership that guides, supports, and inspires others through transitions. Leaders model resilience and adaptability, setting the tone for the rest of the organisation.

T – Transform: Implement change through tangible actions, using structured processes, resources, and training to empower individuals to adopt new ways of working. Transformation focuses on creating measurable impact.

A – Accelerate: Regularly assess progress, feedback, and outcomes to ensure that change initiatives are effective and aligned with goals. Grow and develop change makers to accelerate the change and drive the next wave.

The Delta Model of Change highlights that successful transformation depends on a balanced focus on people and processes, with leaders playing a pivotal role in aligning purpose, engaging teams, and creating a culture of openness and adaptability.

The fundamental choice of every leader

Every leader has a choice in the fundamental mindset and values they bring to their leadership. This choice impacts every decision they make in executing their role including how they lead change and the human experience of transition. This orientation will determine if the impacts on the groups and individuals are positive and the change succeeds, or if the impacts on people are negative and the change fails.

What is this fundamental choice? Leading with fear or leading with love.

Leading with fear

Fear-based leadership assumes the worst about people. This mindset believes people can't be trusted and must be threatened to elicit desired behaviours and performance. Fear-based leadership often views workers as just another input to production, like parts, machinery, systems, software, raw materials, tools, and data. 'Human resources' are just another asset to be managed. This dehumanisation of people often disregards human physical, mental, or emotional needs and pressurises people to perform like machines out of fear of humiliation, demotion, or job loss.

Such threatening approaches, while common at the onset of the industrial era, are now known to be counterproductive to desired worker performance and effective workplace behaviours, such as speaking up, sharing ideas, pointing out problems, testing and learning, collaborating, and productively disagreeing.

We can benefit now from widely shared advances in neuroscience research that illuminate the impacts of threats on people. It is easy to see why triggering the following neurophysiological response is so harmful to effective teams and workplace contributions.

When we perceive danger, whether it is physical or psychological,
our sympathetic nervous system is triggered so that we can deal
with the threat. This happens faster than we are even aware,
quickly releasing adrenaline and cortisol into our bloodstream
and causing activation of certain systems and deactivation of

others. These protective shifts are meant to prepare us instantaneously for either fight or flight, sweat increases, digestion is suppressed, twitchy muscles are activated, and pupils are dilated with the heart pumping oxygenated blood to prioritised areas of the body. If the threat continues and we cannot get away or defend ourselves, then the dorsal vagal system is triggered and we freeze or appease, becoming numb and playing dead, or offering the source of the threat whatever they want.

(Porges, 2025)

In short, fear-based leadership and threatening organisational practices cause people to withdraw, withhold, and underperform. Threats and fear are directly linked to poor organisational outcomes including lower productivity, lower engagement, decreased creativity, increased turnover, poor customer service, and lower job satisfaction (Seppala & Cameron, 2025; DeSmet, Rubenstein et al., 2021).

Leading change with fear

The same negative impacts apply to times of change and transition too. Leaders who approach change with threats and demands for compliance ignore and push against these two human responses at the same time. Their threats trigger the fight-flight-freeze-appease-fear response, making it difficult for team members to adapt and learn, while also ignoring the natural transition response automatically triggered by the change itself. Our experience suggests that this, typically, results in scared team members often demonised for being so resistant to change, when they are experiencing a perfectly reasonable response to fear-based leadership unwilling to understand and guide the process of human transition.

But it doesn't have to be this way!

Leading with love

The alternative to threatening, fear-based leadership is simple. It is love.

It used to be shocking to invoke love as a leadership value, but love is now understood to be the essential quality and experience that underpins all other performance factors needed during change.

Love can be defined in many different ways, for example, as care, compassion, human kindness, unconditional positive regard, and sometimes self-sacrifice.

The definition of love offered by Moshe Engelberg in his book *The Amare Wave* is universally useful (Engelberg, 2019). He defines love as 'energy that uplifts and connects'. Extending that definition, we can easily define fear as 'energy that oppresses and divides'. With this, it becomes even clearer why fear-based leadership is so ineffectual.

But does love really belong at work?

Consider this. The 'energy that uplifts and connects' is expressed uniquely in different relationships and contexts. This energy that uplifts and connects has one set of expressions, romance, commitment, time, or affection, for example, in our personal relationships between spouses or partners, family, closest friends, and pets. This love is expressed in other ways for our neighbours or even between strangers in public with kindness or helpfulness for example. And the energy that uplifts and connects is expressed in still other ways for our colleagues or customers. We will explore this further below.

But make no mistake, such expressions of love belong everywhere, and are needed in every relationship in every part of society and human experience.

How is love expressed and experienced at work?

Renée has been conducting qualitative research since 2017 (Smith, 2025), gathering and analysing stories of love and fear at work. Through her research, she asked people to share stories of times when they felt loved at work. Their examples reveal the operating definition of love at work. These stories of uplift and connection at work begin with empathy. Empathy can be understood as being aware of, sensitive to, and feeling with another person.

Compassionate action follows next taking on many different forms depending on what's needed. For example, compassionate action may take the form of respect, trust, kindness, listening, investment in growth, clarity, challenge, fairness, opportunity, and appreciation. Love is expressed in moments that matter to people, some big and ongoing, some small and fleeting, but all creating uplift and connection.

When people experience such love, they feel acceptance and a sense of belonging. This enables them to contribute their very best and work becomes truly meaningful. This virtuous progression enables organisational outcomes that are essential: productivity and engagement, creativity and innovation, problem solving and learning, loyalty and stability, customer satisfaction, profitability and sustainability.

The good news is that love does not come at the cost of performance. There is no trade off here. Love enables performance. So why wouldn't we lead with love?

A deeper look at loving leadership

At its core, loving leaders centre the full person in their leadership, creating psychological safety. In such an environment, people feel comfortable expressing their ideas, testing solutions, and learning because they know they'll be supported, not punished. In today's rapidly evolving workplaces, this kind of leadership is essential. We're no longer operating in environments where people want to simply show up, do their job, and leave. People seek purpose in their work; they want to feel connected to something bigger than themselves. And loving leadership creates that connection.

Empathy and compassion are at the heart of this leadership style. It's not enough to intellectually understand what others are going through; we must take the time to step into their shoes, feel their experiences, and respond from that place of empathy with compassionate action. When we practise such loving leadership, we build trust. We create relationships where people feel safe enough to show up as their full selves. Through this approach, we create workplaces where people are accepted, feel they belong, contribute, and find meaning in their work.

But loving leadership doesn't stop at empathy and compassion. Loving leaders build strong relationships — real, human connection. In an age where technology often depersonalises our interactions, it's easy to forget the importance of sitting down face to face, listening fully, and building relationships based on trust and respect. As loving leaders, we prioritise that connection. Not only is it the right thing to do for people but when people feel connected to one another and their leaders, they are more engaged, more creative, and more willing to contribute. We create cultures where feedback isn't something to be feared, but something to be valued because it's rooted in trusting relationships.

Finally, support is the backbone of loving leadership. Loving leaders lift people up, providing the resources, encouragement, and guidance that people need to succeed professionally and sometimes personally as well. Supporting our teams means looking out for their well-being in every sense: mental, emotional, and physical. When people feel supported, they go the extra mile — not because they have to, but because they want to. They feel seen and appreciated, which inspires their loyalty and commitment.

Workplace dynamics are becoming increasingly complex. Loving leadership offers a human-centred approach that fosters connection, creativity, and success. It's not just about what we achieve, but about how we achieve it – by caring for the people who agree to work with us and join in our shared endeavour. Loving leadership is the key to creating workplaces where individuals can thrive, teams can collaborate, and organisations can grow, all enabled by honouring the humanity of everyone involved.

Leading change with love

If leading with love is so effective, it only makes sense then to lead change with love.

A key component of managing change through loving leadership is communication. Leaders must be transparent and open about the reasons for change, the expected outcomes, and the impact it will have on the organisation and its people. By involving their teams in the change process — soliciting input, addressing concerns, and providing regular updates — loving leaders foster a sense of ownership and collaboration. This human-centred approach not only reduces resistance but also enhances the likelihood of successful change implementation.

While change sets off a natural fear response and triggers a psychological process, a loving leader can meet these reactions to organisational change with practical support that helps people manage their fight-flight-freeze-appease fear response and return to a sense of safety and connection. Loving efforts to create psychological safety trigger the parasympathetic nervous system, known as the rest and digest response. In this condition, we feel calm, contented, and composed. We are able to access our higher-level thinking. In this state, we can hear, consider, communicate, and learn.

Embracing the DELTA Model of Change and intentionally leading that change with its guidance, is a loving approach. Love is found in the clarity, engagement, compassion, structures, and feedback loops represented by each phase. At the root are empathy and understanding of the human experience to meet people where they are to help them move forward confidently.

Likewise, in each phase of the transition process, leaders can act with love to support successful change.

In the ending phase, compassion looks like the chance to talk about feelings without judgement, opportunities to ask questions, and the chance to remember what was and commemorate what is being lost. Love is also the chance to anticipate what might be.

In the neutral zone phase, a loving leader will be patient with a time of lower performance as people adjust to new systems, relationships, process steps, or cultural norms. A loving leader will welcome creativity and trying out new ways of doing things or giving opportunities to learn or expand experience. This is a time of possibility to be embraced!

In the new beginning phase, a loving leader will celebrate progress and acknowledge efforts, both large and small, to make the change successful. They will solidify and stabilise the team helping them to feel sure of where they are now. And, a loving leader will celebrate the change and transition skills the team developed as important growth too.

However, leading through change requires more than managing the phases of transitions and of the DELTA Model with compassion, care, and connection. It requires energy – a unique type of energy that sustains leaders and their teams through the ups and downs of transformation. This energy is fuelled by a deep sense of purpose and a commitment to creating a better future for the organisation and its people. Loving leaders tap into this energy by staying grounded in their values and continuously seeking ways to inspire and motivate their teams, even in challenging times.

Loving change is supported by The GC Index

To harness the energy required for leading change with love, organisations can turn to The GC Index, a framework that helps individuals and organisations identify the specific energies that drive impact. The GC Index is based on the idea that everyone has the potential to make a unique and valuable contribution to their organisation, but that contribution will differ depending on their natural Energy for Impact.

The GC Index identifies five types of impact that individuals can have within an organisation:

Game Changer: People who challenge the status quo and initiate change with original ideas and possibilities. Game Changers are essential for organisations looking to disrupt industries and create transformational change; they see what is possible in ways that others typically don't.

Strategist: These individuals, at their best, see how the patterns of the past shape the present and the future based upon their search for meaning and need for purpose.

Implementer: Action-oriented individuals who get things done. Implementers bring the energy required to make change happen.

Polisher: Polishers have energy for learning that can underpin continuous improvement and the 'pursuit of excellence'. They can be perfectionists with the things that they care about.

Play Maker: Collaborative individuals who have energy for bringing people together. Play Makers can excel at building relationships and creating environments where teams can thrive. They are often the glue that holds organisations together, especially during times of change.

Each of these proclivities – Energies for Impact – brings a different type of energy to leadership and to individuals contributing to a change. Loving leaders understand the importance of recognising and harnessing these energies within their teams. By aligning the right people with the right roles, and by welcoming these energies into the phases of change and transitions, leaders can ensure that their teams have the energy and resources needed to navigate change successfully.

Moreover, The GC Index provides a framework for leaders to better understand their own impact and how they can best contribute to their organisation's success. Whether they are driving creativity with Game Changer energy, providing direction with Strategist energy, or fostering collaboration with Play Maker energy, loving leaders can leverage their unique strengths to lead their teams through change and transitions with compassion and purpose.

Tapping into The GC Index energy for loving change

As we've seen, change is a constant within our lives, and the ability to lead it and contribute to it effectively is a hallmark of successful leadership. The GC Index provides a framework for understanding the different energies that drive impact within organisations, offering valuable insights into how to harness these energies to lead change or to contribute to change individually.

Each energy type identified by The GC Index – Game Changer, Strategist, Implementer, Polisher, and Play Maker – contributes uniquely to a successful change and transition process, especially when rooted in love. By recognising and leveraging these energies, leaders and individual contributors can create transformational, thoughtful, and sustainable change that can benefit everyone.

Love recognises that everyone has a role to play. But those roles are not the same. By embracing these energy types and the desire for contribution by all, groups and organisations not only unleash the highest possibilities for change, but embody a loving culture of respect, inclusion, and belonging where everyone can contribute their best.

Game Changer energy for possibilities

The Game Changer embodies energy for original ideas, the basis for transformational possibilities and with it hope for the future. Individuals who bring this energy are constantly pushing the boundaries of what is possible, challenging the status quo, and seeking creative solutions. They are driven by a desire to initiate significant, often revolutionary, changes. In the context of loving change and transition, this energy is particularly powerful because it is not just about change for change's sake – it is about change that is rooted in compassion and the desire to create a better, more meaningful future for everyone involved.

Game Changers, when anchored in love, use their possibility-centred energy for transformational change that is both impactful and sustainable. When their ability to envision possibilities is encouraged as a part of the neutral zone phase of transition, their contributions can accelerate adaptations as well as expand the benefits of the change to other opportunities. Welcome Game Changer energy to envision and explore! Love when paired with Game Changer energy, fosters a culture of hope where bold ideas are encouraged, but always with the understanding that these ideas must serve the greater good.

Strategist energy for thoughtful change management

While Game Changer energy provides hopeful new possibilities and options, Strategist energy brings the meaning, purpose and structure necessary to turn ideas into reality. Strategist energy is rooted in seeking an understanding of how we got to the present and what this means for our future. At their best they are the ones who create the roadmap for change.

In the context of loving leadership, Strategist energy is essential for ensuring that change is managed thoughtfully and with care throughout the entire DELTA Model Change Process. Loving Strategists take into account the human side of change, recognising that people are not just resources to be managed but individuals with emotions, concerns, and aspirations. Their approach to change management is holistic, considering both the technical and emotional aspects of the transition.

By combining strategic thinking, the application of Strategist energy, with empathy and care, loving Strategists ensure that change is not only purposeful but also human-centred. They co-create environments where people feel valued and supported and with a sense of purpose and certainty. These thoughtful contributions to change build trust and engagement, making it easier for people to embrace and adapt to new ways of working.

Implementer energy for action

Possibilities and strategy are essential, but without action, they remain just ideas on paper. This is where the energy of the Implementer comes into play. Implementers are action-oriented individuals who can turn possibilities and strategy into reality. They are focused on execution, ensuring that plans are implemented effectively and that goals are achieved.

In loving leadership, Implementer energy is particularly valuable because it provides the stability and consistency needed during times of change. Loving Implementers are not taskmasters; they are leaders who care deeply about the people involved in the execution of change. They recognise that successful implementation requires more than just following a plan, it requires motivating and supporting individuals to perform at their best.

Loving Implementers understand that change can be stressful. As both leaders and individual contributors, they work to create an environment where people feel supported and confident in their ability to succeed. Their action-oriented energy ensures that change initiatives are not only completed on time and within budget but also in a way that fosters a positive and supportive workplace culture.

Polisher energy for learning, continuous improvement and excellence

While Implementers focus on getting things done, Polishers bring a different type of energy, one that focuses on learning, continuous improvement and excellence. Polishers are driven by a desire to refine and perfect, ensuring that every detail is considered and that the final result is of the highest quality.

In the context of loving leadership, Polisher energy is invaluable because it creates environments where individuals feel supported to grow and develop continually. Loving Polishers are not focused on perfection for perfection's sake; they are focused on helping people reach their full potential. They take the time to provide constructive feedback, offer development opportunities, and encourage a mindset of continuous learning.

Polisher energy from both leaders and team members creates a culture of continuous improvement where people feel empowered to take ownership of their development and their work. This not only leads to higher-quality outcomes but also fosters a sense of pride and accomplishment within the team.

Play Maker energy for collaboration

Finally, the Play Maker brings collaborative energy to change. Play Makers, at their best, bring energy to building relationships, fostering teamwork, and creating environments where collective success is prioritised over individual achievement. Individuals steeped in this energy can be the connectors within an organisation, bringing people together to work towards common goals.

In loving leadership, Play Maker energy is essential for cultivating a sense of belonging and shared responsibility. Loving Play Makers can understand that collaboration is not just about working together, it's about creating a sense of community where everyone feels valued and supported. At their best, they go out of their way to build relationships, resolve conflicts, and create a culture where teamwork is celebrated.

Loving Play Maker energy from both leaders and individuals can create a workplace where people feel connected and engaged. This sense of belonging can drive higher levels of motivation and commitment, leading to collective success.

Reacting to change: the role of loving leadership

Understanding how the different GC Index proclivities react to change is essential for guiding individuals through transitions with compassion and purpose. Loving leaders recognise that each person's inherent energy will shape their response to change, and they tailor their leadership to meet individuals where they are, using their unique proclivities to foster resilience and adaptability.

Game Changers often view change as an exciting opportunity to create and disrupt the status quo. They are natural initiators of transformation. However, without structure, their energy may lead to frustration or disconnect with more pragmatic team members. Loving leaders engage Game Changers by validating their ideas while guiding them with empathy, ensuring their contributions align with broader organisational goals without overwhelming the team.

Strategists approach change methodically, often pausing to evaluate risks and consider the long-term implications. While this careful consideration is invaluable, it can also manifest as hesitation or resistance to rapid changes that lack sufficient thought. Loving leaders recognise the importance of involving Strategists early in the change process, offering reassurance through structured planning and thoughtful risk analysis that respects their need for clarity and alignment with the organisation's purpose.

Implementers tend to focus on execution and can become unsettled by change if they don't have a clear direction. Their proclivity for action needs certainty and stability, and sudden shifts may cause anxiety. Loving leaders provide the support and clarity Implementers need, offering detailed plans and well-defined roles to help them navigate change with confidence. By providing consistent guidance, loving leaders reduce Implementers' discomfort with uncertainty, empowering them to turn change into successful execution.

Polishers value refinement and excellence, and their initial reaction to change can be cautious if it threatens established processes. Loving leaders address this by involving Polishers in the refinement stages of the change process, allowing them to apply their attention to detail to improving new methods. This not only helps Polishers feel engaged but also ensures that the quality of the change initiative is enhanced, transforming resistance into a drive for continuous improvement.

Play Makers thrive on collaboration and inclusivity, and their primary concern during change is often how it will impact team dynamics and relationships. Loving leaders foster an environment where Play Makers can maintain team cohesion by involving them in team discussions and ensuring open communication. This ensures that Play Makers can leverage their natural ability to connect people, facilitating smoother transitions while reinforcing the emotional and social bonds within the team.

By understanding and anticipating these diverse reactions to change, loving leaders can tailor their approach to support each proclivity, fostering a culture where change is not feared but embraced as a path to growth and collective success.

Conclusion: the enduring impact of loving leadership

Throughout this chapter, we have explored the transformative power of loving leadership and how it is fuelled by a unique type of energy that combines compassion, emotional intelligence, and the willingness to connect deeply with others.

Loving leadership is not just a set of behaviours or techniques; it is an intentional approach that places humanity and care at the heart of leadership. By leading with compassion, emotional intelligence, and a focus on connection, loving leaders create environments where people feel valued, respected, and empowered. This type of leadership fosters trust, encourages collaboration, and promotes innovation, all of which contribute to the long-term success of an organisation.

The energies identified by The GC Index — Game Changer, Strategist, Implementer, Polisher, and Play Maker—offer a powerful framework for understanding how individuals contribute to the success of groups and organisations. By recognising and harnessing these energies, loving leaders can drive meaningful and lasting change. They create workplaces where people feel supported and motivated to give their best because they know their leaders genuinely care about their well-being.

Change impacts people in many different ways and is a complex thing to lead. Complex because it involves people, with myriads of different responses. Individuals transition through the phases of change at different rates and with different levels of energy. By recognising the ways people experience change through the lens of the Transitions Model, engaging them effectively with the aid of the DELTA Model, and encouraging them to contribute in ways that energise them as measured by The GC Index, people feel seen, respected, and supported to drive the change themselves and make their greatest impact.

As we look to the future, the need for loving leadership has never been greater. It is a leadership style that not only drives results but also leaves a legacy of care, connection, and human-centred success. Loving leaders create workplaces where individuals can thrive, teams can collaborate, and organisations can grow, all while honouring the humanity of everyone involved.

Ultimately, loving leadership transforms the way we approach our work and the people we work with. It challenges us to lead with our hearts, to prioritise relationships, and to cultivate environments where everyone has the opportunity to succeed. By embracing the energy of loving leadership, we can create lasting positive change — for ourselves, our teams, and our organisations.

References

Bridges, William, 2009, *Managing Transitions: Making the Most of Change*, Perseus Books Group

DeSmet, A., Rubenstein, K., Schrah, G., Vierow, M., Edmondson, A., 2021, *Psychological Safety and the Critical Role of Leadership Development,* McKinsey & Company

Engelberg, Moshe, 2019, *The Amare Wave: Uplifting Business by Putting Love to Work*, Angel Mountain Press

Kübler-Ross, Dr Elisabeth, 1969, *On Death and Dying,* Macmillan

Phillips, Simon, 2007, The DELTA Model – 5 Steps To Transform Your Change Management

Porges, Stephen, 2025, *What is Polyvagal Theory?,* The Polyvagal Institute, https://www.polyvagalinstitute.org/

Seppala, Emma and Cameron, Kim, 12/1/2025, *Proof That Positive Work Cultures Are More Productive*, Harvard Business Review

Smith, Renée, 2025, *A Loving Workplace: The Case for Shifting from Fear to Love*, whitepaper published by Center for a Loving Workplace, www.LovingWorkplace.org

Section 3:

Recognising the Power and Potential of Neuroenergy

Our work with The GC Index has given us many new insights about the ways in which human beings differ when it comes to the expression of energy. The chapters in this section explore the unique ways in which energy can be expressed by individuals, adults and children with neurodiverse characteristics.

Chapter 8

Understanding Neurodivergence Through the Lens of The GC Index

In their research, Dr John Mervyn-Smith and Reem Prakkash explore the relationship between neurodivergence and The GC Index profiles. Their findings support an asset-based perspective that highlights the potential strengths of neurodivergent individuals.

This chapter posits that neurodiversity, akin to biodiversity, is essential for human adaptability and survival. Despite the growing acceptance of various forms of diversity, neurodivergence often remains negatively perceived due to traditional academic frameworks that focus on deficits rather than strengths.

An overview of this chapter:

- Critique of the medical model: The authors explore the limitations of a prevailing medical model approach that pathologises neurodivergent characteristics, arguing it fosters a narrative of deficiency compared to a 'normal' standard. They advocate for the neurodivergent paradigm which redefines neurodivergence as a natural variation in human cognition.

- Definition of neurodivergence: Neurodivergence encompasses individuals whose cognitive processes, and associated behaviours, differ from societal norms. The authors emphasise the importance of clear definitions to avoid confusion in academic discourse.

- Neurodivergence and GC Index proclivities: The research found that individuals with ADHD were, typically, Game Changers in GC Index terms, a proclivity that suggests an obsessive need for creative expression. Conversely, these individuals exhibited lower scores for the Implementer proclivity which suggests little energy for practical and routine tasks.

- Implications for individuals and organisations: The findings suggest that individuals with ADHD and dyslexia have the potential to drive innovation and original thinking within organisations. By recognising and leveraging the potential strengths of neurodivergent individuals, organisations could enhance team performance and foster a culture of creativity.

By understanding neurodivergence through the lens of The GC Index, organisations can unlock the potential of neurodivergent individuals, fostering a culture of innovation and adaptability essential for navigating the complexities of a fast-changing world. The authors call for continued research and dialogue to promote the rights and recognition of neurodivergent individuals, highlighting that diversity in thought is a powerful asset that can drive meaningful change.

In summary, the paper advocates for a shift in perspective regarding neurodivergence, urging an inclusive approach to embracing neurodiversity as a vital asset rather than a deficit. Building on this understanding, it becomes crucial to highlight three key considerations when reviewing this paper:

1. While this study confirms correlations between certain GC Index proclivities and neurodivergence through statistical analyses, these relationships should not be interpreted as direct or exclusive causal links.
2. Although this paper adopts a strength-based approach, it does not intend to diminish or overlook the challenges and struggles faced by neurodivergent people.
3. Given the individual differences and unique intersectional experiences of neurodivergent individuals, this paper does not generalise strengths or challenges. Instead, the focus is on the prevalent strengths and a greater tendency of leveraging certain abilities.

Introduction

Consistent with the Darwinian view of the importance of human adaptability for the survival of the human species, we are assuming in this paper that biodiversity is a necessary feature of the process of adaptation to change so vital for survival. The functioning ecosystem within which we all exist relies on this simple fact of nature, and without biodiversity, human societies would lack, we would argue, what is needed to survive.

So, when many forms of diversity are widely embraced in this regard, why is neurodivergence viewed, on balance, in such a seemingly negative light?

Traditional academic research on neurodivergence, which has been strongly influenced by a 'medical model' view of pathology, has seemingly created this negative account, placing focus on the deficit between these divergent traits and what is deemed 'typical' or 'normal' (Dwyer, 2022; Shields & Beversdorf, 2021). An alternative viewpoint, titled 'the neurodivergent paradigm', has emerged from the criticism of the medical model and it aims to change the current academic narrative on neurodivergence. Throughout the process of understanding neurocognitive functions, we find it surprising that there even is a 'norm', leading to the question 'is anyone really neurotypical?' (Russell, 2022).

In this paper we will:

- Seek a definition of neurodivergence. This is a difficult task because it is constantly evolving, with many terms used interchangeably.
- Present a summary of the research themes already established regarding neurodivergence which includes the manifestation of neurodivergence.
- Outline those areas of enquiry which remain contentious.
- Present the findings from our research that has sought to understand neurodivergence through the lens of The GC Index.

What is neurodivergence?

In order to build upon the current literature and research on neurodivergence, it would be useful to define the term. However, it is apparent that the definition is consistently evolving, with writers often disagreeing on how to define this term and with differing views spanning the academic literature (Dwyer, 2022; Pellicano & den Houting, 2021).

For the purposes of our research, we have kept our definition relatively simple to enable an open engagement with our data presented below. More specifically, we take the view that neurodivergence refers to individuals whose brains function differently from what is understood as the societal 'standard' and that these differences are manifest in discernible differences in behaviour.

We take this term to be synonymous with neurodivergent and neuroatypical. While the basis of the term neurodivergence appears to be similar across the literature, a common issue, according to Legault (Legault et al., 2021, pp. 12845), is that some terms are often mixed up and utilised interchangeably in a way that is, potentially, unhelpful.

For the sake of clarity here, we take the view that 'neurodiversity' simply refers to the 'range of natural diversity that exists in human neurodevelopment' (Pellicano & den Houting, 2021). As Walker noted in 2014, it is often stated that an individual 'has' neurodiversity, or that there are 'forms' of neurodiversity, neither of which are possible (Walker, 2014).

They would instead be referred to as neurodivergent individuals or a form of neurodivergence. It is important to make this distinction to ensure our own defining of the necessary terms is comprehensive, but also to point out the missteps that occur too often when researching neurodivergence. 'Neurodiversity is an atypical neurological development' (Houdek, 2022, pp. 1849), and simply refers to the fact that 'diverse minds and brains exist' (Dwyer, 2022).

Rosqvist also makes the point that an incorrect viewpoint of neurodivergence has become entrenched in academia (Rosqvist et al., 2023). Researchers have been 'trained' to understand the diversity of neurocognitive function as a disorder (Pellicano & den Houting, 2021), one that prohibits an individual's abilities and therefore their prospects. This is a view that has been challenged as limiting, a viewpoint that itself limits neurodivergent individuals, as many researchers point out neurodivergence is not a disorder that disables individuals (Brown & Fisher, 2023; Buckley et al., 2024; Pellicano & den Houting, 2021).

The problem here seems to be less to do with definition but more to do with the consequences of that definition. More specifically, the risk with the notion of deviation from the norm, whether called diversity or divergence, is that that deviation has implied negative consequences.

Some would prefer the view that each recognised 'condition' has its own individual challenges, but there may be unique benefits. For instance, autism can 'lead to higher levels of innovation and productivity within organizations' (Houdek, 2022, pp. 1849).

What do we know about neurodivergence?

There is a considerable and growing body of literature about neurodivergence, however a consensus view of the manifestation of neurodivergence is difficult to determine from the current literature.

Neurodivergence, at present, encompasses a wide number of neurocognitive 'conditions', including but not limited to: attention deficit hyperactivity disorder (ADHD), autism, attention deficit disorder (ADD), schizophrenia, depression, dyslexia (Rothstein, 2012, pp. 99). Each 'condition' has 'traits' that it can be associated with, and primarily used to support an official medical diagnosis.

However, these are not exhaustive, and each 'condition' manifests itself uniquely in every individual. For instance, it is considered that the three major symptoms of ADHD are hyperactivity, impulsivity, and inattention (Rothstein, 2012, pp. 103). While these may often manifest similarly, there is a significant gap between the age at which males and females receive a diagnosis due to how it displays differently in women. According to the 5th edition of the *Diagnostic and Statistical Manual of Mental Disorders* (DSM-5) the total number of specific diagnoses is 157 (Houdek, 2022, pp. 1849).

It is hard to grasp how many individuals would fall into these categories with recent studies estimating that 1 in 88 people are autistic (Rothstein, 2012). The sheer number of neurocognitive conditions, as well as the number of individuals with these conditions makes it incredibly hard to determine how neurodivergence manifests in a way that is meaningful let alone practically useful. One could argue that every individual is unique thus making their condition unique as well.

There has been a relatively recent shift in general enquiry into neurodivergence. As mentioned, traditionally, atypical developmental research has been conducted within the framework of the medical model (Dwyer, 2022, pp. 73). This research focuses on the 'deficit' in behaviour between neurodivergence and neurotypical behaviours (Heasman & Gillespie, 2019, pp. 910; Houdek, 2022, pp. 1842; Pellicano & den Houting, 2021), with an unnecessary focus on 'causation and cure' (Rothstein, 2012, pp. 112).

This approach considers that the disabling features of neurocognitive differences are inherent to those conditions (Shields & Beversdorf, 2021). This approach also sees neurodivergence as a disability rooted within individuals, thus limiting them at a base cognitive level (Pellicano & den Houting, 2021). It assumes that disabilities are pathological in nature, which means they are 'medical disorders' of the mind and body causing individuals to have potential deficits which in turn lead to functional limitations (Dwyer, 2022; Russell, 2022, pp. 298).

The 'solution' inherent in this approach is to bring that individual's abilities into the accepted norm in order to transform them into typically developed individuals (Dwyer, 2022; Pellicano & den Houting, 2021). Predictably, this model has been criticised heavily, with the majority of the frustration being the need to find a cure or transform individuals to function in a 'typical' manner (Dwyer, 2022).

The inherent assumption of the existence of a typical level of ability that holds as the 'ideal state of health' is problematic, but in particular for neurodivergence as it comes back to the question 'is anyone really neurotypical?' (Russell, 2022; Pellicano & den Houting, 2021).

The conventional medical approach, these writers argue, places too much emphasis on cognitive deficits, thus having the unintended consequence of highlighting what these individuals may struggle with, rather than the unique assets that may also accompany these conditions (Pellicano & den Houting, 2021). There are four primary issues with this conventional medical approach:

- An overfocus on deficits.
- An emphasis on individuals rather than the social context.
- A narrowness of perspective (Pellicano & den Houting, 2021). While the conventional medical model assisted researchers in shaping neurodivergence science, its narrow-minded approach and fundamental issues has meant that it has been more damaging than useful, as it potentially excludes and alienates those individuals that it seeks to explain.
- This approach is beginning to shape approaches to managing neurodiversity in the workplace in the sense that it is seen as something to compensate for rather than harness in a positive way.

More recently, perhaps in reaction to the medical model, an alternative view has emerged, known as the neurodiversity paradigm.

This movement aims to change the narrative on the current approach to neurodivergence. It aims to advance the rights of neurologically atypical individuals (Shields & Beversdorf, 2021, pp. 127). The primary focus is upon changing the view that neurocognitive differences are not diseases that need to be treated, but instead they are simply variations in human functioning 'that must be equally respected' (Ortega, 2009).

This view, fundamentally, rejects the point that 'divergence from the norm is a flaw requiring correction' (Pellicano & den Houting, 2021), instead placing focus on how neurodivergent behaviours simply differ from what is deemed as neurologically typical (Legault et al., 2021; Rothstein, 2012). These neurocognitive conditions are not disorders that afflict individuals, but instead are merely differences in cognitive function (neurocognition). The medical model of approaching neurodivergence pathologises individuals (Russell, 2022, pp. 298), whereas the neurodiversity paradigm pushes the fundamental point that these individuals have unique differences (Rothstein, 2012, pp. 112). It may be misleading to suggest that there are no disadvantages to these 'conditions', but this blinkered approach ignores the potential advantages. The findings of this research described below, seek to bring some balance to these contrasting viewpoints.

There are two key assumptions within this paradigm that also need to be outlined. First, divergent neurocognitive development is neither superior nor inferior to 'typical' neurocognitive development (Pellicano & den Houting, 2021). If diversity within neurocognitive development can be valuable, then neurocognitive typically does not represent the 'right' way to develop (Pellicano & den Houting, 2021). Second, this paradigm is inclusive of all neurodivergent people, aiming to encompass and promote rights for every neurodivergent individual (Pellicano & den Houting, 2021).

The neurodiversity paradigm aims to reframe neurocognitive diversity simply as a normal manifestation of biodiversity (Chapman, 2021), with the main point being that minds and brains, no matter the functional differences, should all be valued (Dwyer, 2022, pp. 77). It is imperative that neurodivergent individuals are viewed as unique and worthwhile persons, whose lives hold meaning and purpose (Pellicano & den Houting, 2021). It is damaging for them to be understood as individuals who have neurocognitive 'deficits' that inhibit their abilities and their lives. There are, of course, clear parallels with the changing narrative that we have experienced around physical differences over the last four decades.

It is also important to note that while research into neurodivergence has had a reasonable amount of collaboration between academics, the neurodivergent community is often left out of these efforts (Pellicano & den Houting, 2021). It is necessary to bring neurodivergent individuals into the academic narrative surrounding this topic, as researchers themselves, rather than simply including them in the research effort more generally.

An understanding of neurodivergence through the lens of The GC Index

The origins of this enquiry

In 2018, we started to make note of anecdotal observations from GCologists[4] of a possible relationship between reports of dyslexia and certain GC Index profiles (please refer to Appendix 1 for the GCI model). More specifically, we tentatively noted a relationship between dyslexia and high Game Changer scores within GC Index profiles.

---

[4] People accredited to use The GC Index.

An initial pilot study in 2021 supported the view of such a correlation. In 2024 we determined to broaden our approach by including a broader range of neurodiverse 'conditions' in our enquiry.

To guide this research, the following three key questions have been identified:

How does neurodiversity correlate with proclivities measured by The GC Index?

What are the associations between specific neurodiverse conditions and each GC Index proclivity, and are these associations statistically significant?

How might insights from these connections inform strength-based interventions and identify growth areas for individuals to reach their potential?

Our findings are presented under the following headings:

- Methodology
- Research findings
- Summary of findings
- Discussion
- Conclusion.

Methodology

Research methodology

A briefing note (Appendix 5) and questionnaire were circulated to 835 GCologists – accredited practitioners of The GC Index (See Appendices 1 and 2) in May 2024.

We received a total of 396 completed responses to the questionnaire: 258 women and 138 men from 36 countries and in the age range of 18 to 70+.

These data were subjected to a number of statistical analyses to determine possible statistically significant differences relative to the following variables: a formal diagnosis of a neurodivergent 'condition', the subjective report of identification with a neurodivergent 'condition', GC Index profile, age and gender.

Statistical analysis

The relationship between GC Index proclivities (See Appendix 1 for a detailed description of each GC Index Proclivity) and neurodiversity was explored through an initial analysis examining each proclivity in relation to various neurodivergent conditions.

The study investigated the relationship between GC Index proclivities – namely, Game Changer, Implementer, Strategist, Polisher, and Play Maker – and various neurodivergent conditions, specifically ADHD, autism, dyslexia, Asperger's syndrome, dyspraxia, and dyscalculia. Neurodiversity was further categorised based on diagnostic status: formal diagnosis (professional practitioner), informal diagnosis (self-reported), and no diagnosis.

Research findings

The tables and chart below present the numbers and percentage of respondents in each category of neurodiversity

The number of those people with a formal diagnosis of neurodiversity:

Report	Dyslexia	ADHD	Asperger's	Autism	DYSP	DYSC
N	19	34	0	1	0	1
%	4.8	8.6	0	0.3	0	0.3

Table 1: Formal diagnosis respondents

Those reporting a self-diagnosis neurodiversity:

Report	Dyslexia	ADHD	Asperger's	Autism	DYSP	DYSC
N	21	42	2	10	6	10
%	5.3	10.6	0.5	2.5	1.5	2.5

Table 2: Self-reported respondents

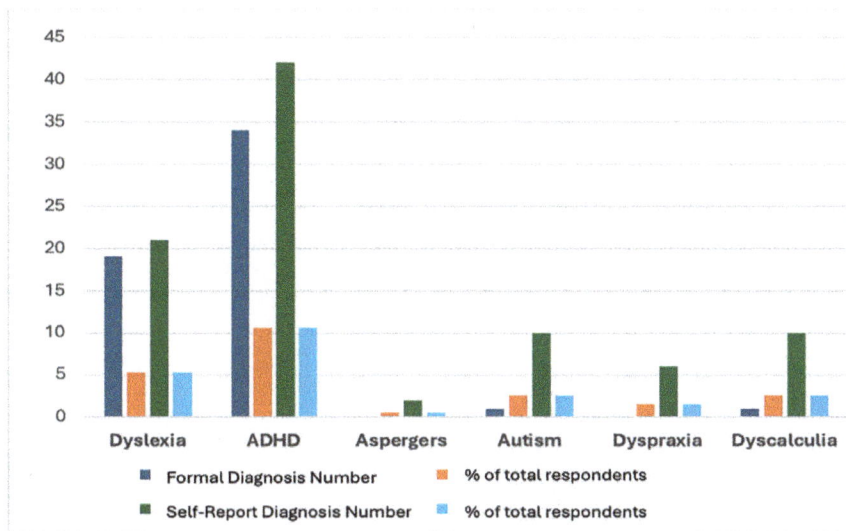

Chart 1: Neurodivergence by category, comparing numbers of those with a formal diagnosis with those with a self-reported diagnosis

Analyses of data: Game Changers and ADHD

The analyses of these data show that while not all individuals with a high (7–10) score for Game Changer report a formal diagnosis of ADHD, a statistically significant number of those with a formal diagnosis are, in GC Index terms, Game Changers. See Chart 2 overleaf.

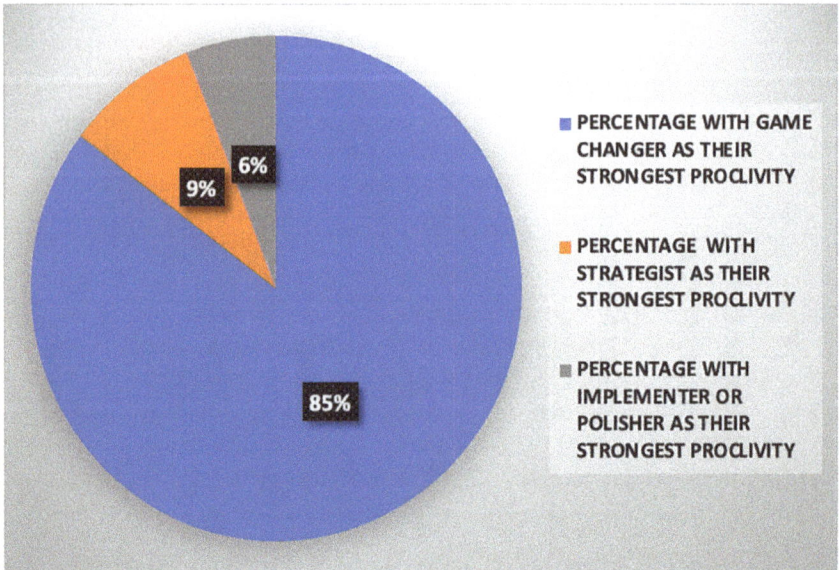

Chart 2: Percentages (of a total of 34) of people with a formal diagnosis of ADHD relative to their strongest GC Index proclivities

The average GC Index Game Changer score for this group of 34 was 7.67. This compares to a general population average on a 10-point scale of 5.5.

With reference to the underlying constructs of The GC Index this means that people with ADHD see themselves as significantly more obsessive and imaginative than the general population.

Game Changer energy would appear to be consistent with some of the characteristics of ADHD, as listed by NHS, UK (attention deficit hyperactivity disorder – ADHD – symptoms, 2017) such as:

- restlessness and edginess
- taking risks in activities, often with little or no regard for personal safety or the safety of others.

Our statistical analyses also revealed that this group also had significantly weaker Implementer energy with an average score of 3.27. As we expected, the frequency of the combination of a strong Game Changer proclivity with a weaker Implementer proclivity was also statistically significant. We were observing data that, statistically, was unlikely to occur by chance and, therefore, needs an explanation. This, we hope, will be the subject of further research.

A lack of Implementer energy would also appear to be consistent with some of the characteristics of ADHD (attention deficit hyperactivity disorder – ADHD – symptoms, 2017) such as:

- continually starting new tasks before finishing old ones
- poor organisational skills
- inability to focus or prioritise.

A strong Game Changer energy taken together with a weak Implementer energy then, would appear to be consistent with these symptoms noted on the same website (attention deficit hyperactivity disorder – ADHD – symptoms, 2017):

- carelessness and lack of attention to detail
- continually starting new tasks before finishing old ones
- poor organisational skills
- inability to focus or prioritise
- restlessness and edginess
- extreme impatience
- taking risks in activities, often with little or no regard for personal safety or the safety of others.

If we take an asset-based view of this combination of Game Changer and Implementer proclivities we would expect people to be:

A potential source of original thinking that can be the basis for creative and transformational ideas that are not constrained by the 'tried and tested' and 'received wisdom'.

Consistent with this, Game Changers, by definition, have the potential to see possibilities in ways that others often don't.

Moreover, The GC Index database shows that business owners as a group have statistically significantly higher Game Changer scores than the general population. This finding may be consistent with the view that ADHD is associated with risk-taking but not always of a reckless nature unless we see recklessness as 'in the eye of the beholder'.

Anecdotal evidence of Game Changer business owners suggests that their perceptions of loss are related to not doing something, rather than doing something and 'failing'. So, we could argue that a 'risk-taking' nature can underpin cultures of innovation and experimentation in the workplace.

Analyses of data: Game Changers and dyslexia

The analyses of data for those individuals reporting a formal diagnosis of dyslexia also revealed a statistically significant relationship with the Game Changer proclivity.

More specifically, this group had higher average scores (6.9) than we would expect to occur by chance.

So, in GC Index terms, dyslexic individuals are significantly more likely than the general population to see themselves as obsessive and imaginative.

If we take an asset-based view of this observation we would expect people with dyslexia to be:

- A source of original thinking that can be the basis for creative and transformational ideas that are not constrained by the 'tried and tested' and 'received wisdom'.
- Consistent with this, Game Changers see possibilities in ways that others often don't.

Discussion

The findings from our analyses of these data allows us to suggest an asset-based view of both ADHD and dyslexia that compares and contrasts with a 'condition' and 'deficit' view more in keeping with the medical model approach.

Our data shows that both ADHD and dyslexia are, in GC Index terms, associated with Game Changer energy, which in turn, reflects self-perceptions of imagination and obsession. As noted above, this energy is significantly associated with business ownership and individuals who, in organisational settings, can bring ideas that transform organisations.

Anecdotally, we notice in our work with Game Changers that their original ideas (imagination) are a product of non-linear thinking, with Game Changers reporting that they are seen as people who:

'Can see around corners.'

'See things that other people don't.'

'Join up "dots" that others don't see.'

'Don't think in "straight lines".'

Given these observations it's interesting to note that dyslexia can be seen, in some respects, as a struggle to process data – letters and words – in a linear way.

Furthermore, the imaginative and obsessive qualities inherent to ADHD can challenge the traditional understanding of 'attention deficit'. Individuals with ADHD frequently demonstrate hyperfocus on specific tasks or interests, suggesting a capacity for intense concentration. While this observation is anecdotal, it prompts us to reconsider the concept of 'normal' thinking and the role of unconventional thought processes in fostering creativity and originality. Scientifically, research has established a connection between ADHD and enhanced creativity. A review of behavioural studies revealed that individuals with high ADHD scores tend to exhibit heightened divergent thinking and creative abilities (Hoogman et al., 2020).

We can take the view then, that those individuals with ADHD and dyslexia have the potential to make a positive contribution to, and impact upon, their world with their Game Changer energy. Moreover, we could take the view that as the pace of change in many aspects of life increases and that that change is increasingly non-linear, that Game Changer energy is needed to both change and adapt to the world in which we live.

It is important to note that this research does not aim to establish a direct solitary correlation between neurodiversity and creativity, nor does it imply that neurotypical individuals lack creative abilities. Rather, the aim is to shift the focus from a 'condition' label towards a strengths-based approach within personal, social, and occupational settings, without diminishing the challenges associated with neurodiversity.

If, and we can't answer this question, the frequency of ADHD and dyslexia has increased over the last 50 years, then we might speculate upon the evolutionary value of these neurological changes. Our findings offer some thoughts on this for discussion and continued research.

Discussion: future research and possible applications of these findings

Future research

In the fields of psychology and broader medical science, exploring neurodiversity through the lens of positive psychology is a relatively new area of research. This study represents one of the initial efforts to approach neurodiversity from a strengths-based perspective, strongly advocating for diversity, equity, and inclusion (DEI).

Moreover, it extends this perspective by examining neurodiversity through an intersectional lens of gender, thus aiming to establish a more nuanced understanding of the topic and promote inclusivity.

Extensive studies in the field have consistently shown that ADHD diagnostic tools tend to be biased, starting with the criteria used for diagnosis (Martin, 2024; Tighe, 2021; Willcutt, 2012). According to data from the Centers for Disease Control and Prevention (CDC, 2022; Danielson et al., 2024), only 8% of girls in the United States are diagnosed with ADHD compared to 15% of boys. Building on this discussion, several questions arise for future research.

One area of exploration is the investigation of gender-based diagnostic disparities with larger samples of working adults. Such research could aim to determine whether there are any statistically significant patterns and identify specific areas of concern. Additionally, future studies could examine how these insights might inform strategies for creating more inclusive workplaces, particularly through the lens of neurodiversity and gender. Neurodiversity could also be explored further from an intersectional perspective, analysing potential correlations with factors such as geographic regions or age.

Another potential avenue for research involves expanding the sample size using The GC Index to examine neurodiverse conditions beyond ADHD and dyslexia, which were the primary focus of this study. A broader dataset could help identify statistically significant strengths and proclivities associated with various neurodiverse conditions. Such findings could enhance the understanding of neurodiversity from a strengths-based perspective, contributing to decision-making processes at individual, social, and organisational levels.

We also noted that some of those individuals who reported a formal diagnosis of ADHD had completed The GC Index before they had received their formal diagnosis and informal conversations with those individuals suggests that their GC Index profile may have been distorted by 'masking' ADHD characteristics. If this is the case then it supports the potential value of a qualitative approach to explore the lived experiences of neurodivergent individuals.

Such investigations could provide valuable and nuanced insights into the unique strengths and challenges faced in both personal and occupational contexts. By integrating qualitative findings with quantitative data, researchers could achieve a more balanced understanding of the relationship between GC Index proclivities and neurodiversity.

These directions emphasise the need for continued exploration of neuro-diversity through inclusive and intersectional lenses, paving the way for more equitable and comprehensive frameworks to support neurodiverse individuals.

Possible applications

For individuals

At the individual level, this research aims to shift the narrative around neurodiversity away from a deficit-based lens.

By presenting statistically validated data and observations, the study aspires to empower neurodivergent individuals to embrace their potential strengths. Encouraging them to leverage these inherent abilities can help them to 'put their best foot forward' in both personal and professional contexts.

> *'I'm at my best when allowed to focus on ideation and strategy, ideally with support in place to manage the routine tasks required for implementation. Recognising this has been essential to managing my work in a way that leverages my strengths and builds in practical support for areas that don't naturally align with my ADHD tendencies.'*
>
> *Andy (Appendix 2)*

Drawing insights from Andy's story (Appendix 2), two prominent themes emerge: the need for support and the value of independent space for productivity and flourishing for those with ADHD. ADHD dynamics can present challenges, not only for the individual but also for stakeholders such as the team, manager, and organisation. However, our research, along with anecdotal experiences, underscores the critical importance of fostering independent thinking to enable individuals with ADHD and strong Game Changer energy to thrive in professional environments.

For society

On a societal level, this study seeks to contribute to the gradual acceptance and normalisation of neurodivergence, akin to other psychological phenomena. It advocates not only for full acceptance but also for the appreciation of the distinctive strengths that neurodiverse individuals could bring to society. By fostering awareness and appreciation, this research aims to challenge stereotypes and pave the way for a more inclusive culture.

For organisations

From an organisational standpoint, the findings of this study can be leveraged to create mutually beneficial opportunities for both employees and employers. These insights can inform the structuring of teams and the overall organisation in ways that optimise the strengths of neurodiverse individuals. While accommodations and adjustments may be necessary for some, this research seeks to advance the narrative of individual strengths through the paradigms of DEI and positive psychology.

> '... yet my manager saw something in me and gave me respon-
> sibilities.
> I feel it was at this point in my life that the team I worked with
> could see what I was capable of.'
>
> Claire (Appendix 3)

Claire's story (Appendix 3) highlights the critical role that managers, teams and organisational support play in identifying and nurturing an individual's strengths. Moreover, her experience underscores the value of granting employees — particularly those with ADHD or a strong Game Changer mindset — the freedom and space to leverage their creativity and 'think outside the box'.

> '...low scores are not a bad thing and self-awareness is a key
> leadership skill. Understanding my low Implementer energy and
> high Polisher energy has helped me identify a need to delegate
> to "happy Implementers", and a need for people to implement
> who have high Polisher scores too.'
>
> Dr Judith (Appendix 4)

Dr Judith's insights in Appendix 4 highlight the importance of balancing a team with diverse strengths and proclivities. Our findings show that most neurodivergent individuals, particularly those with ADHD, tend to score high as Game Changers but low as Implementers. Understanding this can help organisations and individuals to build teams or assign tasks in a way that balances different strengths. As Dr Judith highlights, delegating tasks to Implementers can ensure a well-rounded team contribution and a high-quality output.

Through the Person-Job Fit (PJF) model (French & Caplan, 1972), organisations can identify roles that align with the specific strengths highlighted by The GC Index, such as originality, imagination, creativity, and risk-taking.

Conversely, areas with weaker proclivities such as Implementer, often associated with ADHD and dyslexia, can be addressed through targeted interventions. These interventions can support individuals in overcoming challenges while maximising their GC-Indexed proclivities, thereby enhancing alignment between individual capabilities and job demands.

Conclusion

This research aimed to explore the correlation between neurodiversity and GC Index proclivities. With a total of 396 respondents, three groups were divided into formal diagnosis, informal diagnosis, and no diagnosis of different neurodiverse 'conditions'.

While all the means of all four diagnosed 'conditions' – ADHD, autism, dyslexia, and dyscalculia were associated with high GC Index Game Changer scores, only those scores for people reporting formal diagnoses of ADHD and dyslexia revealed results of statistical significance.

The findings suggest that ADHD and dyslexia are associated with a higher subjective perception and report of original thinking and imagination. These findings, along with the anecdotes, can help inform future strength-based interventions within organisational settings.

Further qualitative studies are needed to shed more light upon the relationship between ADHD and dyslexia and the manifestation of GC Index proclivities. In particular, this would provide an opportunity to investigate the patterns and implications of high Game Changer and low Implementer proclivities which we have observed in individuals with ADHD.

Acknowledgments

The authors would like to express their sincere gratitude to Nigel Evans, chartered psychologist, for his invaluable guidance in shaping the research methodology during the early stages of this project. We are deeply thankful to Andy Cracknell, Claire Elston, and Dr Judith Mohring for sharing their personal stories and insights. Our sincere appreciation also goes to all the participants who generously dedicated their time and efforts to contribute to this research.

Ethical statement

Participation in this study was entirely voluntary, and all participants were informed of their right to ask questions or withdraw from the study at any point without any consequences. Informed consent was obtained from all participants prior to their involvement, and their privacy and confidentiality were strictly maintained throughout the research process. Further details, including the briefing note provided to participants, can be found in Appendix 5.

APPENDICES

APPENDIX 1: The GC Index

The GC Index is an organimetric with psychometric properties. Its origins, underlying constructs and research are presented in detail in the following publications and documents:

- *Coaching Me Coaching You,* Mervyn-Smith, J., and Ott, N., 2018, self-published, The GC Index Ltd, ISBN-13: 978-1-5272-2713-2, ISBN: 1-5272-2713-8
- *The GC Matrix: The Research & Science Behind The World of GCology, Version 3.0.* Mervyn-Smith, J., Ott, N., Evans, N., & Furnham, A., 2020. Available on request from: info@thegcindex.com

The GC Index is a unique language and framework for understanding and profiling individual differences when it comes to Energy for Impact.

Since its development and launch in 2017, The GC Index has been used by coaches, psychologists and consultants to help individuals and organisations understand and develop their Energy for Impact.

Fig. 1: The GC Index model at research phase 3

The framework describes five proclivities that reflect individual differences when it comes to channelling energy, the basis for making an impact.

The GC Index, then, measures proclivities not competence.

These five proclivities suggest individual differences in the following ways:

Strategists

- Bring energy to making sense of patterns and trends in events and data, looking for causal relationships.

Game Changers

- Bring energy to new ideas and possibilities, to original thinking.

Play Makers

- Bring energy to seeking consensus in groups that leads to a sense of cohesion.

Implementers

- Bring energy to delivering tangible outcomes.

Polishers

- Bring energy to review, learning, continuous improvement, and the pursuit of excellence.

APPENDIX 2: A New Diagnosis and an Old Profile: Rethinking my Strengths with ADHD

Andy Cracknell

Strategic Marketing Consultant
Be Seen Media Ltd, Marketing, Branding and Communications
5 November 2024

Recently, I received an ADHD diagnosis, a revelation that's reshaped how I understand my approach to work, decision-making, and relationships. This diagnosis has provided clarity about why I operate the way I do. Interestingly, it also casts a new light on an assessment I took over a decade ago. My GC Index profile:

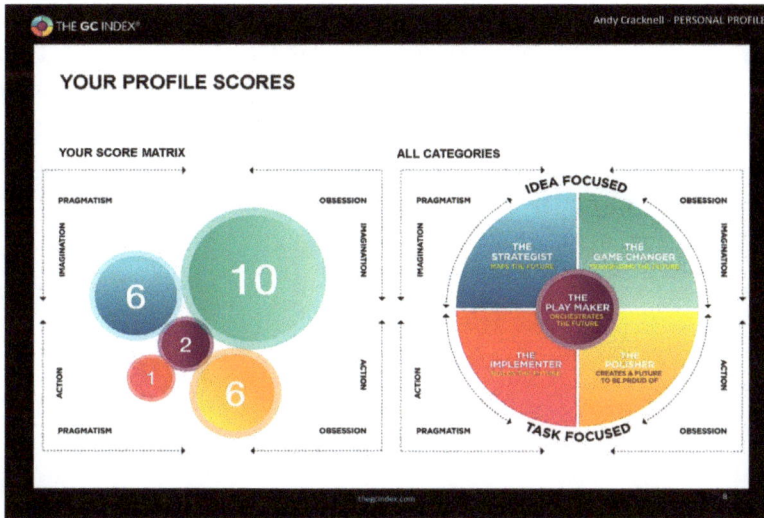

Back then, my GC Index results identified my strong Game Changer proclivity as well as energy for both Strategist and Polisher proclivities. My Implementer energy was seen as low.

At the time, these insights were eye-opening, yet I didn't fully understand why they resonated so strongly. Now, with my ADHD diagnosis, these descriptions of my creative drive, strategic focus, and challenges with routine tasks make even more sense. Looking at my GC Index profile through the lens of ADHD has helped me understand not only my strengths and potential strengths, but also how my approach can be an asset when properly supported.

Game Changer: the creative drive of ADHD

The GC Index maps Energy for Impact and, Game Changers are seen within the model as people with a strong need for creative expression that reflects their capacity for original thought and seeing possibilities that others often miss.

My experience of being a Game Changer, in GC Index terms, is that I thrive on new ideas and possibilities with a drive to question the 'tried and tested', accepted norms and fixed boundaries — characteristics that resonated with me years ago but now align even more closely with my experience of ADHD.

My ADHD feels part of a restless curiosity and the constant urge to explore, challenge, and reimagine. Like many Game Changers I have talked to, individuals with ADHD can see potential where others may not, driven by a unique perspective that flourishes when given the freedom to explore. Far from being constrained by conventional approaches, both ADHD and the Game Changer proclivities capture a need to innovate and imagine possibilities that might not be obvious to others.

The Game Changer - 'Freedom is the Oxygen of Possibilities'

IMPACT

THE GAME CHANGER
TRANSFORMS THE FUTURE

DRIVERS

POSITIVE IMPACT

- They are possibility-centred. They see possibilities in ways that others often don't.

- Generate original ideas that can be creative, supporting transformational change.

- They can help organisations to reinvent themselves with their creative ideas.

NEGATIVE IMPACT

- May see things with such clarity that they can become fixated with turning an idea into a reality.

- Might struggle to accept that an idea may not be relevant or timely.

- They can lose interest and become visibly bored.

A GAME CHANGER'S DRIVERS

The need for creative expression; to express their ideas, thoughts and feelings in an uncensored way.

- They see possibilities which might seem unrealistic or intangible to others.

The freedom to be expressive in a way that can bring about change.

- Game changers work best in a 'safe to fail' cultures that encourages experimentation in innovation and creativity.

Hyperfocus: the determination of the Strategist

One often misunderstood aspect of ADHD is hyperfocus: the intense, almost obsessive concentration on topics or projects that resonate deeply.

For me, this ability to zero in with laser focus aligns directly with the Strategist aspect of my GC Index profile. Strategists bring a strong desire to put ideas into a larger context, analysing possibilities within a broader vision. This ability to focus intently and strategically is a potential strength, I would argue, of both ADHD and the Strategist proclivity, especially when I'm passionate about a goal.

As a Strategist, I'm motivated to think through how to achieve impactful outcomes, and ADHD's hyperfocus enhances this ability to stay locked into a vision. The combination of ADHD and the Strategist mindset gives me the discipline to bring ideas into a strategic framework and sustain focus on long-term impact – especially when I believe in the mission and feel there's real value in the work.

The Strategist - 'The Past Shapes Our Future'

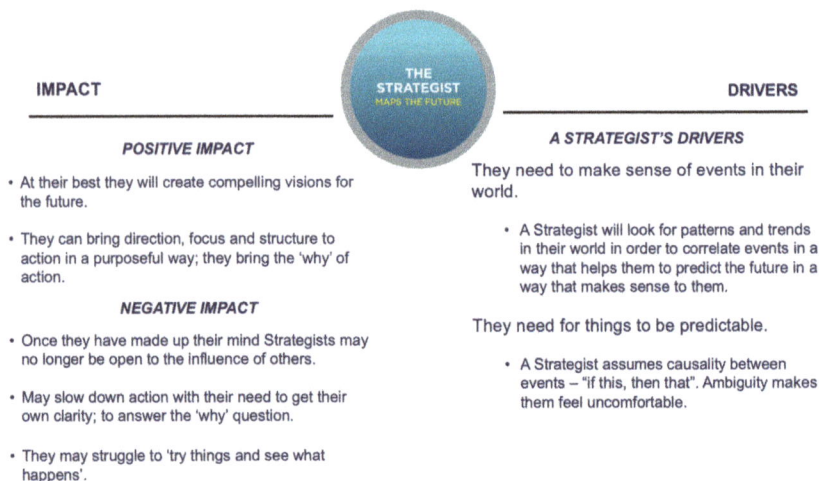

THE STRATEGIST
MAPS THE FUTURE

IMPACT

DRIVERS

POSITIVE IMPACT

- At their best they will create compelling visions for the future.

- They can bring direction, focus and structure to action in a purposeful way; they bring the 'why' of action.

NEGATIVE IMPACT

- Once they have made up their mind Strategists may no longer be open to the influence of others.

- May slow down action with their need to get their own clarity; to answer the 'why' question.

- They may struggle to 'try things and see what happens'.

A STRATEGIST'S DRIVERS

They need to make sense of events in their world.

- A Strategist will look for patterns and trends in their world in order to correlate events in a way that helps them to predict the future in a way that makes sense to them.

They need for things to be predictable.

- A Strategist assumes causality between events – "if this, then that". Ambiguity makes them feel uncomfortable.

Low Implementer score: managing routine and execution

Not all Game Changers or Game Changer/Strategists report a formal diagnosis of ADHD. But, as the research of Dr John Mervyn-Smith, Nigel Evans and Reem Prakkash (2024) shows, over 90% of people with a formal diagnosis of ADHD who have taken The GC Index, profile as Game Changers.

There has been an interest, given this in the influence of other variables and what's emerging, is the relevance of Implementer energy or, more specifically, a lack of it.

While the Game Changer and Strategist proclivities align well with my experience of ADHD my GC Index also revealed a low Implementer score, a characteristic that has emerged from the work of Mervyn-Smith et al., as a statistically significant feature of individuals with ADHD.

Implementers are described as those who bring energy to getting things done in an action-oriented, task and outcome-focused way. They are comfortable with routine tasks, follow-through and repetitive execution.

However, my understanding of people with ADHD, consistent with my own experience, is that they can struggle with routine tasks, follow-through, and repetitive execution — especially when the work doesn't feel novel or creative.

For me, this low Implementer energy means that, while I can be 'deeply committed' to strategic goals and big ideas, the day-to-day, routine aspects of execution can be challenging.

ADHD for me brings a tendency toward mental fatigue in the face of repetitive tasks, and without novelty or purpose, motivation can dwindle. This aspect of my GC Index profile reinforces that I'm at my best when allowed to focus on ideation and strategy, ideally with support in place to manage the routine tasks required for implementation. Recognising this has been essential to managing my work in a way that leverages my strengths and builds in practical support for areas that don't naturally align with my ADHD tendencies.

The Implementer - 'Just Do It!'

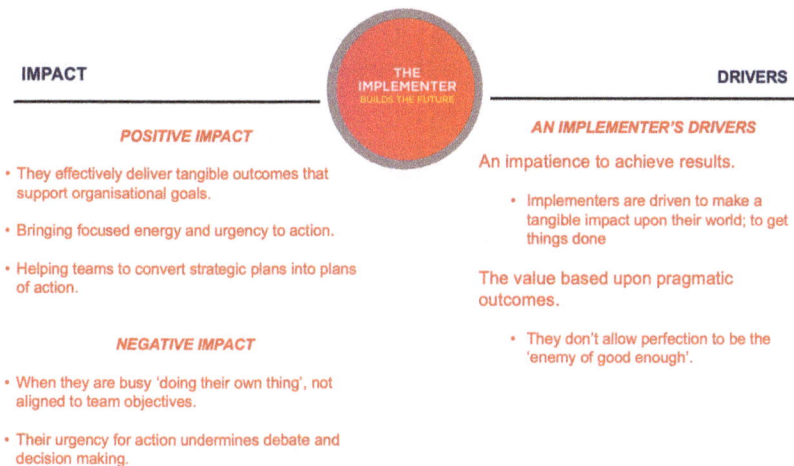

IMPACT

THE IMPLEMENTER
BUILDS THE FUTURE

DRIVERS

POSITIVE IMPACT

- They effectively deliver tangible outcomes that support organisational goals.

- Bringing focused energy and urgency to action.

- Helping teams to convert strategic plans into plans of action.

NEGATIVE IMPACT

- When they are busy 'doing their own thing', not aligned to team objectives.

- Their urgency for action undermines debate and decision making.

AN IMPLEMENTER'S DRIVERS

An impatience to achieve results.

- Implementers are driven to make a tangible impact upon their world; to get things done

The value based upon pragmatic outcomes.

- They don't allow perfection to be the 'enemy of good enough'.

Creative problem solving: the ideal environment for ADHD

The GC Index also identifies me as a creative problem-solver, a focus that is naturally aligned with many people with ADHD The GC Index research would suggest.

My understanding is that individuals with ADHD can excel in dynamic environments with complex, layered challenges and possibilities. I've found that, far from feeling overwhelmed by these challenges, ADHD can actually fuel the creative problem-solving process.

The high level of stimulation that comes with ADHD means I'm often engaged by intricate problems, and this energy helps me approach issues from fresh perspectives. Both ADHD and the creative problem solver in me thrive on stimulation, novelty, and the freedom to explore complex situations without constraint.

Together, they make dynamic problem solving an ideal fit for me, reinforcing that ADHD isn't a barrier – it's an asset when allowed to operate in the right environment.

Embracing neurodiversity in the workplace

Reflecting on my GC Index profile through the lens of ADHD highlights the value of neurodiversity in the workplace. ADHD, combined with the Game Changer and Strategist mindsets, shows how 'non-linear thinkers' can drive innovation, provide vision, and bring a creative edge to problem solving; to seeing possibilities that others don't.

For workplaces, supporting individuals with diverse cognitive styles isn't just beneficial, it's essential for building well-rounded, forward-thinking teams. My GC Index profile provided clarity years ago, and my recent ADHD diagnosis has added even more depth to that understanding. Together, they remind me – and I hope they remind you – that diversity in thought is a powerful asset. Neurodiversity isn't just something to accommodate, it's a force that can unlock potential and drive meaningful change.

APPENDIX 3: The Game Changer: Embracing ADHD to Redefine Success

Claire Elston

Managing Director and Senior HR Business Partner
Elston HR Ltd
20 January 2025

When I was younger although I wasn't naughty, I struggled to sit still and was always talking or playing on my chair at school. I was put into the bottom sets when I moved to secondary school, the teachers spent most of their time dealing with the 'naughty' kids and so, therefore, I had very little support or help.

I was predicted to fail all of my GCSEs, and it was only when I visited a local college and got my sights set on doing a Leisure and Tourism GNVQ that I knuckled down. I needed 5 GCSEs and, in the end, I passed all 10 by cramming my revision in.

Around the age of 20 I went out to France to work on campsites as a rep. I was one of the youngest in our team of reps with the least experience, yet my manager saw something in me and gave me responsibilities. Each summer season I went back to France, I received a promotion becoming Area Manager and then onto Regional Manager covering half of Europe.

I feel it was at this point in my life that the team I worked with could see what I was capable of.

After my time in France, I worked for a large UK hotel operator as Operations Manager. I found this job really hard as the company required you to follow the rules. To do things the way it had set up and not to deviate from this. Being someone who likes to add flare and do things differently I really struggled with this. Now knowing my Game Changing status, I know why I didn't enjoy working in this way. I felt they wanted you put in a box and I just squeezed into this box!

Receiving a diagnosis of ADHD at the age of 41 has given me a lot of clarity, now this all makes sense. I have spent my life berating myself, thinking badly of myself and being overly sensitive to criticism. I deeply care about people and what people think. I am a true people-pleaser, when speaking to people I often get told 'Yes, I am people-pleaser, too.' However, this really is extreme, I can overthink what someone in the supermarket said for weeks on end.

I feel I have spent my life being told what I can't do and what I am not so good at, but now working for myself I get to work and use my strengths. I absolutely love a 'firefighting' style scenario, I love to swoop in and solve all the issues, to set people up for success and then leave. The life of a consultant suits me well.

What is most interesting is when I first did The GC Index I came out as a Strategist/ Implementer. Even when I completed the assessment I was trying to fit in and people-please as it was one of my clients that told me all about The GC Index. I have recently redone my assessment and have come out as a Game Changer/Strategist which feels much more me! My motto is I genuinely believe there is a better way of doing things, we must think out of the box!

This is my GC Index profile:

APPENDIX 4: Beyond the Box

Dr Judith Mohring

Organisational Psychiatrist and ADHD Educator
www.thenaturalpsychiatrist.com

What have I learned from my profile?

My GC Index profile is presented below and came sometime after my diagnosis of ADHD. It has resonated with my understanding of myself as someone who can't sit still, has relentless energy for new ideas and is incapable of confining thoughts to 'inside the box'.

My vision in my work as a psychiatrist has always been 'outside the box'. I know that medication and therapy are effective tools in improving mental health, but I can't help obsessing over 'everything else' from lifestyle, psychiatry to education as effective, evidence-based interventions to improve mental well-being and more. It's why my business now provides training and education as the mainstay of improving employee and individual mental health.

I've also realised that low energy scores are not a 'bad thing' per se and that awareness of self in this regard is key to self-acceptance. Knowing my low Implementer energy and high Polisher energy has helped me identify a need to delegate to 'happy Implementers' who have energy for routine tasks.

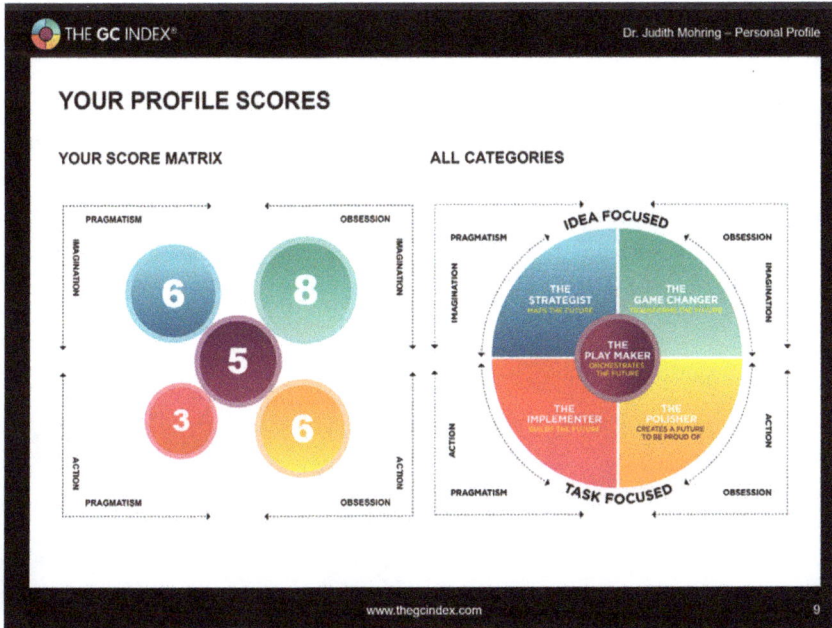

GC Index profile: Dr Judith Mohring

APPENDIX 5: Briefing Note

GC Index and Neurodiversity
23rd April 2024

BRIEFING NOTE (To be sent to all GCologists)

We need your help

Neurodiversity and The GC Index – A Research Project

The Action

If you're interested in furthering our understanding of neurodivergence through the lens of The GC Index, please complete the attached questionnaire.

Your responses will be treated in strictest confidence, and I will be correlating your responses with your GC Index profile. Please do not complete the questionnaire if you have any concerns in that regard.

Headline results from this research will be presented to our GCologist community by the 30th September. No one's individual data will be revealed at any point.

The Context

Many in our GCologist community have an active interest in neurodiversity and working with neurodivergent individuals.

For some years we have been collecting anecdotal data that suggests a relationship between certain GC Index profiles and neurodivergence.

This project will bring some science to those anecdotal observations.

Please get in touch if you have questions and/or would like to be involved in this initiative in any way.

The Questionnaire

Please complete each row with a ✅

Your Name:

Your contact Email address:

		YES Please Tick ✅	NO Please Tick ✅
Have you received a formal diagnosis for any of the following:	Dyslexia		
	ADHD		
	Asperger's		
	Autism		
	Dyspraxia		
	Dyscalculia		
	Other: Please specify		
While not formally diagnosed, do you strongly identify with having any of the following:	Dyslexia		
	ADHD		
	Asperger's		
	Autism		
	Dyspraxia		
	Dyscalculia		
	Other: Please specify		

References

Attention deficit hyperactivity disorder – ADHD – symptoms, 2017, October, Nhs.uk. https://www.nhs.uk/conditions/attention-deficit-hyperactivity-disorder-adhd/symptoms

Austin, R. D., & Pisano, G. P., 2017, 'Neurodiversity as a Competitive Advantage', *Harvard Business Review,* 95(3), pp. 96–103

Brown, M. I., & Fisher, H. R., 2023, 'Promoting neurodiversity without perpetuating stereotypes or overlooking the complexity of neuro-developmental disorders', *Industrial and Organizational Psychology*, vol. 1, no. 16, pp. 36–40, available at: <https://doi:10.1017/iop.2022.97>

Buckley, E., Sideropoulos, V., Pellicano, E., & Remington, A., 2024, 'Higher levels of neurodivergent traits associated with lower levels of self-efficacy and wellbeing for performing arts students', Neurodiversity, 2, available at: <https://doi.org/10.1177/27546330241245354>

Chapman, R., 2021, 'Neurodiversity and the Social Ecology of Mental Functions', *Perspectives on Psychological Science*, vol. 16, no. 6, available at: <https://doi.org/10.1177/1745691620959833>

Danielson, M. L., Claussen, A. H., Bitsko, R. H., Katz, S. M., Newsome, K., Blumberg, S. J., & Ghandour, R., 2024, 'ADHD Prevalence Among US Children and Adolescents in 2022: Diagnosis, Severity, Co-occurring Disorders, and Treatment', *Journal of Clinical Child & Adolescent Psychology*, pp. 1–18

Dwyer, P., 2022, 'The Neurodiversity Approach(es): What Are They and What Do They Mean for Researchers?', *Human Development*, no. 66, vol. 2, pp. 73–92, available at: <https://doi.org/10.1159/000523723>

Dyck, E., & Russell, G., 2020, 'Challenging Psychiatric Classification: Healthy Autistic Diversity and the Neurodiversity Movement. *Healthy Minds in the Twentieth Century: In and Beyond the Asylum,* pp. 167–187

French, J. R., & Caplan, R. D., 1972, Organizational stress and individual strain. The failure of success, 30(66), pp. 61–77

Glenn, D., 2022, Review of *Neuroqueer Heresies: Notes on the Neuro-diversity Paradigm, Autistic Empowerment, and Postnormal Possibilities:* Walker, N., *Neuroqueer Heresies: Notes on the Neurodiversity Paradigm,*

Autistic Empowerment, and Postnormal Possibilities, Fort Worth, TX: Autonomous Press, 2021. *World Futures,* 78(5), pp. 339–341

https://doi.org/10.1080/02604027.2022.2094194

Heasman, B. & Gillespie, A., 2019, 'Neurodivergent intersubjectivity: Distinctive features of how autistic people create shared understanding', *Autism,* 23(4), May, pp. 910–921, available at: SAGE Journals

Houdek, P., 2022, 'Neurodiversity in (Not Only) Public Organizations: An Untapped Opportunity?', *Administration & Society,* no. 54, vol. 9, pp. 1848–1871, available at: <https://doi.org/10.1177/00953997211069915>

Legault, M., Bourdon, J. N., & Poirier, P., 2021, 'From neurodiversity to neurodivergence: the role of epistemic and cognitive marginalization', *Synthese*, 199, pp. 12843–12868, available at: <https://doi.org/10.1007/s11229-021-03356-5>

Martin, J., 2024, 'Why are females less likely to be diagnosed with ADHD in childhood than males?', *The Lancet Psychiatry*, 11(4), pp. 303–310

National Center for Health Statistics, National health interview survey: methods, US Centers for Disease Control and Prevention https://www.cdc.gov/nchs/nhis/methods.htm

Ortega, F., 2009, 'The Cerebral Subject and the Challenge of Neurodiversity', *BioSocieties*, 4(4), pp. 425–445, available at: <https://www.cambridge.org/core/journals/biosocieties/article/abs/cerebral-subject-and-the-challenge-of-neurodiversity/63B14E8F528A660AF0312B70311AB1EB>

Pellicano, E., & den Houting, J., 2022, 'Annual Research Review: Shifting from "normal science" to neurodiversity in autism science', *Journal of Child Psychology and Psychiatry*, 63(4), pp. 381–396

Rosqvist, H. B., Botha, M., Hens, K., O'Donoghue, S., Pearson A., & Stenning, A., 2023, 'Cutting our own keys: New possibilities of neuro-divergent storying in research', *Autism*, 27(5), July, pp. 1235–1244, available at: <https://doi.org/10.1177/13623613221132107>

Rothstein, A., 2012, 'Mental Disorder or Neurodiversity?', *The New Atlantis,* no. 36, pp. 99–115, available at: <http://www.jstor.org/stable/43152738>

Russell, G., 2022, 'Critiques of the neurodiversity movement', in Kapp, S.

K. (ed), *Autistic Community and the Neurodiversity Movement: Stories from the Frontline,* London: Palgrave Macmillan, available at: <https://doi.org/10.1007/978-981-13-8437-0_21>

Shields, K., & Beversdorf, D., 2021, 'A Dilemma for Neurodiversity', *Neuroethics,* no. 14, pp. 125–141, available at: <https://doi.org/10.1007/s12152-020-09431-x>

Tighe, A., 2021, A Neglected and Untreated Population: Addressing the Systemic Underdiagnosis of Females with ADHD

Walker, N., 2014, Neurodiversity: Some Basic Terms & Definitions

Willcutt, E. G., 2012, 'The Prevalence of DSM-IV Attention-deficit/hyperactivity disorder: a meta-analytic review', *Neurotherapeutics*, 9(3), pp. 490–499

Chapter 9

ADHD and The GC Index – is There a Link?

Dr Judith Mohring builds upon the research detailed in Chapter 8 that describes a relationship between ADHD and GC Index profiles. She explores a specific question: how might we understand the relationship between ADHD and strong Game Changer energy coupled with weak Implementer energy?

Why is there a pattern of high Game Changer and low Implementer scores in people with ADHD?

What do we make of the findings Dr John and Reem have made that there is a significant relationship between having ADHD traits and a combination of high Game Changer scores alongside low Implementer scores? As an expert educator in the science, understanding and treatment of ADHD, what do I make of this? Is it a surprise? If not, why not?

Who am I and what is my interest?

I've been a psychiatrist for 25 years working everywhere from Holloway Prison to Harley Street. I now lead two businesses. In the first, The Natural Psychiatrist, I work as an expert trainer and coach to businesses and individuals. We design and deliver evidence-based educational workshops exploring the science of well-being, leadership, resilience and neurodiversity. In early 2025, we launched ADHDEd., a programme of evidence-based, practical education and groups for successful adults with ADHD and the professionals who support them.

I'm a clinical expert in ADHD and train doctors in its diagnosis and treatment as part of the UK Adult ADHD Network. I'm also on the advisory board for the Centre for Neurodiversity at Work at Birkbeck University, and a visiting lecturer in Organisational Psychiatry at King's College, London.

I trained as a GCologist in 2024 having first been introduced to it through my coach on the government's 'Help to Grow' management course. I use The GC index in my own team, in my leadership coaching practice and in organisational consulting as an aid to fast awareness. I'm a Game Changer/Polisher with a low Implementer score and I also have a diagnosis of ADHD.

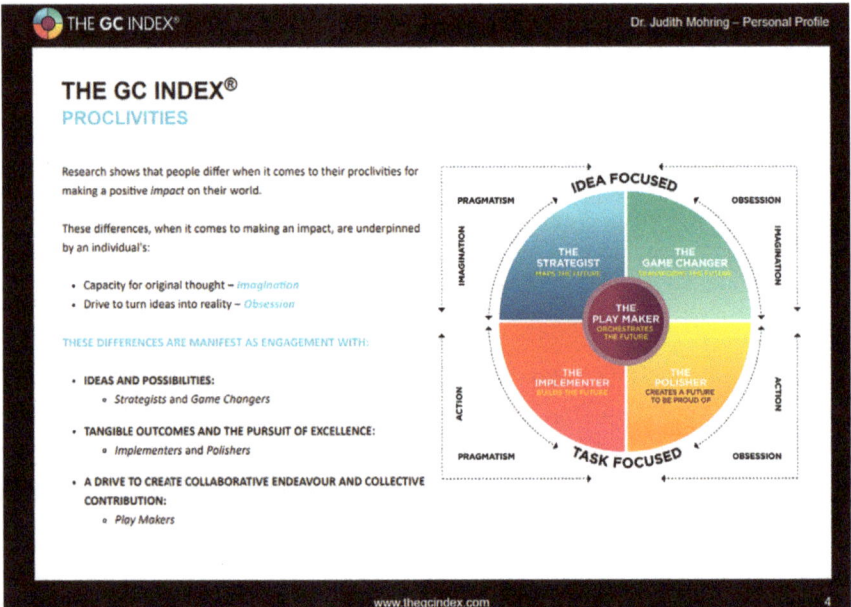

What does The GC Index measure?

The GC Index grew out of a practical need by corporations to identify Game Changers (Mervyn-Smith et al.,2020). These are the individuals who have the potential to transform corporate/business functioning to some degree; to initiate and drive transformational change.

The preliminary research (see Appendix 1) suggested that Game Changers, compared to C-level executives and high-potential executives, were perceived as significantly different relative to these characteristics:

- More likely to 'see the bigger picture'
- More driven and obsessive
- Risk-takers

- More creative
- Less strategic.

Within this group of characteristics are features we would expect to see in neurodivergent people – particularly those with ADHD and/or dyslexia. Research in neurodivergent people suggests that creativity and an ability to see the bigger picture are common strengths in dyslexia, and being driven, obsessive, creative and able to take risks are common strengths of ADHD. There is significant overlap in diagnoses of ADHD and dyslexia with around 40% of each group having the other diagnosis. So, it appears that from the very beginning of The GC Index research, neurodivergent traits were being recognised by people in their colleagues, but being identified as Game Changer energy.

Flipping Neurodiversity on its head: from diagnosis to difference

Neurodiversity refers to a constellation of differences in the way that people experience the world through thinking, sensation, social interaction, information processing, communication and behaviour. The term was originally coined by Judy Singer and is now used to describe a group of different ways of being (Singer, 2017).

Traditionally diagnosis of these ways of being was seen as the focus for formal medical diagnosis: and the ways of being were categorised as quite separate conditions. Now we understand them more as a constellation of differences. The diagnostic categories used for neurodivergent conditions include autism, attention deficit hyperactivity and specific learning disorders.

As we learn more about neurodiversity it is becoming apparent that as well as certain difficulties, there can be characteristic cognitive strengths in being neurodivergent. We are moving from a diagnostic construct to one of recognising differences, including both strengths and strains.

What is ADHD?

ADHD is a form of neurodiversity, a developmental difference in the way the brain functions which impacts how we experience, behave and operate in the world. People with ADHD may struggle with attention and concentration, motivation and focus, organisation and implementation.

In psychological terms, their executive function, the ability to use the brain to get things done, or implement, is impaired compared with people without ADHD, and this means they may struggle to order and implement action. They may be very mentally and physically active, energetic and busy sometimes to a degree which causes them, or others, problems. They can also seem impulsive and have difficulties with powerful emotions.

ADHD 'runs in' families and is associated with not one but many different genes (Faraone & Larsson, 2019) and commonly co-occurs with other forms of neurodiversity including autism, dyslexia, dyspraxia and dyscalculia. ADHD is not a mental illness it's a way of being, rather like personality. But it does predispose to many common mental health conditions including anxiety, depression, insomnia, eating disorders, OCD (obsessive compulsive disorder) and PTSD (post-traumatic stress disorder).

ADHD is caused by differences in a number of brain networks and neurotransmitters and ADHD traits exist in a normal distribution in the population, meaning many of us will have some traits.

The graph below is from a Danish study (Hoeffding et al., 2018) showing how a population of adults showed some features of ADHD.

The ASRS is the Adult ADHD Self-Report Scale and the diagram below plots the scores on this scale for this population. You can see from the curve that symptoms of ADHD are common, but only a few people have so many symptoms that they would meet the diagnostic threshold for ADHD with a score of 37+.

Distribution of the ASRS scores in the cohort

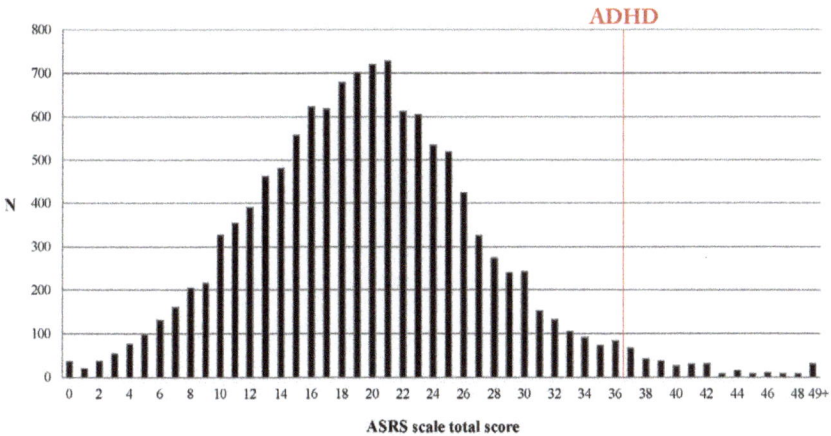

Hoeffding et al., 2018: Sociodemographic characteristics of adult blood donors with ADHD in Denmark

ADHD strengths

Although ADHD has been described using a deficit model, and is diagnosed using a disease model, in many people it is linked to significant strengths. Jane Sedgwick, Andrew Merwood and Philip Asherson interviewed a group of high functioning adults with ADHD for their 2019 paper (Sedgwick et al., 2019).

They identified six core strengths within this group:

- Cognitive dynamism
- Courage
- Energy
- Humanity
- Resilience
- Transcendence.

Four of these six strengths map directly onto the 20 core strengths identified by Martin Seligman in his 'positive psychology' research and discussed by Sedgwick et al. (2019).

These are highlighted in green in Table 1 below. But a subset of six strengths were unique to ADHD, highlighted white in the table below.

These were:

- Divergent thinking
- Hyperfocus
- Non-conformism
- Adventurousness
- Self-acceptance
- Sublimation – putting others before oneself.

COGNITIVE DYNAMISM	COURAGE	ENERGY	HUMANITY	RESLIENCE	TRANSCENDENCE
Divergent Thinking	Non-Conformist	Spirit	Social Intelligence	Self-regulation	Appreciation of beauty and excellence
Hyper-focus	Adventurous-ness	Psychological	Humour	Sublimation	
Creativity	Bravery	Physical	Self-acceptance		
Curiosity	Integrity		Recognition of feelings		
	Persistence				

Table 1: Core themes and defining sub-themes that represent the positive aspects of ADHD

We can clearly see here how the ADHD strengths of divergent thinking and non-conformism map onto the idea of imagination, and how hyperfocus and energy map onto obsession. These are the two core aspects of the Game Changer construct (Sedgwick et al., 2019).

The dyslexic advantage

Dyslexia is a specific learning difficulty which affects the processing of both written and auditory language. Dyslexia has traditionally been seen as a disability, but increasingly there is recognition that it is a difference in cognitive style and function.

Dyslexia has been shown to be associated with certain cognitive strengths as well as difficulties and these are outlined in the book *The Dyslexic*

Advantage by Brock and Fernette Eide (Eide, 2011). They describe strengths in four areas of reasoning: material, interconnected, narrative and dynamic. They also note Dr Julie Logan's research into entrepreneurship and dyslexia (Logan, 2003). Her Cass Business School Study of 2003 showed that between 20 and 40% of entrepreneurs had dyslexia, compared to a diagnostic estimate of around 10% of the general population. It's worth noting, however, that some of these 'dyslexic' entrepreneurs may also have had ADHD as around 40% of people with dyslexia have ADHD and vice versa.

'Big picture thinking' is a classic dyslexic strength; the ability to see a situation in a visual, dynamic, interconnected way is characteristic both of Game Changers and also those with dyslexia.

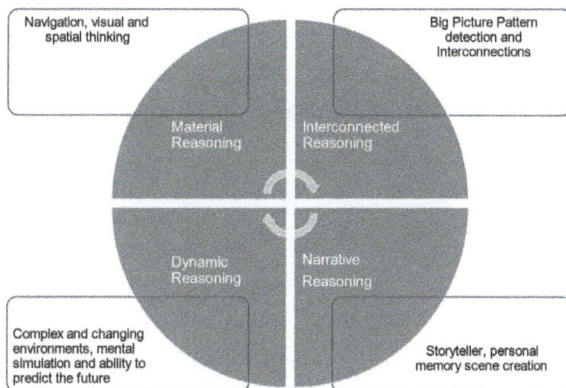

Proclivities, noradrenaline and energy

The GC Index was developed very specifically with a focus on energy, not competence or skills. This distinguishes it from other profiling tools. In practice, I ask people where their attention will naturally flow, given free choice over how to spend their time. ADHD is at its heart a difference in patterns of energy, attention and flow and The GC index helps us understand how these patterns operate.

Noradrenaline is a neurotransmitter which helps regulate attention alertness and stress. It also has roles to play in the sleep-wake cycle, memory and mood. People with ADHD show differences in the way noradrenaline circuits function in the brain (del Campo et al., 2011). With lower noradrenergic activity we see the inattentive symptoms of ADHD: poor memory, focus, concentration, listening and learning. With higher noradrenaline activity we see the hyperactive symptoms of impulsivity, restlessness, impatience, urgency and lack of forethought. Noradrenaline activity is 'geared' through the locus coeruleus and in ADHD it appears to be harder to get the brain into the right gear, we're either underactive in too low a gear and zoned out, or overactive, in too high a gear, hyperfocused and running late to make things happen (Robson, 2024).

Within the strengths-based research of Sedgwick et al., energy came across as a significant positive feature of ADHD. That being able to operate at much higher levels of arousal and stress than others is a core feature of ADHD and both a strength and a strain. This was also demonstrated in the work of Sibley et al., published in 2024.

Default mode network, dopamine and imagination

Another relevant feature of ADHD with respect to imagination is the functioning of the default mode network or DMN. This network was only identified around 20 years ago, it's the 'mind wandering' or daydreaming part of the brain which is active when we're not engaged in a task-focused activity (Vinod, 2023). In people with ADHD this part of the brain struggles to switch off, when we're doing one cognitive task, the mind continues to wander and lead us off track.

ADHD medicines which increase central nervous system dopamine levels have been shown to improve the ability to switch out of DMN function and focus on completing the task in front of us (Faraone et al., 2024). But the DMN has many functions beyond mind wandering, it is the network involved in autobiographical memory, thinking about the past and thinking about the future. It is the home of the divergent, non-conformist, humane and imaginative ADHD strengths, and it also underpins the imagination of the Game Changer.

Low Implementer scores and weaker executive function

So, if people with ADHD have energy, imagination and obsession what stops them being able to implement? Why might GC Index Implementer scores be lower in this group as noted by Reem Prakkash and Dr John Mervyn-Smith in Chapter 8? Can we understand this in terms of impaired executive function?

Executive function is the ability to use the brain to get things done, or implement (Diamond, 2013). To plan, motivate, organise, execute, avoid distraction and complete a task in a timely and sequential manner is definitely not what most people with ADHD would identify as a strength! People with ADHD can often do something if it is urgent or a cause of shame (higher stress and noradrenaline) or if it's very interesting (dopamine driven hyperfocus), but for straightforward, routine, business-as-usual tasks the energy and focus just isn't there. Which explains the low Implementer energy that we see in GC Index profiles.

Can you use The GC Index as a diagnostic tool?

You might ask then, if we can use The GC Index as a diagnostic tool for ADHD or dyslexia, but it wasn't designed for this purpose. ADHD should ideally be diagnosed by clinicians experienced in diagnosing and distinguishing between mental health conditions, so that the right interventions can be suggested (NICE Guideline NG 87, ADHD Diagnosis and Management, Section 1.3.1).

Many of us have ADHD traits as they are common in the population and are normally distributed. To reach the diagnostic threshold according to the DSM-V, we need more than five traits of hyperactivity, impulsivity and inattention with evidence of several of these since the age of 12 in multiple settings, they should be causing distress to a degree requiring specialist intervention and support and the symptoms shouldn't be better explained by another condition like depression or post-traumatic stress disorder.

If you're interested in helping people raise their self-awareness however, and their potential for developing self and relationship management, then The GC index is excellent. So too is Professor Amanda Kirby's DoItProfiler (https://doitprofiler.com/) work on understanding neurodivergence without a formal diagnosis.

A side note on The GC Index and neurodiversity at work

Many neurodivergent people think in pictures, and a picture can convey more information in a more memorable form than words or numbers for many of us. It is interesting that The GC Index gives a visual output representing a person's profile, which is memorable through the use of colour and relative circle size across the diagram.

For me, it makes recalling individual profiles very easy and for neurodivergent colleagues the tool is easy to interpret and remember. In addition, I've found The GC Index useful when coaching teams with neurodiverse colleagues as, without discussing any diagnoses, it's easy to show relative strengths in different areas of business.

What have I learned from my profile?

My profile is below and came sometime after my diagnosis with ADHD. It has supported my self-understanding as someone who can't sit still, has relentless energy for new ideas and is incapable of confining thoughts to 'inside the box'. My vision in my work as a psychiatrist has always been outside the box.

I know that medication and therapy are effective tools in improving mental health, but I can't help obsessing over 'everything else' from lifestyle psychiatry to education as effective, evidence-based interventions to improve mental well-being. It's why my business now provides training and education as the mainstay of improving employee and individual mental health.

I've also realised that low scores are not a 'bad thing' and self-awareness is a key leadership skill. Knowing my low Implementer, high polisher scores has helped me identify a need to delegate to 'happy implementers', and a need for people to implement who have high polisher scores too.

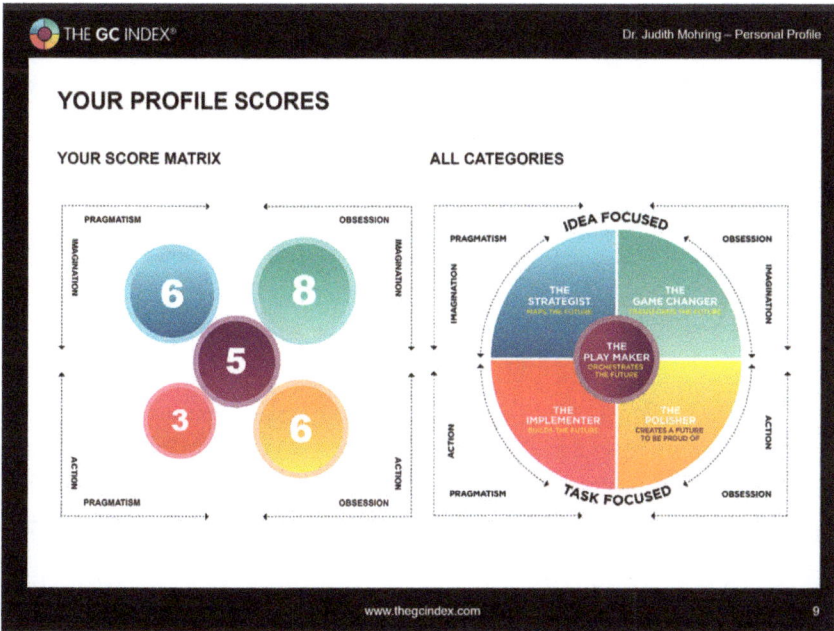

Concluding remarks

The relationship between ADHD traits and The GC Index highlights the unique cognitive strengths and challenges that neurodivergent individuals, particularly those with ADHD, may experience in the workplace.

High Game Changer scores alongside low Implementer scores reflect the natural tendencies of individuals with ADHD to be innovative, energetic, and driven by big picture thinking, yet struggle with the implementation of routine tasks due to their impaired executive function.

While The GC Index was not designed to diagnose ADHD, it can serve as a valuable tool for fostering self-awareness and helping neurodivergent individuals better understand their strengths and areas for growth. By embracing these differences and leveraging The GC Index, organisations and individuals can harness the full potential of neurodivergent talent, enabling them to thrive in environments that value creativity and transformational change.

References

del Campo, Natalia et al., 2011, 'The Roles of Dopamine and Noradrenaline in the Pathophysiology and Treatment of Attention Deficit Hyperactivity Disorder', *Biological Psychiatry*, Volume 69, Issue 12, pp. 145–157

Diamond, A., 2013, 'Executive Functions', *Annual Review of Psychology,* 64, pp. 135–168. doi: 10.1146/annurev-psych-113011-143750. Epub 2012 Sep 27. PMID: 23020641; PMCID: PMC4084861

Eide, B. & F., 2011, *The Dyslexic Advantage: Unlocking the Hidden Potential of the ADHD Brain,* New York, Hudson Street Press

Faraone, S. V., Bellgrove, M. A., Brikell, I., Cortese, S., Hartman, C. A. et al., 2024, Attention-deficit/hyperactivity disorder, *Nature Reviews Disease Primers*, Feb 22, 10(1):11. doi: 10.1038/s41572-024-00495-0. Erratum in: *Nature Reviews Disease Primers,* Apr 15, 10(1):29. doi: 10.1038/s41572-024-00518-w. PMID: 38388701

Faraone, S. V., & Larsson, H., 2019, 'Genetics of Attention Deficit Hyperactivity Disorder', *Molecular Psychiatry,* Apr 24(4), pp. 562–575, doi: 10.1038/s41380-018-0070-0. Epub 2018 Jun 11. PMID: 29892054; PMCID: PMC6477889

Hoeffding, L., Nielsen, M., Didriksen, M., Schow, T. et al., 2018, 'Socio-demographic Characteristics of Adults with Self-reported ADHD Symptoms in a Danish Population of 12,415 Blood Donors', *Journal of Psychiatry and Behavioral Sciences.* 1. 10.33582/2637-8027/1012

Logan, J., 2003, 'Dyslexic Entrepreneurs: The Incidence; Their Coping Strategies and Their Business Skills', Cass Business School

Mervyn-Smith, J., Ott, N., Evans, N., & Furnham, A., 2020, *The GC Matrix: The Research & Science Behind the World of GCology*

NICE Guideline NG 87, ADHD Diagnosis and Management, Section 1.3.1

Robson, David, 2024, 'Take Control of Your Brain's Master Switch', *New Scientist*, Oct 9

Sedgwick, J. A., Merwood, A., & Asherson, P., 2019, 'The Positive Aspects of Attention Deficit Hyperactivity Disorder: A Qualitative Investigation of Successful Adults with ADHD, Attention Deficit Hyperactivity Disorder',

11(3), pp. 241–253, doi: 10.1007/s12402-018-0277-6. Epub 2018 Oct 29, PMID: 30374709

Sibley, M. H., Kennedy, T. M., Swanson, J. M. et al., 2024, 'Characteristics and Predictors of Fluctuating Attention-Deficit/Hyperactivity Disorder in the Multimodal Treatment of ADHD', (MTA) Study, *Journal of Clinical Psychiatry,* Oct 16, 85(4):24m15395. doi: 10.4088/JCP.24m15395. PMID: 39431909

Singer, Judy, 2017, *Neurodiversity: The Birth of an Idea,* ISBN-10 : 064815470X,

ISBN-13 : 978-0648154709

Vinod, Menon, 2023, '20 Years of the Default Mode Network: A Review and Synthesis', *Neuron*, Volume 111, Issue 16

Chapter 10

Helping Game-Changing Children to Thrive in the World of Education

Helen Rivero talks to educators and young people about their experiences of being Game Changers in the world of education in the UK. This thought-provoking piece asks us to think about how we can adapt to meet the needs of individuals with very particular talents.

Introduction

In his video 'Here's to the crazy ones', Steve Jobs offers the view that people who want to change the world for the better, Game Changers by definition, are the ones who do. And yet, in my experience, the world of education often doesn't get the best from young Game Changers. What can be done? The case studies in this chapter give us some ideas to explore and build upon.

Game Changer energy and education

We know from our work with The GC Index (see Section 1, Chapter 2) and with The Young People Index, The GC Index equivalent for 13–18-year-olds, that there are people in the world with strong Game Changer energy. These individuals, typically, have a strong need for creative expression, they bring original ideas to their world and will often question 'tried and tested' approaches to doing things.

Game Changers often propose bold, unconventional ideas that challenge existing norms.

In the world of education, this energy is often an uncomfortable fit but, at the same time I would argue, we need these individuals to be the catalysts for change in the world of education.

Enhancing their communication skills enables them to articulate their vision clearly and persuasively, resonating with others. This clarity is crucial for gaining buy-in and support, building teams, and forming friendships. Collaborating with individuals who have different proclivities, especially those who can provide a pragmatic approach, can be highly beneficial for Game Changers.

The argument that education needs to continually evolve is supported by a long list of individuals who have struggled to 'fit into' existing education systems. Most of us will know someone 'failed by the system'; these are high-profile individuals who, we might guess are, in GC Index terms, Game Changers. Here are some examples.

Albert Einstein dropped out of high school at the age of 15 because he felt traditional schooling left little room for questioning or thought. After leaving high school, Einstein failed the entrance exam to the Swiss Federal Institute of Technology. He then completed his education at a Swiss school in Aarau.

Richard Branson is dyslexic and dropped out of high school at the age of 15. He started Virgin Records and rapidly grew the Virgin brand during the 1980s. Forbes listed Branson's estimated net worth at $5 billion dollars as of 2015.

Walt Disney began drawing in high school. After dropping out at the age of 16 to join the army, Disney was rejected for being underage and joined the Red Cross instead. He was sent to France, where he became an ambulance driver. After returning to America, he became a newspaper artist and eventually one of the most influential animators the world has ever seen.

When we delve into this topic, it becomes evident just how many remarkable and accomplished individuals faced challenges within the school system: try googling 'successful school drop-outs' as a starting point.

On a very personal note, my colleague, co-author and inventor of The GC Index, was 'thrown out' of school at the age of 17, feeling 'written off' by his teachers.

Game Changers in education

In the first part of this chapter, I will explore real stories of Game Changers including pupils, teachers and adults who have had struggles navigating their way through the education system in the UK.

In the second part, I will discuss how we might better support these young people in schools, and at home. I hope this short chapter will provide some useful support for schools, teachers, parents, and young people.

Let us begin with where it all started: The Young People Index. I am writing this first-hand because it is relevant to the history of The Young People Index, and I too, am a high-scoring Game Changer/Strategist.

'I wish I had known this when I was younger'.

Have you ever heard yourself say this? I know a lot of people who have, and continue to do so, as I did nearly eight years ago when I attended a GC Index Accreditation.

Some years before, I'd always dreamed of working for myself, but it felt like a distant 'dream' that perhaps wouldn't become a reality. Entrepreneurship was not discussed at my school as an option, and at the time only 18% of people passed their GCSE exams. We were advised to get a job, and as I wanted to travel after school, my career advice was to become a travel agent!

After some 'negative' experiences in my world of work, I decided now (2016) might be the time to 'try it out' and become my 'own' boss. I'd decided I'd had enough of working within organisations, where they simply wouldn't listen to good ideas!

This would be something that I found out to be common in my world as I started a journey of self-discovery with The GC Index. To interpret GC Index profiles, you must be trained to do so, so training was my first experience of The GC Index. During the GC Accreditation Programme with Dr John, all I kept thinking about was whether this insight would have made a difference to the decisions I made when I was younger. I kept asking myself, would I have had this Energy for Impact when I was at school?

The more I questioned myself, the more I realised that it was present, or at least emergent during my school years. I was compelled, a feature of Game Changer energy, to know if The GC Index could be used with young people or in education, and that was what compelled me to take this innovative and insightful tool into education back in 2017.

The GC Index makes you reflect almost instantly about yourself and your life. My reflection began with considering how I liked to learn, and what things I struggled with. It made me question why I'd moved from one job to another in my early career, getting bored with routine and always gravitating to new projects to work on.

The GC Index changed my perspective and impacted my career trajectory. From the moment I discovered my Energy for Impact, to this present day, I haven't looked back since gaining a new sense of purpose and obsession to change the way young people view themselves during their formative school years.

My observations during the past eight years as co-visionary of the YPI are anecdotal, but the stories are captivating. As I have said, although much of what I discuss in this first part is anecdotal, only down to my observations during my work with young people, I believe that what we measure with The Young People Index can help support young people who find the education system challenging. I am specifically talking about young people with Game Changer energy, as well as teachers within education and their take on this topic.

You might say that every young person agrees that school can be 'challenging', but for some, my son included, it is simply awful (his words not mine!) and not 'fit for purpose' for some. I have listened to many stories from adults who found school challenging, so my hope is that we can positively change this moving forward for young people with Game Changer energy. After all, it is these young people who have the potential to change the world for the better.

What follows are five case study examples of Game Changer energy in three young people and two educators.

Game Changer energy in young people

Case study 1: Game Changer energy or 'disruptive'?

David is a successful entrepreneur. He left school at the age of 15 without any qualifications. Below is David's GC Index profile. He described his time at school as a place where he felt lonely at times, disengaged and lacking purpose in the sense of why it was important to pass RE, or French (as his examples) when they didn't relate at all to his future. I have presented his YPI profile below.

When we discussed his profile, it was evident that his natural proclivities were present at school. He described, on reflection, that he wished that school was a place where you could be more creative, where you had time to 'polish' your work. Unable to satisfy his Game Changer and Polisher proclivities during school made David feel demoralised and he disengaged from his education.

Here are a few snippets from our conversation:

'I was thrown out of the class for being disruptive … But all I wanted was more information, more clarity.'

'I didn't see the purpose in a few subjects and how they related to my future. I wanted to leave and get a job, not go to college or university … That didn't seem to be an option discussed at the time.'

'I didn't have time to "polish" my work leading to feelings of frustration.'

'I thrived in chemistry because my teacher was amazing. He involved everyone in the discussion.'

'I loved coursework over exams.'

'I didn't know I was different back then.'

Case study 2: A young Game Changer learning to adapt to their world

Tom, aged 17, was part of a YPI (The Young People Index), programme with a group of 25 other students. The programme focused upon helping these students think about career choices related to where their energy was. As you can see from his profile below, he has high Game Changer energy, as well as Polisher energy. Tom is a self-aware individual and was able to apply his profile to his studies and what he wanted to do in the future, which was to join a large company in marketing. This is Tom's YPI profile:

During our second visit to the school for workshop 2, Tom told us he had gone for an interview for a part-time job and that he had shared his impact and contribution as part of the interview process. He told us that he had got the job and that he felt that the insight had helped him articulate his impact at the interview. This was great to hear.

Tom told me a little more about how his GC proclivities impact his school experience, including his learning environment. He noted that it's sometimes been a struggle to get people to listen to his ideas. To support Game Changers in school he would like to see teachers include more discussion time in lessons; he's really motivated by conversations, participation, and humour.

Case study 3: A young Game Changer finding their 'sweet spot'

Harry is 15 years old and interested in design. This is Harry's YPI profile:

He related to his Game Changer and Polisher proclivities. He also related this to his interest in graphic design: coming up with new ideas – Game Changer – and making them brilliant – Polisher.

He found that within the school environment there wasn't much time for thinking about concepts and time for discussion. He also found that time was an issue for him because he had a desire to finish things off well, and sometimes that time wasn't available.

He described himself as having a small group of friends, and that at times making friends was difficult, especially if they did not 'get him'. His lower energy for Implementer was difficult for him to manage, especially when things were not clear to him in class; what was expected of him. Clarity (Strategist) and detail (Polisher) were important for him: he needed to understand the 'why' and the 'what' of a task to be able to motivate himself to get things done.

He wasn't overly bothered by working in groups all that often but understood the importance of this. This he said was related to the ideas that he shares and sometimes people don't understand them. Game Changers often report that they don't feel understood in this way.

When we discussed strategies to help him at school, and with friends, we discussed how teachers who involved him in discussions got the best out of him, and teachers who were clear with their instructions, but who also explained 'the why' they were doing things. He had been told previously by teachers that he was easily distracted from the task, and that he was often talking in class and that sometimes he didn't hand in his work on time. We talked about sharing his profile with his teachers, especially the ones who he did not 'gel' as well with. He identified some of them as 'high Implementers' which didn't get the best out of his Game Changer energy.

Harry would like to run his own graphic design business, but the school does not teach much about becoming an entrepreneur, or what opportunities might exist outside university, or getting a job. The YPI review helped Harry to validate his feelings about himself and helped him to understand the environments within which he will thrive in the future.

Summary of themes for young Game Changers

David's narrative exemplifies the disconnect between traditional education and the needs of Game Changers. Despite his entrepreneurial success, school failed to nurture his innovative spirit, leaving him disengaged and unfulfilled. It suggests that offering diverse educational pathways, including direct entry into the workforce, could help students find relevance and motivation in their studies.

Tom, with an understanding of his high Game Changer energy, is navigating his educational journey with self-awareness, leveraging his profile to articulate his impact and secure a part-time job. It reinforces the view that human beings can be hugely adaptable when given opportunities to develop insight and self-awareness; the basis for growth and development.

Harry's story highlights the challenges of aligning with the traditional school framework for creative individuals, underscoring the importance of tailored educational support that recognises these individual differences when it comes to approaches to learning.

All of these examples illustrate that understanding and accommodating different proclivities can lead to more engaged and successful students; they reinforce a common-sense view that people learn in different ways and, therefore, approaches to education cannot be a 'one size fits all'.

Enlightened educators know this and have, probably, know this for years. The following case studies illustrate this point.

Game Changer energy in educators

Case study 4: Ex-head teacher Andrew Roberts-Wray with 17 years of experience in education

This is Andrew's GC Index profile:

Andrew was an educationalist for many years in various roles from teacher, subject leader, pastoral leader, and careers leader to head teacher.

He took the view that being a Game Changer helped when working with students. However, it can be much more challenging when working with senior teachers, senior leaders and governors.

> 'I have taught at primary and secondary level in mainstream and special education and have always aimed to provide as individualised an education as possible for my students, even in classes of over 30 students with a broad range of abilities and no support. Being a Game Changer/Polisher helped because I had the

energy for the creative practical problem solving needed in that environment: finding solutions to teaching your subject in different ways to allow students to access the curriculum in the way that suits them best.

'It also seemed to help me to look for relevance of the topic for my students by looking for applications of examples from real life where possible. This same creative approach helped me to analyse my students: constantly giving me an intuitive understanding of their needs and how to meet them. For me there is a constant internal dialogue and self-reflection that comes from being a Game Changer/Polisher looking for interesting solutions to problems.

'As a Game Changer I also had a need to keep looking to the future and planning for it in my teaching, seeking to give 16+-year-old students the advantage of "reading beyond the curriculum". I wanted to increase their motivation for the topic and subjects I taught. Often this has led to improved exam results. At times this approach would feel at odds with the standard curriculum guidelines.'

Consistent with our understanding of Game Changers, Andrew's approach did not sit well with those educationalists who value the 'tried and tested'. Those with new ideas and new ways of doing things can be seen as a threat to the status quo as they may 'rock the comfortable boat'.

Case study 5: The possibilities for teaching Game Changers – Andy Elliott, Director of Learning

Andy Elliott a Director of Learning in a sixth form at a secondary school in Dorset, UK.

Andy commissioned an external YPI GCologist to work with his sixth form classes after completing his own GC Index profile.

Andy told us that understanding his profile has encouraged him to be more creative and try new things in the school environment. He takes the view that the YPI helps students to understand how their own proclivities could be an asset to them in the workplace of the future. It has also given him a way to understand students' strengths and weaknesses outside of the curriculum content. He embeds a flexible approach to working with students and adapts his approach to what students need.

His advice for working with Game Changer students is 'Give them novel tasks. Give them space to explore answers themselves and opportunities for creativity.'

His observations align with the work of Natalee Holmes, a GC Partner at Conscious Connections in South Africa with a background in teaching. Natalee's work with young people, incorporating The Young People Index and The GC Index within education, supports the notion that the most critical factor in determining the quality of education is the quality of the teacher and quality is defined as the ability to adapt to the individual learning needs and styles of students.

Natalee emphasises the importance of aligning teaching styles with learning styles. Educators, ideally, should be capable of teaching one lesson to an entire group while engaging all learning styles, while recognising the pressures that teachers are under to conform to fairly regimented approaches with large groups of young people.

Our proposal is that when teachers understand themselves and their students, they can significantly improve student performance by recognising and supporting each student's unique contributions and potential. Natalee suggests:

> 'Imagine a system that aligns teachers and students, creating a common language that fosters real learning. By utilising The GC Index and The Young People Index, we enable educators to identify and nurture young people's key talents — the future leaders and workforce. These assessments empower young people by highlighting their natural preferences and show how they are best engaged. They also provide teachers with tools to engage all learners based on the five different proclivities.

> 'Education is central to preparing current and future generations to thrive. It is crucial to develop an education system that fosters human potential.'

Case study summary

Natalee Holmes' findings reinforce the critical role of teachers in education and the need to align teaching styles with learning styles. By using tools like The GC Index and The Young People Index, we can enhance educational outcomes by empowering both students and teachers. This approach can enable a system that values teachers, supports diverse learning styles, and prepares students for future success.

Educators like Andrew Roberts-Wray also recognise the pivotal role that Game Changers can play in education: developing creative approaches to teaching and learning, and challenging the education system more broadly to invite game-changing ideas into the world of education.

Sadly, while fostering creativity and adaptability among students, educators like Andrew often encounter resistance from entrenched systems focused solely on examination outcomes.

Andy's story is, however, an inspirational one: a forward-thinking educator who has leveraged The YPI and GC Index to create inclusive learning environments tailored to students' diverse strengths and aspirations.

Proposals for continued change: what can we do to make things better for Game Changer students in education?

The case studies presented above suggest the following themes for continued focus:

1. The power of *developing self-awareness.*

    a. Helping young people to understand their energy and how they seek to express and channel it for impact
    b. Giving them ways to understand and manage their frustrations when their energy does not align to the process of learning and work.

To support Game Changer energy, YPI insights can help budding entrepreneurs, or intrapreneurs. From the adult world we have seen that the most common The GC Index profile for those starting their own business is Game Changer/Polisher. We have learned much from that world that can help us to take student's entrepreneurial ambitions seriously and help them to think about those people that they need around them to achieve their ambitions.

Developing this self-awareness also helps young people to appreciate the work environments within which they will thrive and almost every young person I speak to tells me how useful they find this understanding. Typically, young and older Game Changers thrive in environments that give them the freedom for creative expression: to challenge the 'tried and tested' and to bring ideas and energy to new ideas and possibilities.

2. Giving them *the confidence to express* their energy by validating and 'normalising' it.

   a. Helping young people to develop those skills needed to express their energy effectively; to have the impact that they want to in their world.

Game Changers often have bold and unconventional ideas that may challenge existing norms and ways of doing things. Consistent with this, a big challenge for Game Changers, again young people and older people, is to build effective skills around communicating their ideas. So, building skills in this area is vital for young Game Changers if they are going to have the impact upon their world that they want to.

An important part of this skill set is understanding how, in terms of the five YPI/GCI proclivities others are similar to, or different from them. This knowledge helps them to tailor their communication in quite specific ways, enhancing their ability to engage and influence others. Our experience suggests that young Game Changers readily grasp, for example, the need to present the practical value of their ideas to Implementer friends and colleagues if they are to be taken seriously.

Developing the confidence to express ideas comes from the development of associated communication skills.

3. Creating the *right learning conditions* for Game Changers.

Using the wonderful insights from a diverse range of people from inside and outside The GC Index community, we have a growing understanding of those conditions that are conducive to learning for Game Changers.

There's more to explore, however, what we have learned to date is already proving useful for teachers, parents, families, and schools.

Consistent with the case studies presented above, these are key ingredients to Game Changer learning:

- The freedom to give expression to possibilities; to play with ideas.
- The freedom to question the 'tried and tested' and 'received wisdom'.
- Being encouraged to take the view that, in principle, no idea is a 'bad idea' but that in the world we live, Game Changers need to develop those disciplines needed to communicate their ideas and help others to evaluate their merit.
- Appreciating that they will have ideas that others don't and that's okay.

Conclusions

The narratives of the Game Changers in this chapter serve as a poignant reminder that each of us has the power to contribute uniquely to our world.

While this chapter focuses upon the educational experiences of Game Changers, my hope is for all young people to develop the self-awareness and confidence needed to learn effectively and, as a consequence, make informed choices about their lives.

Let's offer young people a fresh perspective, one that celebrates their unique Energy for Impact and without confining them to labels or boxes; let's provide them with a window through which they can see endless possibilities.

Thank you to everyone who gave up their time to add in their stories and experiences, Andrew Roberts-Wray, David Store, Andy Elliott, Natalee Holmes and our young Game Changers: David, Tom and Harry.

Personal Journeys from Surviving to Thriving: Understanding the Relationship Between Energy and Well-being

Many of us will have grappled with the challenge of the 'work-life' balance: being productive in a way that pays the bills and, at the same time, feeling that we have time for those activities that 'feed us', giving us the energy that we need to sustain us through the tougher times.

But do we know what 'gives' us energy? Do we know what depletes us? Do we always know what has left us feeling exhausted at the end of a day's work? Do we know what it takes to 'recharge' our energy?

Many of us lose sight of these questions as we seek to meet the complex and competing demands of our lives.

Chapter 11

What Happens when we 'Freeze'?: A Journey of Healing from the Depths of Post-traumatic Stress Disorder

Leticia Dollennga brings to this chapter a personal and compelling story of trauma supported by an academic understanding of what trauma means for people. Her journey of healing was profound but, in some sense, fragile. Her knowledge of The GC Index helped her to understand and trust her journey of change.

Introduction

Two years ago, I discovered The GC Index, which shed light on how I influence my world. It revealed my Implementer energy, and my drive to achieve tangible goals.

Fig. 1: My GC Index profile at April 2021

Shortly afterwards, I experienced a traumatic event which, ultimately, led to a fundamental shift in the way I felt and thought about the world and my relationships in particular. This shift was evident in my GC Index profile when I completed the questionnaire for a second time and helped me to make sense of, and trust, the healing process I had been through.

This chapter explores this change and what prompted it and my experience of a therapeutic approach called Somatic Experiencing (SE); a therapeutic approach developed by Dr Peter Levine and designed to heal trauma and regain emotional balance.

The Nature of Trauma

It is important to start with an understanding of trauma. According to Dr Peter Levine (1997), trauma, can be linked to an internal restraint formed when an intensely distressing moment gets 'trapped' in our psyche, hindering the natural flow of our life. Levine (1997, p. 1) proposes that trauma:

'disconnects us from ourselves, others, nature, and spirit'

impeding our progress in life. In times of overwhelming danger, our instinctual survival energies may become immobilised, creating a sense of being 'stuck' and unable to take action.

This 'freezing' is dramatically evident in the animal world and often described as 'playing dead', Levine (1997, 2015b), explains why a wild animal, displaying this intense physiological shock response, will either become prey or, if spared, return to its normal life after the near-death experience. In other words, when faced with a threat, most animals can defend themselves or run away (fight-or-flight response) from a predator, triggering a considerable physiological response in their bodies, but when these responses are not employed, the prey may resort to a freeze response in an attempt to deceive predators and to save its life.

Similarities between the responses of wild animals to threats and the reactions of individuals when they experience frightening events, started to become evident to Levine in his work with traumatised clients (Rick, 2019). His observations suggested a human equivalent associated with this third survival reaction to a perceived life threat, involving 'freezing' and collapsing.

In situations where neither fight nor flight is possible, both wild animals and humans may 'freeze' and become immobile, resembling a state of 'playing dead' (Levine, 2015b). Should the immobility phase fail to conclude, the accumulated energy remains confined.

In our lives, and possibly in our careers, achieving our aspirations may remain elusive if we neglect to address and reconcile past experiences that continue to manifest in the present. While some find this process clear and easily achievable, others may face more formidable challenges. Nevertheless, navigating these challenges is a natural part of life and we all must confront our fragmented selves as they have the power to shape our reality. This perspective reinforces my belief that each of us holds an inherent potential to excel by embracing our individuality, our history and, more important, our core nature.

A traumatic event

Not long ago a painful and challenging personal experience acted as a reminder of my past traumas. It triggered a resurgence of traumatic stress and reactivation of traumatic symptoms placing my beliefs about the world and life's purpose in a state of suspension.

I went through a heart-wrenching breakup of a relationship that felt like a sudden and unexpected blow. The relationship ended abruptly, leaving me with an overwhelming sense of emotional neglect and abandonment.

For a more comprehensive understanding of how a traumatic event can influence an individual's emotional well-being, Dr Levine's work (SE-MANUAL, 2022) suggests exploring the timeline, events preceding the traumatic event, the event itself, and the experiences that follow. I will provide some context to address this, with the purpose of shedding light on the matter without delving too much into the details of the associated drama.

I met someone through a close friend in whom I confided. Our connection felt secure and committed, a perfect connection given the background, that supported the potential for a fulfilling relationship. During this time, I believed I was living my 'desired life', filled with happiness and promising prospects. In my mind we only had a few practical challenges to address and we would be committed to the relationship. One day, without warning, everything suddenly fell apart.

Shortly before the breakup, I was, without warning, characterised as 'cold and logical'. This left me feeling that my core beliefs and values, such as honesty, trustworthiness, integrity, responsibility, confidence and intimacy were under scrutiny. I experienced a sense of judgement and condemnation that I felt I could never 'shake off', as I was told that my past was the determinant of how I was. I recognise that I may occasionally draw upon these characteristics, especially at work, but I see myself as an inherently sensitive and compassionate individual with a strong ethic, dedicated to others in a cooperative and empathic way. I would say that I embody a tolerant nature, remaining mindful of my responsibilities and the impact I exert on others. I diligently strive to bring positive outcomes in my connections, naturally radiating affability, friendliness, and kindness. Truthfulness is integral to my character, and I inherently aspire to assist others.

Growing up in a dysfunctional environment and losing my father at a very young age, I have little doubt, led to the development of some coping mechanism in life: I have frequently taken on the role of a caregiver to the extent of sacrificing my own well-being. I either yearned to give endlessly or sought escape to avoid feeling too much. Either way, it is, paradoxically, the same subjective experience: the ways in which I express and manage my energy. I would say that I used to become so attuned to those around me that I used to lose sight of myself and my needs, seeking validation, affection, and love.

Consistent with many relationship breakups, perhaps, this proved to be challenging. I had to contend with emotions of abandonment, rejection, and a sense of inadequacy. While I recognise that not all relationships are designed to be everlasting, and people enter and exit our lives, this breakup was different. What stood out the most was the manner in which it ended, similar to my father's passing – abruptly – and mirroring, controversially, what I believed most, that our life cannot be defined or condemned by our past.

I was devastated when my hopes and aspirations crumbled on that fateful day. I felt overwhelmed with guilt and loss, experiencing a sense that I had committed something profoundly wrong. In that tough situation part of me worried that it was all my fault. I was viewed as responsible for another's suffering without any explanation. As days passed, my distress deepened, making it extremely challenging to comprehend what was unfolding.

In my perspective, the world often presents situations where power imbalances lead to abuse. However, when individuals with similar power levels blame each other I would suggest that they're usually avoiding 'real issues'. I wanted this relationship to be different. I chose to be open about my life, childhood traumas, and insecurities, perhaps sharing too much with an individual who lacked experience to accept my past as a part of my history, but saw it as a constraint for my future growth, development and identity. While I had mentally acknowledged that the relationship was over, I bore the weight of the emotional impact of separation.

Often, traumas believed to have been conquered, lie dormant, waiting for a trigger to resurface. This relationship represented a mirror of my past and seemingly offered a solution to resolve everything from the past – 'a perfect match'. With this narrative, past pains were meant to stay behind, and perhaps, I hoped to uncover a solution to my past void. It may sound illogical, but our brains have the capacity for seeking such 'solutions', and this person, consciously or not, represented that 'solution'. Contrary to my hopes, it ended up retraumatising me, forcing me to revisit the pain of a young person who experienced abrupt loss, regressing to my young-self, seeking safety, love and connection.

Today, I've come to the realisation that I'd been in what I experienced as a toxic relationship. It's important to note that my emphasis here is not on labelling individuals as 'bad actors' but recognising that the dynamics and situations themselves can be unhealthy. This wasn't the first instance of encountering such dynamics in life. While each of my previous relationships had its unique circumstances, the outcomes were surprisingly consistent. I found myself grappling with feelings of disappointment and regret leading to a pervasive sense of loneliness and confusion, a feeling reminiscent of what I experienced after my dad's passing.

When a significant event deeply affects us, recognising that we've experienced a traumatic event can be a challenging endeavour. Nonetheless, it's essential to engage in introspection and investigate why it has had such an impact. When we are prepared to undergo a transformative change, toxic relationships can offer abundant information and valuable insights.

I found myself overwhelmed by emotions such as shock, confusion, a sense of danger, as well as intense physical and psychological distress. The conventional therapy I was undergoing at that time did not respond at the pace I required. Instead, it seemed to overstimulate my nervous system, keeping me in a 'frozen' state, hindering the transition to a more effective approach for resolving my post-traumatic reactions.

On the day it happened I tried to hold back the tears, telling myself to 'pull yourself together'. However, within the next hour, I felt really shaken and teary. This continued in the following days. I felt depressed and anxious. I couldn't stick to my usual routine and the uneasy feeling remained for the next few weeks.

I remember the following week: as I attempted to return to my normal self, I decided to take a long walk by the Thames river, near the Queen's Walk, one of my favourite spots in London. Everything seemed perfect; the weather, the sky, the autumn colours. But as I began walking, I experienced a severe panic attack, something I didn't recognise at the time, until I went to a nearby hospital and had it confirmed. I felt completely disconnected from myself and my body was collapsing.

During this period, I alternated between anxiety, depression, angry outbursts, and tears. This took a toll on my work and personal life. My heart raced, I had a knot in my stomach, and my head felt fuzzy, the pain was visceral. Stress levels soared, leading to more panic attacks, sleep troubles, and severe headaches. Even simple activities became a challenge as I found myself unable to focus.

Everything felt tangled and confusing; distinguishing between what belonged to me and the other person's responsibility proved perplexing. Initially I accepted the words spoken to me as the only truth, convincing myself that I was unworthy of being in that relationship due to my past. Simultaneously, thoughts like 'I shouldn't be reacting this way; it's not rational, after all, he called it off, and I just need to accept it' echoed in my mind, yet I felt utterly powerless to alter my emotions. I was in a state of denial.

While recognising the need for adaptive behaviours, my emotions were tumultuous too. I grappled with cognitive dissonance: an internal conflict between my pre-trauma values and the distressing experience I had endured. While honesty, trustworthiness, integrity, and responsibility still hold significance, their application became distanced. The pillars of justice, decisiveness and knowledge wavered under the weight of my emotional turbulence. Appreciation and faithfulness, once seamlessly built, now face the challenge of adapting to the changing structure of my connections. Confidence and stability became elusive. In any relationship the struggle to reconcile these conflicting emotions adds complexity to my interactions.

Another element of trauma present in my experience was dissociation. Dissociation is a component that comes into play when we encounter a threat or experience pain. It involves a profound mechanism that distances us from fear or suffering, creating a rupture in our sense of continuity (Levine, 1997). This disconnection can make us feel detached from time and space, as though we are observing the situation from an external perspective. In the context of trauma, dissociation serves as a coping mechanism, allowing individuals to temporarily endure overwhelming experiences. Levine (1997) also highlights its role in helping manage experiences that would otherwise be unbearable at that moment. In my experience, I believe this disconnection acted as a shield, isolating the constrained energy.

Notably my beliefs were also thrown into turmoil during this period. I consider myself a passionate individual when it comes to understanding people and human behaviour. I believe that each of us has the potential to thrive in all aspects of life by embracing our uniqueness. In my professional path, this conviction drives my dedication to work towards creating a more compassionate world that actively contributes to societal development. However, at this point in time I began to question the potential for personal transformation and growth, which, in turn, challenged my ability to cultivate my personal development and support others on their journey; another aspect of 'freezing' on reflection.

The confined emotions and behaviours within my body were a response to how the trauma was retained. The process of the 'freeze response' was embodied, not verbal. These unsettling impressions, deeply imprinted into my essence, have a profound ability to evoke not only unpleasant but, at times, seemingly insufferable emotional and physical reactions that persist relentlessly.

What is intriguing about these imprints is their mysterious ability to resurface in response to incidents reminiscent of the past wounds or triggered by subtle sensations tapping into hidden parts within the depths of our psyche. They can also manifest when we feel something similar to what we felt in the past, even if we can't quite 'put our finger' on it or describe it with words or thoughts.

In both situations, we end up feeling like we are in danger and exposed, making us go through the same painful experiences all over again. It's like the past keeps coming back and it makes us feel upset and uneasy.

At times, trying to understand things logically, make sense of them, or dwell on the past would not substitute for the importance of getting my body moving and engaged in the healing process. It was during this period that I embarked on my journey with Somatic Experiencing, a therapeutic approach developed by Dr Peter Levine.

Somatic Experiencing (SE) – A look at Peter Levine's work on unlocking our energy

When confronted with trauma it becomes imperative to take a holistic view of the triggering experience and the resultant impact. This holistic approach involves not only 'psychological recovery' but also addressing the sensations and physical impact of a traumatic experience. This was the reason my focus and curiosity led me to explore the fascinating Somatic Experiencing world.

As my SE professor and practitioner Sérgio Oliveira once said in his classes:

> 'Even though we can't change certain facts, the good news is
> that we have the power to take care of our inner selves. It's worth
> exploring the marks that pulse deep within us in this regard.'

Allow me to employ an analogy to illustrate how SE comes into play. Imagine having a car that you have been driving on a challenging road. Over time, the car starts making strange noises and encounters unidentified issues. While you know you need to repair the car, you're uncertain about the exact problem. It won't start and there's a leak. Trying to fix the tyres won't address the presented issues. Instead, you must investigate which specific part(s) is/are affected.

Over the last 45 years, Peter Levine (1977, 1997, 2010, 2015a) devoted himself to building this innovative form of therapy. Levine's work is a body-centred approach rooted in natural phenomena for healing trauma. It is 'a method that is highly effective in dealing with the effects of overwhelm on our nervous system' (Levine, 2015a).

In his interview with *Psychotherapy Networker* Simon Rich (2019), Levine shared his fascination with exploring the origins of trauma and its pathways.

During his investigation into stress on the nervous system, he realised that:

'animals in the wild are constantly under threat of death from predation, yet rarely show symptoms of trauma'.

(Levine, 2015, SE-MANUAL, 2022)

As we established in the beginning of this chapter, animals faced with a threat typically activate a fight-or-flight response to defend themselves. However, if these responses prove ineffective they may resort to a 'freeze response', attempting to trick predators and protect their lives by 'playing dead'.

To complete its full cycle this response must follow its natural progression, enabling the substantial energy generated for fight or flight to release through spontaneous, gentle inner shaking and trembling (seen in animals) suggests Levine (1997). If the immobility phase remains incomplete the stored energy persists as 'locked' and, from the body's viewpoint, it still perceives the world as a threat, causing a continued physiological imbalance. Therefore, trauma can be assumed as an intense and unresolved biological/physiological reaction to a threat that remains suspended or stuck in a particular moment, unable to complete its natural course of response (Payne et al., 2015).

This distressing mechanism is inherent in every mammal, including humans, according to Levine (1997). Unlike wild animals that naturally shift between responses, we, as humans, tend to retain this shock reaction becoming trapped in a harmful and unending cycle. Our stomachs can knot up, our muscles can tense, and our heartbeats can accelerate or, on the contrary, slow down to a low level (Porges, 2009, SE-MANUAL, 2022). These physical sensations, like the gut twisting, cold hands, and a pumping heart send signals back to the brain, which then reinforces and intensifies the initial perception of danger and threat (Porges, 2009).

An essential element of trauma renegotiation entails the completion of these incomplete survival responses, including orienting, fight, flight, and freeze responses. Levine (SE-MANUAL, 2022) emphasises that these responses are governed by our autonomic nervous system, particularly influenced by our reptilian brain and the limbic circuit. This highlights the significance of comprehending the role of survival responses in the framework of traumatic stress within the SE model. The specified responses are detailed below:

Fight

'Fighting is the defensive response initiated in situations that call for aggression, or when it seems necessary or possible to overcome a threat directly, or when flight seems unavailable or was unsuccessful. If the defensive response cycle is interrupted in the fight stage most typically there will be a linking (coupling) of aggression and powerlessness. The strong urge to fight will have been overcome but not eliminated. When the fight response is prevented, and flight s unavailable, the freeze response will be the natural result.' (SE-MANUAL, 2022, B2.11)

Flight

'Flight is initiated when the perceived magnitude of the threat is such that fighting seems unlikely to succeed, when fighting has failed, or when the threat is non-specific enough that direct confrontation is unavailable. If the response cycle is interrupted in the flight stage, the person is more likely to move into an immobility response/freeze state. The strong urge to flee is incomplete. When flight is unavailable either the freeze response will be followed or a final attempt to fight will sometimes be provoked.' (SE-MANUAL, 2022, B2.14)

Freeze

'The freeze, or immobility, response is not a conscious choice in the hierarchy of the threat response cycle; it happens automatically when excitation or activation reaches a certain physiological threshold. The freeze is like a circuit breaker that shuts down the physiology when it is overloaded. The freeze is a profound physiological state, and has a tremendous amount of activation contained within it.' (SE-MANUAL, 2022, B2.16)

Freeze mode then, is the sense of immobility that is associated with feelings of helplessness. It is not an ordinary sense of helplessness that we experience from time to time; it is a visceral experience, leaving us with the subjective feelings of collapse, brokenness and powerlessness.

Levine (1997, p. 142) compares it to a car's functioning:

'if hyperarousal is the nervous system accelerator, the sense of immobility, freezing and overwhelming hopelessness is the brakes'.

Then the survival mode is in operation using both accelerator and brakes at the same time responding to threats that are no longer in the present moment. It's important to note that this doesn't necessarily mean the threats are real. Our body and mind 'freeze' in the high alert mode as it is still anticipating a threat.

Remaining in this 'frozen' state for an extended period allows the accumulated energy to persist. The continuous response, fuelled by elevated levels of cortisol and adrenaline, endures until the body has the opportunity to finish what it initiated during the traumatic experience. It's less about the trauma's initial cause and more about concluding the response. In this 'release phase', the nervous system can restore its 'balance' once again.

One of the crucial understandings from Levine's research is that each of the three components of the nervous system:

'evolved to protect people from the injury of violation and thus should be valued as maintaining and communicating certain survival skills'

(Helsel, 2015, p. 685).

Moreover, according to Payne and colleagues (2015), individuals who have undergone trauma display physical signs that act as snapshots, reflecting their unsuccessful attempts to defend themselves in moments of threat and injury.

To explain this complex circuit, Somatic Experiencing has incorporated the Polyvagal Theory (PVT), developed by Stephen Porges (1998, 2003, 2011, 2017a), a distinguished researcher in his field.

The PVT is a neurobiological theory which proposes that our vagus nerve, a key component of the autonomic nervous system, holds the possibility to examine the dynamics of the body and the nervous system. It is a neurological, physiological and biochemical mechanism that monitors our physiological, psychological and social behaviours. This interconnection is what Stephen Porges calls Neuroception.

Neuroception refers to the nervous system's ability to detect and evaluate cues in the environment, like a radar, to determine whether a situation is safe, dangerous, or offers risk without conscious awareness. It posits that physiological state plays a crucial role in influencing the spectrum of behaviour and psychological experiences (Porges, 2003, 2004, 2009). It's seen as an effective way to identify safety in the environment that we are in and with whom we are connected. It is a process translated into our autonomic nervous system (ANS).

Porges in his book *The Pocket Guide to the Polyvagal Theory* (2017b) reconceptualises the ANS as a hierarchical structure, with newer circuits inhibiting older ones. When challenged, the system sequentially shifts to older circuits as an adaptive survival response. While the world assumes voluntary actions, neural regulation shifts are often involuntary, triggered also by specific environmental reminders.

We may be unaware of these cues, but we are able to notice in our body reactions like increased heart rate or sweating hands. To transition from defensive to social engagement, the nervous system assesses risk and inhibits primitive limbic structures if the environment is considered safe.

To elucidate how neural platforms operate and describe how our own bodies contain the wisdom, strength, flexibility, vitality and resilience to unlock the constrained energies, I will present a brief, but not limited, dialogue between these platforms using the principles of the Polyvagal Theory by Porges (1998, 2003, 2011, 2017b,2022).

Here is the Polyvagal Theory and evolutionary model of our autonomic nervous system:

The autonomous hierarchy is composed of three evolutionary circuits. The latest being the ventral vagal nervous system (VVNS): a 200-million-year-old connection essential for mammalian and human well-being. It is known as the social engagement system. When activated, it promotes feelings of harmony, safety, joy, mindfulness, open and curious to the present moment, free from fear and stress. The VVNS activates human connections, communication, fostering empathy and providing well-being. It also serves as our anchor, borrowing from two other older systems for functioning. In challenging situations, the VVNS can paralyse us, removing the desire to act, serving as self-defence.

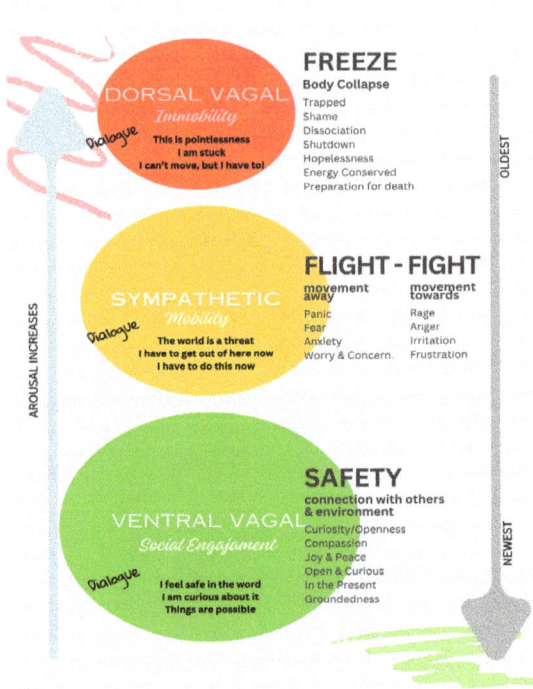

FREEZE
DORSAL VAGAL
Immobility

Body Collapse
Trapped
Shame
Dissociation
Shutdown
Hopelessness
Energy Conserved
Preparation for death

Dialogue
This is pointlessness
I am stuck
I can't move, but I have to!

OLDEST

FLIGHT - FIGHT
SYMPATHETIC
Mobility

movement away
Panic
Fear
Anxiety
Worry & Concern

movement towards
Rage
Anger
Irritation
Frustration

Dialogue
The world is a threat
I have to get out of here now
I have to do this now

AROUSAL INCREASES

SAFETY
VENTRAL VAGAL
Social Engagement

connection with others & environment
Curiosity/Openness
Compassion
Joy & Peace
Open & Curious
In the Present
Groundedness

Dialogue
I feel safe in the word
I am curious about it
Things are possible

NEWEST

While it is useful temporarily, prolonged shutdown in stress or fear may lead to immobility, making it difficult to regain a sense of well-being.

Sympathetic nervous system (SNS) is known as the mobilisation system. It senses threats and triggers a mobilising response, channelling energy to either flee or confront the danger. Activation on this channel brings a surge of energy, vitality and desire for coping in life. During periods of stress, it embodies the instinctive fight-or-flight response.

The most ancient circuit is known as dorsal vagal system (DVS), 'the immobilisation system'. It's a state where one loses vitality, feeling drained, physically and emotionally. When we are operating in this system our face loses colour, muscles ache, and the body redirects blood to protect vital organs. Cold hands, cold feet, weak voice, and dull eyes are characteristics of this state, creating a sense of worthlessness and disconnection from the world.

When stuck in dorsal vagal energy there's an inward turn of awareness, dissociating from the external world. The brain's oxygenation decreases, making it challenging to think clearly. It's a survival mode where one becomes highly suggestible, enters a state of shock, and the nervous system collapses, impairing the ability to reason about it. Criticism hits harder, internalising negative remarks, and memories become vague, often favouring positive ones while forgetting the bad experiences.

Moving from one to another during the day is natural and healthy. Sometimes, we need to be energised to respond in an invigorating manner. Other times, we need to be calm and dormant to relax. However, it is not healthy to be stuck in either state, as our bodies autonomously navigate between these channels without conscious awareness.

According to Porges (2017b, 2022) the hierarchy is structured based on evolution, where newer circuits suppress older ones. This model aligns with the idea that, when faced with challenges, the crucial inquiry is: how and why do we transition between these diverse circuits? In challenging situations, the regulation of the autonomic nervous system progressively reverts to older circuits, serving as an adaptive mechanism for survival. What prompts or triggers this process?

Unfortunately, there is no straight answer. What the Polyvagal Theory elucidates is that our nervous system employs various defence strategies, with the decision between fight, flight or freeze not being a conscious choice. This theory is the science of connection and serves as a roadmap for our nervous system. It is where we interact, and it is where we can exit a state of depression and/or anxiety, step out of a stressful moment, interrupt forms of response during an overwhelming experience. It's the realm where interaction happens, and crucially, it's the space where we can break free from unlocked energy.

From my individual experience, addressing this challenge of unlocking our trapped energy requires self-compassion, understanding our reactions, and accepting the process of recovery. Moving away from the dorsal energy involves transitioning to activities that activate the sympathetic system, like physical movement, play, negotiation, connections with nature, to break free from immobility and collapse, and then climbing up to the newest circuit where we restore a sense of connection, safety, and well-being.

In Somatic Experiencing (SE), the PVT advocates for a bottom-up intervention approach, focusing on internal sensations like visceral and musculoskeletal experiences rather than cognitive or emotional aspects. The main goal is to modify the stress response associated with trauma. The approach recognises the interference of the rational brain (neo-cortex) in trauma healing, as it may suppress instinctual reactions needed for recovery when fear and excessive control are present. The PVT emphasises restoring these instinctual reactions for effective trauma healing.

Recognising and incorporating sensory experiences is fundamental, as releasing these sensory fragments effectively removes trauma memories from our system, following Levine's (2015, p. 3) emphasis on 're-establishing core autonomic nervous system regulation'. It's important to clarify that SE does not aim to revive or alter memories but rather focuses on discharging accumulated energy from the body.

My studies and SE sessions

Reading a book called *Necessary Endings* by Dr Henry Cloud, I found these lines that really caught my attention and snapshotted the moment I was in:

'I was living in hell, but I knew the names of all the streets.'

It was time to take some steps toward a balanced life and my journey with Somatic Experiencing began not only as a patient but also as a soon-to-be practitioner.

I had the urge to explore it more and go deep into its roots, address my attachment issues and my indirect traumatic memories. This involved also addressing the completion of fight-and-flight responses to integrate my motor reactions, leaving behind those defensive and unhelpful responses that I could routinely slip into.

With each SE session I was feeling stronger and more capable of facing adversities and also able to sense and tolerate experiences that previously overwhelmed me. I gradually calmed the emotional storm, gaining confidence in myself again.

I had the opportunity to become aware of myself more deeply and to choose how I wanted to respond to my traumatic memories in a therapeutic context, allowing for a resolution of the episode in a secure environment.

Everything I went through was not easy. I went through various grieving processes in a short period of time. I had to strip away the illusions of a relationship I believed to be true, grieving once more my dad's passing. I had to understand that involved relationships would also undergo transformations, and to learn how to navigate out of my typical feelings of confusion. It is what I call today: Life-death-life!

Now, after the storm has passed, I have recovered my 'balance', my essence. It was essential to make a successful transition from defensive reactions to social engagement strategies, while also gaining control over my primitive limbic structure, which was dictating my 'freeze' frequent responses.

I discovered that emotions and sensations aren't essentially good or bad; instead, they serve as sources of information, providing valuable clues for cultivating deeper self-awareness and fostering meaningful connections with others, whether they bring positivity or adversity into our lives. This knowledge empowers us to navigate our social interactions effectively and offers a pathway to shift from states of hopelessness, escape moments of stress, and interrupt habitual responses during overwhelming experiences. The transformative nature of these shifts was notably captured by The GC Index.

The GC Index – the transformation of my GC Index profile

Two years ago, I was introduced to The GC Index for the first time. It was a revelation and validation of certain aspects of my individuality that had, until then, remained hidden beneath the surface. The assessment shed light on how I present myself to the world and the energy I bring to my professional and personal environments. My profile provided a structured insight into how I positively manage and influence my world.

Below I have represented my first GC Index profile:

Fig. 1: My GC Index profile at April 2021

Looking at my profile, you will see that my strongest proclivity was Implementer. Consistent with my comments above, I was very aware of my drive for action, for getting things done. On the flip side, my scores in other areas, like generating ideas (Game Changer/Strategist), refining details (Polisher), and building collaborative relationships (Play Maker) show I had less energy.

Dr John's description of The GC Index in Chapter 2 highlights the fact that the Implementer drive can be different for different people. For some it can reflect a sense of responsibility, for others not wanting to let people down; wanting to be seen as dependable. For me the drive was to prove myself worthy through achievement; to meet the needs of others, often at my own expense. The other weaker proclivities also reflected a quite single-minded focus upon action and often a 'loss of perspective'. I was so devoted to achieving tangible goals and objectives, often immersing myself in the results with a focus upon getting things 'done'. I needed a sense of accomplishment to boost my morale; a tangible and visible manifestation of my worth. You could say that I was a 'human doing' rather than a 'human being'.

My excessive focus on results would often lead to short-term thinking at the expense of long-term sustainability. Basically, my approach channelled energy firstly into action, followed by thought, and then reflective feelings. The dynamic was: act, think and feel. It was a very reactive way to be at the time.

In the days that followed the trauma, my emotions were in turmoil. However, I remained resolute in my determination to address the situation and channelled the Implementer energy I had into finding a way out and forward.

I had no doubt that SE was a pivotal point. It invited me to explore feelings rather than relying solely on action. It encouraged a shift from operating primarily on acting, thinking, and then feeling to a more balanced approach of feeling, thinking, and then acting.

Through my studies and Somatic Experiencing sessions, I gained a deeper understanding of my autonomic nervous system's functions. It dictates how I was responding to various environmental and everyday demands, which includes monitoring potential danger signals, amplifying threats, and processing my internal thoughts and memories. This intricate system played a pivotal role in shaping my responses to social interactions, encompassing both positive and negative encounters all in the service of my self-preservation.

After undergoing the healing process using Peter Levine's approach, I sensed a personal transformation and wondered if this change would be reflected in my profile. Upon retaking The GC Index, I observed a shift in my results. This change wasn't entirely anticipated, but given the transformative journey I underwent, it pleasantly surprised me. I present my GC Index profiles in Figs. 1 and 2 below.

Fig.1: My GC Index profile at April 2021   Fig.2: My GC Index profile at August 2023

During my conversation with Dr John to examine the nuances of my updated profile, he emphasised that while profiles do change, the crucial aspect is whether the change aligns with real-world experiences. It's essential to ensure that the shift is not merely a result of measurement errors as occasionally seen in psychometric instruments.

While the changes are small, our focus lies in assessing their significance and determining if they genuinely reflect real change. This exploration is ultimately more crucial than the five numbers in a profile.

The profile is more balanced and, broadly I feel, reflects the balance that I have achieved in my life. I now have insight into my Implementer drive for action and feel that I have tempered that single-minded drive to achieve in order to please others; I can now 'draw on' this energy in a deliberate way rather than getting 'drawn into it'. In doing so I can also draw upon my

Strategist proclivity to think and gain perspective about events in my life but without overthinking things.

Most importantly perhaps, I have embraced my Play Maker proclivity. From being the dependable and self-sufficient Implementer, I'm more prepared to be vulnerable and depend upon others in an interdependent way that is affirming for me. This, despite my traumatic experience.

After a meeting with Dr John, I was invited to document the process – an opportunity I embraced with enthusiasm. Writing about my trauma served as a crucial step in processing and understanding my feelings. Having reflected on my journey with the help of The GC Index, I am confident that the change I've undergone is tangible and reliable, a transformation I can trust in contrast to something fragile and transitory.

One of the significant lessons I've learned on this journey is that in life, when handed lemons, the outcome isn't determined by the lemons themselves, but rather by how we choose to transform them into lemonade. The fundamental aspect is confronting our shadows, bravely cultivating self-awareness, embracing the process, and being committed to analyse, evaluate, validate and then execute the plan, all of which will shape the results.

Personal development has played a significant part in my life, and, consistent with the human drive to survive and thrive, I firmly believe in our capacity to learn and grow with each experience.

Initially, my curiosity led me to explore human development for personal reasons, delving into unravelling the complexity of life, challenges, and uncertainties. Now, it has evolved into a transformative journey, where the pursuit of personal growth positively influences various facets, guiding me toward a more fulfilling and purposeful life. I view my experiences as opportunities for a fresh start. I acknowledged that change is hard at first, messy in the middle, and gorgeous in the end. If there is an end in this journey! But what it represents to me is that, although I had to grapple with pain, I can encounter my true self, and it was crucial for unlocking my energy.

References

Cloud, H., 1998, *Necessary Endings*: *The Employees, Businesses and Relationships that all of us have to give up in Order to move Forward*, 1st Ed., Harper Collins, New York

Helsel, P. B., 2015, 'Witnessing the Body's Response to Trauma: Resistance, Ritual, and Nervous System Activation', *Pastoral Psychology*, 64, pp. 681–693. DOI: 10.1007/s11089-014-0628-y

Levine, P. A., 2010, *In an Unspoken Voice: How the Body Releases Trauma and Restores Goodness*, North Atlantic Books, Berkeley, USA

Levine, P. A., 1997, *Waking the Tiger: Healing Trauma: The Innate Capacity to Transform Overwhelming Experiences*, North Atlantic Books, Berkeley, USA

Levine, P. A., 1977, Accumulated Stress, Reserve Capacity and Disease, Ann Arbor, MI: University of California, Berkeley, USA

Levine, P. A., 2015a, 'Somatic Experiencing: Definition of the topic: Bottom-up Processing', Ergos Institute of Somatic Education Retrieved from: https://www.somaticexperiencing.com/somatic-experiencing

Levine, P. A., 2015b, *Trauma and Memory: Brain and Body in a Search for the Living Past: A Practical Guide for Understanding and Working with Traumatic Memory*, North Atlantic Books, Berkeley, USA

Payne, P., Levine, P. A., & Crane-Godreau, M. A., 2015, 'Somatic experiencing: Using interoception and proprioception as core elements of trauma therapy', *Frontiers in Psychology*, 6(93), 1–18

Porges, S. W., 1998, 'Love: an emergent property of the mammalian autonomic nervous system', *Psychoneuroendocrinology*, 23, pp. 837–861. 10.1016/s0306-4530(98)00057-2

Porges, S. W., 2003, 'The Polyvagal Theory: phylogenetic contributions to social behavior', *Physiology & Behavior*, 79, pp. 503–513. 10.1016/s0031-9384(03)00156-2

Porges, S. W., 2009, 'The polyvagal theory: new insights into adaptive reactions of the autonomic nervous system', *Cleveland Clinic Journal of Medicine*, 76, S86–S90. DOI: 10.3949/ccjm.76.s2.17

Porges, S. W., 2011, *The Polyvagal Theory: Neurophysiological Foundations of Emotions, Attachment, Communication, and Self-Regulation*, 1st Ed., W. W. Norton, New York

Porges, S. W., 2017a, 'Vagal pathways: portals to compassion', *The Oxford Handbook of Compassion Science*, Seppala, E. M. (ed.), Oxford University Press, New York, pp. 189–202

Porges, S. W., 2017b, *The Pocket Guide to the Polyvagal Theory: The Transformative Power of Feeling Safe*, W. W. Norton, New York

Porges, S. W., 2004, 'Neuroception: S Subconscious System for Detecting Threat and Safety', *Zero to Three: Bulletin of the National Center for Clinical Infant Programs*, 24(5), pp. 19–24

Porges, S. W., 2022, 'Polyvagal Theory: A Science of Safety', *Frontiers in Integrative Neuroscience*, Vol. 16. https://doi.org/10.3389/fnint .2022.871227

Rich, S., 2019, 'An Interview with Peter Levine', *Psychotherapy Networker*, USA. https://www.psychotherapynetworker.org/article/interview-peter-levine/

Somatic Experiencing, 2007, Beginning Year – Module 2 (handout obtained for accreditation), SE-MANUAL, Copyright, B2

Chapter 12

The Wild and Freeing Journey of Connection and Thriving

Nikki Finucan offers us this personal story of her quest to thrive in the workplace rather than just survive. Her story illustrates the drive to channelling her Game Changer energy in a way that gave her the opportunities she needed for creative expression.

Have you ever felt the niggle that something isn't quite right? Have you ever felt that there is a better way to live and work? Have you ever felt the need to step out of the status quo? You live to get to your weekend, and you just NEED to nap. You hit the snooze button time after time because you just do not want to go to work. The thought keeps swirling in your mind, 'I really don't want to go to work today', you're staring down the barrel of a day filled with meetings and an even longer evening of getting your actual work and tasks done.

You aren't sure what your next steps are for your job or career, you are frozen and do not know what to do. You feel a sense of stagnation. At work and at home you are the 'jack of all trades, master of none. Our old friend imposter syndrome rears its ugly head and sends you into a spiral of doubt about what you are good at, and what impact you make in work and life. Maybe you even feel like you don't fit in or belong.

You feel like you are just *surviving;* sometimes just by the 'skin of your teeth'. While your internal landscape and inner dialogue is wrestling with all the above, to the outside world it looks like you are *thriving.* The external world sees that you appear to be making good money, have a nice house and car, you have great friends and a loving family, you go on nice holidays.

The external view shows that you work for a great company and appear to have a good job, you've made career moves that appear to follow the 'appropriate linear career path'. The external world believes you did all the things you 'should' do.

If you have any of these thoughts, you are not alone. I was that person. Those thoughts were all mine, for many years in fact. It is also normal and so many of us go through this and have experienced it first-hand. I am old friends with that inner dialogue that screams into the pillow or the abyss wondering how can I change this? Can I actually change this? Maybe you even have the thoughts that there is more to life than this. All that you feel is 'okay' and normal *and* you can change it.

The fantastic news is that it doesn't have to be this way.

Imagine, if you're a Game Changer, that you get out of bed every day and love going to work. You get dressed and you are excited about the day ahead, you are looking forward to the people you are meeting and connecting with. The initiatives you are working on have you giddy about what a difference it can make to your teammates, the organisation and the customers it serves.

Imagine, if you're a Strategist, that the rhythm you have created for your day creates so much spaciousness and you have more than enough time for all your meetings, connections and tasks.

Imagine, if you're a Polisher, that when difficulties and challenges pop up you handle them with such grace and ease that they didn't even feel like challenges, just something you got even better at.

Imagine, if you're an Implementer and even the most boring of household chores on that 'to-do list' brings a sense of peace and happiness.

Imagine getting to the end of your working day and you have 'energy to burn', so you play a game with your kids on the living room floor, you are all laughing hysterically and revelling in your connection to each other, you feel your Play Maker energy soar.

Maybe you are on a wonderful, romantic date with your 'other half', enjoying the moment just as it is, savouring a bite of delicious and flavourful food with a sip of a full-bodied wine, feeling the love and connection.

Imagine Tuesday night movie club with your friends, a great meal together, lots of conversation righting the wrongs, feeling supported, a really random film that makes you all laugh so hard you cry and your cheeks ache.

Imagine a weekend where on Sunday you enjoy the full day with loved ones, lunch out, a nice walk in nature without Sunday syndrome and the week ahead's to-do list creeping in. If that was the world we lived in, wouldn't it feel much more loving and beautiful?

This chapter is about your connection to you and how that connection can help you to *thrive* rather than just *survive.*

My intention for the work I do with people is to help them to connect to, and step into, themselves at their best; embracing and owning with confidence their most impactful lives.

The exciting part for the 'recovering accountant' in me, is that, with The GC Index, we now have a way to anchor this connection, a language to describe and understand ourselves and our potential to be our most impactful selves; I would like to see this as our 'Super Selves'.

There's a good deal of anecdotal evidence within the GCologist community to suggest that many people have found their GC Index impact profiles to be affirming, confidence building and 'grounding', because there is a language and a framework that can begin to explore and explain who they really are and what they really bring to work and life.

In this chapter I will share my experiences, my journey and some of the rituals and exercises I use every day to keep me thriving, not just surviving.

Connecting to what I have come to call my 'Super Self' has been an exercise steeped in data, science, together with a bit of 'woo magic'. Please know that as you read or listen to these words, it may prompt all sorts of emotions, feelings, thoughts, criticisms, and some resistance; it might make you feel uncomfortable.

You may even be thinking right now, 'What the hell, lady? Woo magic? I am not here to read hippy craziness, I'm out!' Know that whatever comes up is okay and normal. You may even put this down, skip this chapter and come back to it. You are meant to read it or hear it when you are most ready.

The GC Index is based in the research described in Section 1, Chapter 2, of this book, and is one of the 'grounding points' that I talk about in my journey to becoming my Super Self. The experiential aspect is built upon the somatic exercises we use in our work encompassing the *4 different levels of learning and processing* we use to deepen our connection to our most Super Self.

My experience suggests that through using these *four levels of learning and processing* the integration of the data points from The GC Index can be profound and, pardon the pun, be quite literally Game Changing for your work and life.

Again, I want to share that as you read or listen to this chapter, the language and these exercises in the different parts of the chapter may cause discomfort that you can't quite put your finger on. You may think, 'Oh hell, no,' and put it down and come back. Do the exercises that make you feel comfortable as and when. Stretch yourself where you feel it is right to do so, even in those moments of discomfort. On the edge of that resistance and discomfort is your greatest Super Self.

What resistance might pop up while experimenting in this chapter?

Over 100 years ago, in 1920, Freud was writing about the ways in which human beings defend themselves against emotional distress and trauma. These defences take many forms but are, essentially, a denial or distortion of reality that is designed to protect us emotionally. In the short term these defences can be healthy in that protective sense. In the long term they can stifle growth and self-expression. For Freud these defences were the basis for neuroses: the expression of energy distorted by our Superego.

When I write about resistance in this chapter, I am talking about the manifestation of our defences.

Resistance can show up in many different ways. When it shows up, we know that it is perfectly normal but need to explore why it arises. Resistance is created as a result of our fears and limiting beliefs. Resistance is designed to help us survive in the short term, but evident over time, keeps us in that survival mode, stopping us from *thriving*.

Remember, our fears want to keep us safe, they are logical and rational but again they are designed to keep us in survival mode: the emphasis, as psychologists have referred to it over the years, is upon 'avoidance' rather than 'approach'. Through beginning to understand this resistance, we can truly start to shift how we think, how we work and how we thrive.

My proposition in this chapter is that we thrive in the world when we're engaged in those activities that, in GC Index terms, feed our strongest energies (proclivities) rather than deplete through having to apply our weakest proclivities: a Game Changer will thrive when they have consistent opportunities to bring energy to creative expression; a Polisher will thrive when they can bring energy to the pursuit of perfection.

I know I have my own favourite resistance 'go-tos': avoidance (or procrastination) is definitely one of them: I kept conveniently avoiding writing this chapter. I created lots of excuses like 'not enough time, too many client calls, too busy'. Writing this is a creative (Game Changer) endeavour for me, and something I love doing, but resistance can still come up even when it is our natural energy and something we love. It is the fear 'playing through'. In my case the fear of not being good enough; that old chestnut.

Resistance can show up as that sense of 'no choice', being very resigned to your situation. A sense of powerlessness, resignation that you feel you cannot change the situation. It might even sound like this: 'I can't possibly just go off following my joy and my "Energy for Impact"; I am the breadwinner, I have to make the money for our household', or 'It would be lovely to do a job that I loved but I have a mortgage, kids schooling, a family to support.'

I have experienced this kind of resistance. I even went back and did a job I really hated. It could even appear as if: 'This is what I know, I have always done this. I do not know another way to do it.'

Another personal favourite is the 'Inner Critic' who pops up as resistance. The Inner Critic isn't just your critic, they are critical and judging of others as well. 'I can't possibly do that, it's stupid.' I have used this one on many occasions when I was in a place of discomfort. Perhaps the Inner Critic is being critical of someone else, in this instance, your Inner Critic could be thinking: 'This is utter b******s and nonsense, this woman is spouting.'

These are just some of my favourites, that I notice in myself and in some of the work we have done with organisations and individuals.

Key takeaways

We all have resistance in some form or another, please know that this is normal. The secret is being aware of what your resistance is and how it shows up. Start to notice it for yourself. This will help you to begin to tap in more deeply to you and allow you to step into your Super Self.

Here's an exercise that you might find useful at this point:

- Have you noticed any resistance patterns from the above, that you know you use? Making a list of them will help you to be very conscious of them when they do appear.
- Write down when these resistance patterns come up. Situations, feelings and thoughts, any body sensations? This will help you to not feel 'blindsided' by them.

Four levels of learning and processing

At this point I want to introduce you to the four different levels of learning and processing. This model will help you to strengthen your understanding of, and your connection with, you at your best.

1. **Cognitive/mental** – During this experience you will learn new information and data. Our goal is to ensure you retain it and connect it to existing ideas about yourself, your work, your impact. The next piece of the puzzle is to ensure that the new information or data begins to help shift those mental/cognitive ideas about you, your work and your impact.
2. **Emotional** – Effectively processing our emotions is, I would suggest, a 'superpower' of its own accord. The exercises we use in our work, through this chapter and experience helps to connect to our emotions and begin to use them as our internal GPS. All our experiences and interactions with our world can create emotions and these emotions can either give us energy or deplete us dependent upon how we recognise and accept that emotion, what

meaning we give it, and how we might transmute it for the greatest good for ourselves, our work and our impact.

3. **Transcendent/Spiritual** – This level of learning, processing and connecting is exploring our values, beliefs and purpose. Through somatic and experiential exercises, we can begin to understand and align our purpose with our core values, bringing greater meaning to what we do each day. Being aligned will give us energy. Being misaligned will take our energy: with a constant tension between what we say, do and think.

4. **Embodiment** – Showing up every day and embodying all that you are, all that you desire to be as person, a leader, a change maker, creating that more beautiful and loving world. Find that physical place in your body you can come back to, to energise yourself.

Now that I have shared a little of what's to come during our time together, let's start our journey by connecting you to yourself and start to explore the question: 'Am I *thriving* or simply *surviving?*'

'Connect to you' exercise

This is an exercise that will help you to begin to reflect upon the question: 'Am I *thriving* or simply *surviving?*'

Find a comfortable and quite space where you won't be distracted. You will find it easier if you ask someone to talk you through these instructions:

Breathe in and feel that inhale fill you up, now exhale, release what will no longer serve you as you begin to deepen your connection to you. As you breathe in, think the word OPEN, as you exhale, think the word RECEIVE.

As you inhale, you are opening and expanding your body, creating space for yourself. As you exhale, imagine a golden light coming down into your body, you are receiving all that space, that wisdom, that energy, the impact, the skills, the gifts that are you.

Follow that breathing rhythm for just a few moments, with that mantra inhale, OPEN, exhale, RECEIVE.

Now ask yourself:

'Where in my life am I thriving? Work, home, family, friends?

Notice what this sensation of thriving feels like in the body and make a mental log of these feelings.

Where in my life am I surviving? Just getting by? Work, home, family, friends?

Notice what this sensation of surviving feels like in the body and make a mental log of these feelings.

Come back to the space where you feel like you are thriving again, let it permeate all of your body. Really revel in it. Allow yourself to accept your potential to thrive.

Breathe, you are here now, exactly where you are supposed to be in this moment. Breathe in, let the inhale fill your whole being. And exhale, surrender all the tensions that are clutching at you right now. Consciously inhale your perfection, just as you are in this moment, exhale what you no longer want.

Journal exercise

Take some time to write down all you experienced in this exercise. Deepen the connection to yourself through journalling. Here are some prompts:
Where are you thriving? What did it feel like? Where in the body was it?
Where are you surviving? What did it feel like? Where in the body was it?
How does it feel to connect with yourself in a different way? Did any resistance show up? What did the resistance look like if it did show up?

You are in the right place, right now. It's your time to shine, we're here to support you. There is an entire community using The GC Index dedicated to helping people understand their Energy for Impact, with the assumption that that knowledge helps people to know how they can thrive in their world. Our intention is to help at least 10% of the world's population truly live and embody their impact, which will create a more loving and beautiful world.

Uncovering my life script – 'Barely surviving'

My husband often jokes (yeah, not really joking) that when it comes to household tasks I excel at avoiding the ones I hate. When it comes to work though, I have always been the 'Energizer Bunny', I can just keep going and going and going, and I can do all the things, so I do *ALL* the things. I have a lot of energy and stamina so I can work really long hours. I have never left a job where I wasn't replaced by a minimum of two people. Now, logically that level of pure effort is of course going to be an energy drain.

At this point I am going to start to explore in more depth, the connection of emotions, behaviours, fear drivers and our Energy for Impact. Strap yourself in.

For the first ten years of my career, I worked as an accountant. I started in an accounting practice. You can imagine here the woman with a fluffy pen and a sequin notepad – think *Legally Blonde* – and I did not 'fit in'. That job lasted for a year, enough time to get some experience and some foundations and then I was off into the corporate world.

I spent the next five years with two major global players, I worked 18 hours a day and month end felt like it was every week: there was always a report of some description due! It felt like I was stuck in a time loop, like *Groundhog Day.* For me, those repetitive tasks day after day, week after week, were stifling. It made me want to scream. Even as I sit and write this, I can feel the tension in my body, remembering it. I remember getting home at midnight, another 18-hour day for the thirtieth day in a row and thinking 'There has to be more to life than this.' I remember driving over a bridge on my way home thinking 'I could just drive off the bridge, because there needs to be more than this.' This depression, yes it was diagnosed, was really my internal weather system, my emotions, telling me something wasn't right.

As a GC Index Game Changer, this was destroying my soul. I was having to behave like an Implementer, which I'm not, delivering one report at a time. This is not where my energy is. Not only was I drained by the sheer volume of effort, my Energy for Impact was being constantly drained by tasks that I could do but was not engaged by. I know now that that this is a working life that many people choose: they pick a job that they *can do* but don't ask the question: *'do I really want to do it?'*

That midnight moment was my catalyst for moving countries from Brisbane, Australia, to London, UK. Now, I wish I could say that I managed to plug that 'Energy Leak' but alas, it went on for much, much longer. For a little while, after moving to London, working less hours, having more fun outside work, I managed to keep the Energy Leak slightly contained and at bay. Until I took a permanent job, where it was time to get serious again and keep climbing this alleged ladder on this boring linear career path.

I continued down my finance path, the same reports and tasks month after month, lacking any opportunity for creativity. This was me operating in my survival mode applying Implementer energy, that I didn't really have, to repetitive tasks, with a sense of constant urgent action. As I climbed that linear ladder, much more Strategist energy was being needed and expended. I was the one making sense of other people's ideas, creating plans, roadmaps (Strategist energy), figuring out how to make other people's ideas the reality (Implementer energy), very rarely implementing my own ideas. Neither of these proclivities – Strategist and Implementer (see my profile below) are my natural Energy for Impact or my complete Zone of Greatness.

Dramatically, I started to lose my hair, I had weird rashes come up on my face, I had some sort of cold or bug every single month. This went on for five years. Not only was my body saying 'Hey enough of this now, this is not for you', but my emotional well-being was taking the hit again.

This time I was bringing everyone down with me. I showed up for work in ways that are not me, and it was definitely not who I wanted to be, definitely not embodying the revolutionary leader I wanted to be. I was angry all the time, everything frustrated and annoyed me. I was snappy and rude to people. I was known as 'difficult to work with', unmanageable, and definitely too outspoken. But I performed to a high level and high standard, I ploughed through mountains of work; I achieved strong outcomes. So, some of my behaviours were overlooked and certain people were given the responsibility of 'handling' me. I didn't like who I was. How could I be an effective and authentic leader if this was how I was showing up?

All the signs were there, but I had no framework and no language at the time to explain what was going on. I felt I wasn't making the impact I truly wanted to make in the world. In fact, the work I was doing was blocking me from making my greatest impact in the world. I was disconnected and couldn't even see my purpose. Even my body was showing me I was working in the wrong jobs, the wrong organisations. My emotions and behaviours, and who I was showing up as, were showing me that I was in the wrong jobs, the wrong organisations. I was *surviving* … just! I was doing all the things a 'good career woman' should.

Now my logical, rational brain thought I have a respectable job, earning 'good money', climbing the corporate linear ladder, surely this means I am *thriving*. Nope, the writing on the hindsight wall, showed me I was surviving, and barely.

Luckily for me I had respite in the form of secondments to large scale transformation projects. I managed to get two of these. This was a light in my dark tunnel. Finally, through these digital transformation programmes, I got to really shine. Imagine, the woman who was not overly liked, started smiling and laughing at work. I felt energised and happy to go to work. I got a real chance to look under the hood of the organisation and share my most creative ideas on how to fix broken processes and structures. I got the opportunity to really change how people worked and make it better, easier, more fun for them. I loved the new ideas, consistent with how I now understand Game Changers, I could see things that others didn't and felt valued for being able to so do and not just different: I loved the game-changing possibilities of how we could do things differently.

The allies I had in this permanent role helped me to explore this and it started to shift things for me. I could create and each day was different, and this fed and nurtured my Game Changer energy. I could fix things and make them better, improve them and this fed and nurtured my Polisher energy. These are words and language I can use now because I have the framework of The GC Index.

I went through a phase where I really loved what I did every day. I got variety, I really felt like I was making a difference in this kind of work. I finally had that sensation of fulfilment. I laughed more, I smiled more, I was easier to be around, people enjoyed working with me. I started to *thrive* in so many different areas of my life. My career trajectory, that linear path got marginally easier, I was recognised more positively for who I was and my work.

And then I had to go back to my finance work. This time, however, I struck a deal with the new CFO: I would give it six months and set up the business to operate in three different markets, train the teams, get the tech stood up, do all the boring finance and legal bits. If I wasn't enjoying myself, I would wander off into the sunset and go on my merry way. Now, I still had some of the tasks and activities that drained me, after all I had to make sense of this idea of launching into three new emerging markets. There were roadmaps and plans needed to create (Strategist energy) and I had to figure out how I could do all this (Implementer), using some tried and tested practices. I had to keep the international division ticking over with boring finance tasks (Implementer), so month end still felt like it happened every week, not every month. I did, however, get to really start digging into my creative side for all the possibilities for these ventures and events (Game Changer). How could we transform how we did things? I also got to use existing UK organisation processes, ways of working and unleash my Polisher to make them better, more fit for purpose in these locales.

But alas, at the six-month mark, I felt that niggle, something wasn't right. In those six months, I had labyrinthitis, which is constant vertigo, for two months. I had no relief from that as I am severely allergic to anti-vertigo medications. Having vertigo and being on flights for three weeks, in three different countries was quite the challenge. Yet again, my body (a part of the internal GPS) was screaming that something was not right. It all ended up with me blowing up at the MD I worked with at time. I could no longer control those emotions, that anger, frustration and fear. I was drained, depleted and I had nothing left in my tank; I was running on empty.

I called the CFO and said, 'We made it a deal, it's time for you to honour it. I cannot do this any more.' We negotiated and agreed I would finish up in three months to finalise getting the international businesses online and the events started. The relief that the end was in sight, was out of this world. Finally, I could be free.

My exposure to The GC Index has reinforced how important this sense of freedom, freedom for expression, is for Game Changers. This has helped enormously to recognise who I really am and not 'lazy or crazy'. The lens of The GC Index framework and language has also helped me really to understand that I was working in a space that was not my natural Energy for Impact. Through understanding the data points on where I am energised, I have been able to connect the dots to my emotions, beliefs and patterns and my body. This internal GPS is now my guide to support me in the work I do.

Key takeaways

Just because you are good at something, doesn't make it your natural Energy for Impact or even where you can create the biggest impact in your organisation. It is simply you have learned to adapt. So, being good at something is also not the same as being energised, excited or joyful for what you are doing.

Your internal GPS of emotions that leads to behaviours knows the way. Watch your behaviours: are they who you truly wish to show up as, or is there an even greater person in there wanting to be let out?

Now it's your turn for some reflection.

Tuning into your Energy for Impact exercise

> *Put on some meditation music, something at 528Hz. I invite you to sit still for a moment with your feet flat on the floor, feeling your seat beneath you.*
>
> *Inhale through the nose, exhale out the mouth, really sighing it out. Do that again. Now, this time inhale through the nose, exhale out the mouth with an 'aaahhhhhh' sound.*
>
> *Tap into this place of your sense of personal power and confidence. Bring your work to the centre of your being; can you feel how this*

work is impacting you? Can you feel an energy leak or a drain? Or can you feel the excited buzzing of your cells?

Ask yourself, am I making the impact I want to? Explore any body sensations that come up when you ask questions about your work. You do not need to change them, simply allow them to be there and share their wisdom with you.

Energy audit exercise

This exercise is designed to connect you more deeply to yourself and start to work with your internal GPS. Those feelings, body sensations, well-being states are the compass to tell us we are aligned to our Energy for Impact and our purpose.

Note any resistance that pops up as you work through this exercise. Avoidance, the inner critic, powerlessness in your current situation, maybe they are other ones you will find.

Grab your notebook and open it so you have two blank pages. Write at the top of the left-hand side ENERGISED and at the top of the right-hand side DRAINED/LEAKING.

Step 1. Think about all the tasks, activities, meetings, initiatives you have worked on (or avoided) over the last few weeks. Think about each one, were they energising or were they draining?

Step 2. Write each of those tasks, activities, meetings, initiatives in the column most appropriate, ENERGISED or DRAINED/LEAKING.

Step 3. As you look at what you have been working on (or avoiding), going line by line, tap into how you were feeling as you did it. Trust your instincts and what it brings up. Using the word cloud for inspiration, jot down beside each item how it makes you feel now.

Step 4. Try to be really honest with yourself. Jot down beside each task, activity, meeting, initiative, how you have been showing up to work on (or avoid) these activities, tasks, meetings or initiatives? What behaviours have you been displaying?

Step 5. Journal prompts

- *Looking at what you wrote in the exercises above, are you spending more time in tasks, activities, meetings, initiatives that are energising you or draining you?*
- *What grounded action do you want to take to work more in the places that energise you?*
- *Am I being the person I want to be everyday? Showing up as the person that I know I can be?*
- *Am I making the impact I truly desire?*
- *Am I thriving or simply surviving and doing what I SHOULD, what I think others expect from me?*

The journey to surviving

Back to the story of my work journey. I had been engineering my job exit with two of my mentors for some time. It just happened to culminate in the aforementioned emotional outburst. I had decided I really wanted to go out on my own, do contract work in the transformation programme space.

I had even set the intention of creating more freedom in my life through really changing how I worked. More space for rest, holidays and fun. Back then it was the thought that I would work really hard for nine months, have three months off. The 'best laid plans of men and mice' as they say.

Even though I engineered it, the shock of being a free woman bought to the surface so many fears. Even though I knew there had to be a better way, a different way, those old limiting beliefs still came out to play.

I was a free woman in September 2013, so I decided to Eat, Pray, Love a little bit to see if I couldn't reset and give my poor emotional and physical body a chance to recover. I sought solace, strength and wisdom with my best friend in Midwest America. I sought connection to self and my purpose in Bali. I also thought that going back and doing some studies would help me shift into the transformation space I wanted. I got my Prince 2 accreditation and my Lean Six Sigma green belt. Those limiting beliefs calmed a little bit with these accreditations, maybe helped me feel validated that there was a certificate that said I could do it.

It was in Bali, during my three months of Eat, Pray, Love, that I met Sami the healer. Healing had been in his family for generations. I remember the day with such clarity even now, more than a decade on. He did the massage scan, found the places that I was holding onto emotions, where they were stuck, and he did his best to release what was ready and no longer necessary for the next phase of my journey. At the end of the session, we sat by the pool, and he said to me, 'Are you aware you are meant to be a healer, this is your calling? Not like a doctor-style healer, but you are meant to help people heal.'

Little did I know then, that was a defining moment for me in the next phase of my journey. The deep knowing of my purpose, was ignited somewhere deep inside me, I knew this to be true. The emotion in the moment was one of relief, happiness and the sense of joy at the door opening to this purpose. However, a greater part of me resisted it. Surely that wasn't me, I was a corporate woman, I was working on growing my career in the traditional way.

I came back from Bali, having released some of emotions through my physical experiences. I came home with new information about what my life's purpose had the potential to be. I also returned knowing that I couldn't go back to the world of finance. I desperately wanted to work in transformation, as I knew deep inside of me, it was the next move in my expansion of skills and personal growth.

I want to share here that there is no myth of perfection in my world, even today. My fears of not being good enough still played out, so I applied for finance jobs AND transformation programme and project roles because 'good career women' are responsible and shouldn't be without a job. It took me four months to find a new job, which was the longest I had ever been out of work.

I had interviewed for a great permanent Head of Finance role at a very big organisation; great pay, excellent benefits, the boss seemed like a good guy. This was a job I could do with my eyes closed! Month in month out, I knew I could do it. It ticked the boxes on the linear career progression path.

At the same time, I also interviewed for an incredible European Project Manager contract role for an amazing 'go to market' programme, changing all of the sales structures, commission plans and technology stack for an old traditional company. The contract was 12 months. Now, I had a lot of experience with sales structures, sales processes, how to go to market, sales tech stack implementation, I had many transferrable skills as it was all part of what I had done in the projects I had been seconded to. But of course, my friend imposter syndrome, reared its head. I began to doubt myself. Could I really do this? Should I really do this, as it is not as secure as a permanent job?

I was offered both jobs, 30 minutes apart from each other, now I had a decision to make. Should I be the responsible, good career woman and follow this linear path? Or do I throw caution to the wind and change careers and do something which fulfils me, lights the spark in me? Can you guess which one I took?

I threw caution to the wind and took the European Project Manager contract role. Good money, but not stable, it was only a year contract, but I was free, my career change was beginning. Oh, the giddy joy and excitement I felt. If you recall I mentioned earlier, I am not an Implementer in GC Index terms.

This role was very much an Implementer. Getting it done, bringing it to reality. Yes, I was included in the conversations around the design of what was to happen, but my Game Changer energy was not fully engaged, I was there in the capacity of getting someone else's vision done.

The pattern repeated for a few more years. Again, on the outside I got paid lots of money on a day rate, I had more of the chosen time off that I wanted. I was still working in transformation, surely this was thriving right? I was building my consulting business, and I had created a digital sales lead generation business as well. Surely that meant I was thriving too, right? Not so much. That time off, however, was needed to simply recover after each programme. I was still living in Implementer energy. Work still wasn't a joy, it was a necessity, now I also had employees to pay. This was a different level of stress and anxiety.

My behaviours had begun to shift, I was behaving differently, I didn't have the same levels of anger and frustration that I did from finance work. There was still some anger and frustration, but it was different. It was a different feeling. I did have the joy of connecting with people differently. I was being more fulfilled working in this work than I had other in places. My Polisher was energised through continuously improving on my approach to programmes, my Game Changer was curious about finding wild, creative solutions to problems we came up against while helping people move through these transitions, along with designing truly fantastic change in some cases.

While the physical burnout was still something I needed a few months to recover from each year, I didn't have the consistent weird flu bugs and unexplained illnesses that I was having during my finance phase.

I still took consulting jobs even though there was no alignment to my core values and these jobs were certainly not always aligned enough to my Energy for Impact. It probably didn't help that I hadn't figured out my personal core values then either! I often did consulting gigs for money, to prove to the world that I could always do the impossible. I would pick up things where people had failed and turn them around. I was effectively a 'gun for hire' and somewhere along the way that started to be a problem for me, reliant on that level of external validation. This was my Polisher on overdrive.

The Polisher energy in these scenarios was motivated from my fear mind of not being good enough, needing to prove myself, prove my value or my worth. This over-action from the Polisher energy – even though it was part of my personal Energy for Impact – was draining me. Constant 'doing' or action to high quality and standards, with the underlying fear motivation of proving myself.

It became my personal mission to create as much integration and embeddedness in all programmes I worked on. I really wanted to see the shift for people, to make their working lives better and easier. It is what made me curious all those years ago about change, change management and transformation. How do we help people to evolve and grow? How do we help the collective of people in an organisation evolve?

Now after having done some fun and energising work designing a sales playbook with an organisation, I got a message during my fortieth birthday trip from the EVP of Sales Operations globally. 'Call me, we got the funding for the European salesforce programme. We'd like you to run it.' This was in March 2018, when the real shift began.

Key takeaways

Following the breadcrumb trail of what 'lights you up', what energises you or excites you, is the way to begin to uncover your life purpose and career purpose. You can begin to understand what energises you or excites by watching your body for its wisdom. Where in your body do you feel it? What does it feel like? The more you watch this, the more likely you are to keep connecting to those energising and exciting elements. You also attract more of it into your life.

Once you have uncovered some of the areas of excitement or interest, start to notice where the motivation is coming from. The motivation adds another layer of energy to it. When we are motivated by fear we tend to over-compensate, when we are motivated purely from a place of love or joy then we are operating at our most impactful.

This also connected to the concept of core values and how we make decisions. Core values are at the heart of who you are and what is most important to you. They underpin your beliefs, influence your decisions and the actions you take, impacting all areas of your life. Are there times when you know that something feels absolutely right? Or in an instant when something is proposed to you, that it does not sit well?

These are your core values. They give you powerful messages when you are aware of them. They can surprise you, confuse you and when you recognise them, they allow you to see with absolute clarity the decisions you can make.

Now it is time for some more reflections and connection to yourself.

Explore your core values exercise

Understanding our core values means life can be simpler, clearer. It allows you to see the reasons why you are in the relationships you are in, the job you chose, the friends you spend time with (or stopped spending time with), your reactions and feelings to situations and how you make decisions.

Steps to work and feel through (take as long as you need)

1. *Think about your greatest achievement, personal or professional, a moment where you felt you had accomplished something you really wanted. It may be something you worked hard to achieve or had thought about for a long time.*

2. *Can you recall another time you are proud of? This moment might have been competing with number 1 and now you can include it. Who was around you when you achieved it? How did you feel?*

3. *Can you remember a third achievement? What did you enjoy about it? What were you doing? For all three achievements, moments of pride and when you were bursting with joy:*

   ○ *What were the common threads between these?*

   ○ *What were you doing that you enjoyed?*

   ○ *Were there other people that were with you or who helped you?*

   ○ *How did you know they were your moments? What words come to mind?*

4. *Google a list of core values below, read through the entire list. Once you have read through, and only when you have read through, select the Top ten values that resonate with you. If you have printed this, you can either circle them or alternatively write them down.*

5. *Now circle or write down the bottom ten values that you feel no affinity with. That was easier wasn't it!*

6. *Think again about those three achievements. Do the top ten feel right?*

7. *Now think about a time when you felt disappointed, confused or in conflict. It may help to think about a work or personal situation. Has there been a friendship or work relationship that isn't working or hasn't worked in the past? What happened, what were you feeling during those experiences?*

8. *Take your time and now focus on the values that resonate with you. Reduce the top ten to five. Which ones are absolutely vital to your life? Start crossing five off one by one.*

9. *How does that look? Does that feel pretty good? The thing is you can have three values only. They are values that you cannot live without! Think about all the times that you have felt strong connections with a decision. When you reduce down to the last three you will have one of the most important life (that includes work!) tools to guide you. Have you decided which three?*

10. *Now you can write your three values down on a separate page.*

Congratulations! You now have your three values for life and work.

This is key: write down and describe what those words means to you. How can you use each one to make decisions in personal and work situations, in relationships and balancing everyday life?

The initiation begins

Again, it is only with hindsight that I can see where and how my initiation came to be. This initiation was truly the beginning of a new world, a new way of working and living for me, the beginning of a deeper understanding of me and my purpose. As with most initiations you don't get through it unscathed, it is through the hardship that the learning happens.

There are multiple elements to this initiation. There are the events that happened and how that changed me, then there are the emotions that came with it, but that wisdom arrived a lot later!

This was the beginning of the shift, these experiences changed it all and changed me.

The Cluster Impact, April – May 2018

There was a lot that happened in a really short space of time. You can imagine my excitement that a client I really enjoyed working with wanted me to design and deliver with them their new Customer Relationship Management European programme. At the same time, I was working with client on a CRM and an Enterprise Resource Planning implementation as well as getting our digital sales lead generation business off the ground and designing new processes with them.

On a personal level we had a lot of moving parts too: I had just discovered that I was pregnant and my father-in-law had taken a turn for the worse during April 2018.

Now here is an element of the initiation. On 12 May 2018, we lost my father-in-law. It was very sudden and wasn't expected. You can imagine the grief our family was going through. He was a wonderful, loving and kind man and, at the end, we saw suffering in so many different ways and from so many different places. On 29 May 2018, I had a miscarriage with complications. The work I had meant to start in May with my beloved client had to be postponed as I needed to go through some surgery. These two big life events in one month drastically shifted a lot for me.

With hindsight, I realised how much I dimmed my emotions as a result of these events. My internal GPS got a little dimmed just so I could *survive*. When we dim our internal GPS we put ourselves at a greater risk of something very severe happening. What I have since learnt, and fundamentally believe, is that our emotions are designed to help us understand where we are in alignment and where we are not. If it is joyful and exciting, you are aligned and connected. If it is the more challenging emotions, you know it is time to consider the fact you are not aligned to you and your purpose and Energy for Impact.

Sadly, my behaviour was even more motivated by fear to prove myself; there's that Polisher again! Action in perfection!

I took up the challenge of an assignment with an organisation that had never managed to deliver a single global scale tech solution for all countries in its entire history. This became one of the most challenging and difficult times in my career. But also, one of the most powerful, rewarding, connective experiences of my life and it was how and where The Change Tribe consulting firm was born.

I came to work driven and motivated by fear but surrounded by an incredible work family that we created and nurtured. A team of people with whom, finally, I could be myself. In many ways I showed vulnerability despite sometimes knowing those emotions were dimmed.

My vulnerability was sharing my thoughts, my concerns, some of my fears. I asked for help to solve the problems, and slowly I didn't feel like it was all on me to solve everything all the time. I asked for challenge to find the best ways to do things, to get others' ideas and processes. I trusted those around me. I got to operate in my energising space (mostly). I created spaces through unconventional, untraditional methods. We had a people first philosophy. Remember, as a Game Changer, I needed this sense of freedom of expression in all forms.

This team's mottos:

'We've got so much talent in one place we always play our best team. That's how we win.'
'We've done it before we'll do it again.'
'The sum of the whole is greater than the parts.'

Through support and shared vulnerabilities, the team gave freely, everyone was able to show up as their real self, everyone got to live their Energy for Impact. This team created its own micro-culture that everyone was drawn to and excited by. Every country we went to, we got asked, 'Can I join this group?'

Through always playing our best, most aligned team in all situations for the outcomes our clients were looking for, we created balance. There was no judgement for a bad day, the joy of all the good days carried us. The laughter of each day nourished us. Each person in this group evolved so much as a result of how we worked and most importantly how we showed up.

This included the rituals we created, the space we curated and nurtured. Most of the team went onto better jobs with more money, but with a real sense of self, what they were good at and what they really wanted to do and, most importantly, what lit them up.

None of this means I wasn't put under pressure; it didn't mean that my body wasn't starting to give me signs. I could sense when my motivation or drivers for my work were still, primarily, fear.

There came a point in 2019 and the beginning of 2020 where we were on planes, trains and automobiles every week, the programme we were working on got expanded from Europe to include Canada and we were gearing up for the USA as well. Then the pandemic hit in March 2020.

During 2020, my growing awareness of myself and my energy and my willingness to lean on others meant that I had started to no longer operate on fear, I operated on the trust of myself, those around me and more from a place of joy. It is why The Change Tribe exists today and why it felt it could knock on my door to be born.

The Change Tribe exists to change the status quo of work. It is here to help organisations evolve at a human level through deeper work collectively. The Change Tribe exists to support organisations to be high vibe, joyful places

Key takeaways

This continuation of following the breadcrumbs of what lights me up, brings me joy and excitement and having a safe space and freedom to experiment has been a big part of my journey. It was also about me consciously creating that safe space for myself and knowing that when we are vulnerable, people respond to us differently. You see their truth, their fears as well. From that place all of us can move forward together, as one. Through being vulnerable my emotions began to come back, which allowed me to see so much more about myself. The internal GPS came online and began working again.

Earlier I said no initiation leaves you unscathed and while this is true, an initiation always gives you the beginning of something different, of something better. This part of the initiation connected me more deeply to my purpose. Earlier in my journey I learnt that I was a healer. Little did I know then that part of my purpose is to heal organisations; to help organisations become better places for people to *thrive* and not just *survive*.

The next phase of the initiation

It was from this place in the beginning of 2021 that The Change Tribe continued to emerge and grow.

In February 2021, I was introduced to The GC Index. That moment of uncovering my real Energy for Impact. It became so clear! This is who I really am, this is why so much has happened in the way that it did. It was this moment of confidence, that I can really be that person! I am a Game Changer/Polisher. It's why I am so passionate about making a difference, seeing all the transformational possibilities.

It all made sense; all was right with the world now I had this data point that explained so much but gave me clarity. I had a framework and a language that could make sense of it all. My constant need to make everything better, to improve it. All the wild, outlandish ideas I was constantly generating; it all made sense.

Except now came the bumpy road of beginning to figure out what that all meant and why it was important and how did it connect to The Change Tribe.

Fear gripped me once again, this time it didn't motivate me, push me or drive me, it *paralysed me.* I couldn't move forward. The limiting beliefs turning the thoughts in my head into a drumbeat, 'I can't go out into the world and do this, who is going to believe me?' My chest felt so tight; bringing my passions into the world felt overwhelming and extremely scary. I desperately wanted to bring The Change Tribe to life, desperately wanted to change how we all work, to make an impact for people, break these structures and show people there is a better way. But fear of being seen, the fear of being good enough paralysed me.

I began to cultivate my support system. Part of supporting myself was learning through courses and research, finding communities and cheerleaders that were aligned with purposeful work. This passion to change the status quo of work was like a burning inside me and I needed to find a way to release all those fears and all those things that were holding me back. It felt like this was my time to *THRIVE*.

I did some pro bono work for a charity to keep my hand in while I worked through this genius idea. I ended up taking a contract with them to design and architect their community experience and implement all the tech to go with that. This time, however, I was going to be the Game Changer/Polisher, there would be other people to implement.

The ideas and the design were glorious (Game Changer energy), most people were excited. Like all these things there are those who are onboard and those who need some reassurance to move them forward because they are in their fear states.

There were a few challenges in the journey. The people impact data from the GCI team profile showed us that our approximately 100-strong programme team was missing Implementer energy for the implementation phase. In order to bring this transformative programme into reality we needed strong Implementer energy and focus at the point of execution.

I momentarily stepped into that Implementer mode – old habits! But then I chose to move on as the implementation phase took off in earnest; this was not where I could add most value.

Key takeaways

Once again, my physical body, my emotions and my behaviours were my indicators to whether I was surviving or thriving. I was on the road to thriving now because I had made the steps to leave after my Game Changer contribution was done, it was time to pass the baton onto the Implementers without fear.

Motivations exercise

Going back to the Energy audit exercise (above)

Step 6. You can now see the behaviours and the emotions aligned to

each task. Get really honest with yourself, what was motivating you?
Was it fear or was it joy?
Step 7. What limiting belief was driving your behaviours?
Step 8. What new belief would you like to take its place?

The road to thriving

This experience with this client made me realise that my well-being, in all respects, depends upon me having the freedom to be a Game Changer/Polisher. It then became my mission that to heal organisations, I had to heal me first. I had to use all the data points that were being shown to me, to my advantage.

Today my work looks a lot different to what it used to. I am much more creative in what I do, how I do it and who I am *being* when I do it. When I have an idea, you can find me in my meditation room with a sketch pad drawing it (Game Changer). I love to write from my heart about what I do and how I do it (Game Changer). I also tell my story a lot. I have a weekly live show on healing organisations and how we do it, which gets turned into a podcast (Game Changer ideas). I also experiment *a lot* with what work is (Polisher). Some days work is processing my emotional triggers to let go of old ways of being, continually learning and growing myself (Polisher).

The road to thriving is not always easy, it is full of experimentation. It requires us to listen to what is really going on inside us and then take aligned action. It takes work to get still and really hear what's needed vs the many voices of our fears. This is why I work with my toolbox to keep me thriving and to understand when I am wandering off-course and need to come back, but also how I can bring myself back quickly.

The toolbox to thriving

Tool 1: Get to know and understand all your data points

- My GCI profile – it helps me understand where I want to work and live because I know it naturally feels good, and it is a big part of who I want to be and how I want to show up. It takes work to integrate it and this toolbox goes a long way to achieving this.

- My emotions – this is a way of showing me I am not on the right path if I am acting in anger, frustration or annoyance. This tells me the motivator is fear. Sometimes it takes a little while to uncover this. It will get quicker the more you keep connected to yourself. If it feels good, if it makes me happy, free, spacious, joyful or excited I am aligned to the right path.
- My behaviours – my emotions create my behaviours. It also connects back to my motivators. If I am being difficult, hostile, rude, abrasive, manipulative or abrupt, the chances are I am operating from my place of fear. If I am relaxed, open, curious, or intuitive then I am operating from a place of love.
- My core values – getting clear on my core values has supported my decision-making process. It shows me who my people are very clearly, as we have aligned values. It helps me determine alignment to clients as only in the right environments will we all thrive. It also helps me to create the right environments for my clients to thrive too.

Tool 2: Create liberating supportive structure through daily rituals

- Connect to my *being* state every day. Who do I want to show up as each day? Activate that energy through saying those *being* statements out loud. For me, my *being* state is aligned with my GCI profile. It helps me understand through my emotions and behaviours if I am operating in my true *being* state and, therefore, thriving or simply surviving.

Tool 3: Track my activity of what energises me and what drains me

- Keep a journal each day (see the exercise earlier in the chapter) of what activities you've done throughout the day and whether they energise or drain you. I kept this journal for two years. You start to see patterns and trends. I started to see the limiting beliefs underneath my emotions and behaviours. I started to see other people's perspectives and what might have been motivating them.
- Create the list of your breadcrumbs you have been following of topics and activities that light you up.
- Experiment with what lights you up and track it.

Tool 4: Create your support system

- Teammates, family members, friends, coaches, communities can all help you see things from another perspective. They also cheer-lead you when you are experimenting. Fundamentally we were also never meant to change by ourselves, so why try when it is so much more fulfilling to do it together?

Tool 5: Emotional processing tool

- These are the 'big guns' right here. Learning to process my emotions in a healthy way, means that the limiting belief pattern doesn't get stuck; it doesn't stop my progress. I can see it, give it space and allow myself to keep moving forward.

Tool 6: Conscious choice making

- We always have choices. Even when we don't choose, we are still choosing. I know sometimes it feels like we don't have a choice, particularly when it comes to work but we do. We can choose how we show up, we can choose how we respond to people. Ultimately, we can choose to stay in a job or leave; even though that might feel difficult it is true. Being conscious in how I make choices and the decisions I make is a much more powerful place to operate from. It means I can create whatever work life I choose; it means I feel freedom which is aligned to my core values.

The final word

Life is to be enjoyed rather than just endured. Gone is yesteryear where people worked for 45 years in factories, mines and doing hard labour, and then retired.

It is time for the world of work to evolve, there is so much disease, burnout, anger, frustration and discontent. It's time to choose! Are we brave enough for the revolution, or do we maintain the status quo that no longer serves us? The choice is ours. I choose revolution.

Work no longer needs to be a slog, it can be joyful, it can be fun, and your contribution is valuable. You are valuable.

Each one of us belongs, we all have a place we just need to uncover it and live. We can create that sense of belonging through connection to ourselves. When we do this, we truly thrive.

Bibliography

Freud, S., 'Beyond the Pleasure Principle', *Standard Edition,* Vol. 18, Hogarth, London, 1920, pp. 7–64

Maslow, A. H., 'A Theory of Human Motivation', *Psychological Review,* 50, 1943, pp. 370–396

www.ingramcontent.com/pod-product-compliance
Lightning Source LLC
Chambersburg PA
CBHW040144270326
41929CB00024B/3369